CLEAVE TO LIVE

A Practical Guide for Marriage

To Jill Hirst

signature

05/02/2023

AUTHOR AND PUBLISHER
ADEDAYO IGE
c/o Harringay United Church-Baptist
Green Lanes
London N8 0RG.
UNITED KINGDOM

IMAGES
Images from Adedayo Ige 2012 and 2016 ©
Front Cover image used by permission of Val and Helen

All Scriptures except where stated are from:
THE NEW KING JAMES VERSION,
Copyright © 1982, Thomas Nelson, Inc.
All rights reserved.

ISBN: 978-0-9954746-0-4

Cover designed by:
Adedayo Ige

DEDICATION

To God for the grace to mediate between
couples and counsel people for marriage.
To my wife Jadesola and our children for their
longsuffering in sharing my time with others.
And all the married couples who
have benefitted from this service and whose
encouragement led to writing this book.

CONTENTS

CLEAVE TO LIVE

A Practical Guide for Marriage

ACKNOWLEDGEMENTS

Praise and thanks to God for giving me the courage and the inspiration to write this book. People who have benefitted from marriage preparation classes I offered over the years have encouraged me to put my thoughts into a book but I have always resisted the encouragement for two reasons.

Firstly, writing is time consuming and I thought I didn't have time to write; and secondly, I do not like writing because language and especially English is not my strong point. However, since the beginning of 2013, I felt strongly that I should take the challenge. Being helped by the Holy Spirit who motivated me and gave me the courage and inspiration I took to writing and this book is the product. To God be the glory, honour and adoration. Amen.

From the outset, I want to acknowledge all the couples (whom I deliberately withhold their names) that have passed through this course over the years and have benefitted from it before their marriages. I also want to acknowledge couples who while already married took up the opportunity sitting in these marriage classes. I have enjoyed your companies, contributions and encouragements, all these have enabled me to put this course in writing. At last your encouragements have yielded fruit.

I also want to thank the person who has painstakingly read every word of this book and helped edit it. God knows you and I pray that God will reward your secret deed in public. My gratitude goes to other people who have read and commented on it too. I appreciate all of your efforts and pray God's blessings on you and yours.

I appreciate my beautiful wife, Jadesola Ige for her support, encouragement and tolerance over the years and without whose support and understanding this book would not have been possible. Thank you. To my children, Seun, Ope and Tobi though very young when I started counselling people and preparing them for marriage; but now old and independent in your various positions I say thank you for enduring hardship with us and learning to sacrifice by accepting your parents' time to be shared by others.

PREFACE

In these precarious times when the institution of marriage is threatened by ideas of political correctness, by deviation from the normal and universally accepted form of marriage, when people are co-habiting and the rate at which marriages are being dissolved is far greater than the rate at which they are being contracted, it is exciting and pleasing to me to see people who want to tie the knot, who want to commit themselves to living together through the institution of marriage by committing themselves to marriage vows especially before God. It is important that those who want to commit themselves to this course of action be well prepared and equipped for the task ahead of them, of founding a solid and stable home life.

This book is intended to help prepare and guide couples who are about to marry and who have agreed to participate in the preparation. It may also benefit those who are married, whom for one reason or other have not previously benefitted from this kind of preparation. In addition, it may be useful for those who are married and are keen to re-kindle the fire of their marriage and love, to bring it to life again.

This is not an academic writing that is research based; neither is it a spiritual book, hence I am not preaching. Instead, it is just a practical book that highlights first, my previous experiences with couples preparing for marriage, and secondly, my personal experience as a married man and the experiences I have gathered in my pastoral years.

Although the book is intended for Christians who are preparing to get married I envisage it being useful for non-Christians too. I consider it beneficial for everyone who intends to marry and is looking for help and guidance which will prepare them for the world of marriage. The book will also be useful for those who have not met the right person to marry, but are still looking so that they are prepared. It is also intended to guide and not to be taken as a blueprint. Some of the things discussed may not be applicable or workable for everyone. I correspondingly would suggest that those reading this book take the Bible as the foundation of relationships, as I believe this should be the standard for couples to establish their relationships.

Therefore, I am imploring you to read this book with an open mind and I pray that God will help you. If you read it and it helps you, please spread the word, and if it does not work speak to me as it will help me to improve future editions. The majority of the chapters in this book will be useful in developing good relationships with colleagues, friends and bosses. This is because the principles discussed here are universal and can be applied to other relationships. The chapters on making love, children, dealing with in-laws and on preparing for the big day [the wedding day] are specific to familial relationships and therefore central to the marriage institution.

I pray that this book will bless your relationships and help you to enjoy your married life.

Adedayo Ige

INTRODUCTION

Marriage is the first institution God created, even before any form of worship, society or any form of human group. Therefore, marriage is at the heart of God. He is interested in it and invests everything He has in it. Anyone who considers marriage is obeying God and will receive God's blessing whether they are Christians or not.

Over the centuries, marriage has been held in great honour and everyone aspired to marry. However, for the past half a century or so, the desire to marry and the understanding of marriage has undergone a significant shift, to the detriment of the marriage institution.

Within the last twenty years or so, co-habitation instead of marriage has gained ground. Men and women live together, do all kinds of stuff together, buy houses, have children and do everything that those who have regularised marriages do, but they simply do not wish to commit themselves to the vows of marriage. They do not want to go to Church or a registry office to regularise their relationship and attain a legal status. They refer to each other as 'partner', rather than 'husband' and 'wife'. And it is so fashionable that it has entered into public offices, where when you have to complete legal forms where before the designation required was 'husband' or 'wife', you will now find 'partner'.

What could be responsible for this? Writing from British scene, it is increasingly and rapidly becoming a litigious nation where lawsuits are used to settle everything. Divorce has become very expensive because of the litigation culture. People want to take more of their own share of the benefits. It's all about money. Hence people are scared of this state of affairs and therefore wary of committing themselves. On the other hand, other people are pushing hard and putting pressure on the state to recognise their relationships as being equal to those who marry legally.

There are still some people who simply choose that type of relationship because they think it is fashionable and cool. They do not wish to commit to vows and anything as permanent as marriage. It appears that they want to live for the here and now. When the relationship is good they stay and continue; if it is not, they call it quits and there will be nothing to settle because nothing binds them together. It has also become fashionable for people not to want to commit to organisations, establishments or governments; such people are anti-establishment and view marriage as belonging to the establishment.

This perhaps explains why there is a low rate of marriage in England and Wales.

CHAPTER ONE

UNDERSTANDING MARRIAGE

It is always good to start to understand what a thing is in our own way by knowing its definition. That way we master it and make the most of it. So to start to understand what marriage is, I have tried to approach the definition on three fronts.

1. What is marriage according to society?

By society, I mean understanding marriage according to the law of the land for England and Wales. The Oxford online dictionary as at 2014 defines marriage as "the formal union of a man and a woman, typically as recognised by law, by which they become husband and wife."[1]

This is the most widely held view worldwide of what marriage is. However, the form it exists in, in various parts of the world, is a different matter. The shape and length it takes are another matter and this is determined by the society and the individual couples.

I attended a Marriage Registry the other day - the second time in over twenty years. The Registrar defined marriage as "the union between a man and woman according to the law of the land." This is in line with the Oxford English Dictionary.

As at the time of writing, this is still the accepted definition of marriage according to the law in England and Wales.

---

[1] http://www.oxforddictionaries.com/definition/english/marriage

However, pressures are mounting from those who have alternative life styles to change this definition of marriage from its conventional meaning to the permissive one that recognises other forms of relationships. We have to pray for God's mercy on our nation.

When a marriage is being contracted at a Registry office or place of worship, a legal pronouncement must be made before the marriage can be accepted as having been contracted. The question must be asked:
> "If either of you knows of any reason why you may not lawfully marry, you should say so now."[2]

Or any words to that effects are also acceptable but must be asked. The question may also be put to the congregation present as:
> "if anyone knows of any reason why A & C should not be joined together as husband and wife, let him say so now or else keep your peace forever". [3]

Once the question has been answered affirmatively, the vows follow, which can vary depending on where the marriage is taking place and who is getting married, and then the marriage is contracted.

Marriage however, has been defined elsewhere as 'what the society calls it'. A definition that takes cognisance of the various cultures in the world. Going to a registry office or church or any other place of worship for marriage is fashioned after the Western culture, although many cultures contract marriage differently. In bible texts for example, Abraham sent his servant to his relative to get a

---

[2] Gathering for worship, the Baptist Union of Great Britain p190
[3] Ditto

wife for his son Isaac. Whilst Jacob who was Isaac's son, went to his uncle Laban to get his wives.
In the Yoruba land in the western part of Nigeria, where I come from, traditionally the parents of the groom go to the parents of the bride to be and ask for their daughter's hand in marriage to their son. Once the bride's to be parents agree to the proposal, a date is agreed for a public ceremony. The ceremony features invoking blessings from the elders of the two families, eating and drinking and dancing round the homes of two families and relatives. Usually at night, the bride is taken to her husband. This type of marriage is accepted even now in modern Nigeria and it is tagged 'marriage contracted by native law and custom'.

As many cultures as there are in the world, so too are the many varieties of marriage forms that exist. I can only write about the marriages that I am familiar with, nonetheless anyone reading this book will be familiar with other kinds of marriages practiced where you now live and what form of marriage you have in your mind if you are not married. If you are planning a marriage all you need to do is to pray that God will lead you so that your dreams will be fulfilled according to His plan for you as a couple, for the kind of marriage you want to undertake.

2. What is marriage according to God?

Nowhere in the Bible can one point to, to suggest how marriage was defined or how its process was clearly spelt out. Scripture is vague about this topic. There are 83 references to 'marriage', with four different words used. For 'wedding' there are 13 references, 'wife' 12, and 'married' 32 and 'marry' has 21 hits. However, none of these words describe in biblical terms how marriage was conducted. Genesis 29: 21-24 describes a little about Jacob and Leah's wedding that included witnesses by the men in the place, feasting and handing over the wife to her husband at night.

The wedding that Jesus and His disciples attended at Cana in Galilee (John 2:1-12) does not say much about how that marriage was conducted, except that a detailed attention is given to the sign Jesus performed there. Hence, from the biblical texts relating to marriage one can infer that parents were involved and there was a covenant between the couple. The covenant was witnessed by others irrespective who sourced the wife, whether it was the mother like Hagar did for Ishmael in Genesis 21:21, or an intermediary between the wife and the husband like Abraham's servant for Isaac in Genesis 24, or the man who sourced the wife himself, like Jacob in Genesis 29:21.

Marriage according to God is a covenant between a man and a woman to live the rest of their lives together, and is witnessed by people. Genesis 1:27, suggests in part how marriage should be, "So God created man in His own image; in the image of God He created him; male and female He created them". NKJV. It is between a man and a woman and no other pairings such as those which are being campaigned for in recent times.

The modern church wedding is a tradition from the church fathers and a predominantly Western culture practice. It is shaped by the culture in which people lived at that time and by what their society approved as normal or standard. Still, there is no particular model recorded in Scripture.

3. My definition of Marriage:

Over the years of being involved in counselling, in settling issues between couples, and preparing people for marriage I have realised that the conventional dictionary definition of marriage needs modification.
Marriage involves two different people, born and raised in different homes, cultures and sometimes countries coming to live together. Marriage therefore creates a situation that brings challenges, tension as well as joy and excitement too. It is easy to cope with the good aspects of marriage but the challenges and tensions are usually very difficult to deal with and, if care is not taken, these can split a couple.

We are influenced and shaped by our cultures, the people we live with, the schools we attend and our society at large (church, clubs, and other groups). All these aspects of life have great influences on us, however, greatest influences on our lives are our parents. What the father does, the son is likely to do and what the mother does the daughter is likely to do. Our parents are our role models and we are greatly shaped by what we learn from them and what we see them do.

On account that no one is perfect and no one ever will be, we all have our weaknesses, shortcomings and blemishes. Therefore, there is no point blaming others for our weakness or negative behaviour and views. Nonetheless, if we have been born a new and we should by the power of the Holy Spirit be gradually being transformed. That is to say we should have our minds being transformed to do the right things instead of us blaming our parents for our misfortunes.

That being the case, any attempts that a spouse may harbour at the back of his or her mind that she/he is going to change her/his partner to be like them is an exercise that is doomed to failure. You are you and s/he is s/he. You can't change him/her and you never will. In my experience, because couples enter into marriage with this misplaced understanding that they will change their spouses to the kind of persons they want, this understanding changes the conventional understanding and definition of marriage. I have come up with my own definition of marriage

.

"Marriage is the ability to tolerate the inadequacies of your spouse (husband or wife)."

I have argued above that you can't change your spouse, but as you are about to enter into this life-long relationship, it is better that you are prepared for it. It is good and wise that you prepare yourself to tolerate what you can't change. You, yourself you are not perfect and you would want people to take you as you are, therefore, take them as they are because they are just like you are full of shortcomings.

The choice of the word 'tolerate' is deliberate, because of the following definitions from an online dictionary:
- Permit something: to be willing to allow something to happen or exist.
- Endure something: to withstand the unpleasant effects of something.

- Accept existence of different views: to recognise other people's right to have different beliefs or practices without attempting to suppress them".[4]

So, allow people especially your spouse to be who they are and try not to change them is the way forward to wanting to be married and stay in it till death do you part in your very old age.

How are you sure the intended person is the right one?

The last question to be treated under this topic or chapter is: How do you know that the intended person is the right one? (Allow the couple to state why they think he or she is the right person)

This is a very good question because you must know why you want to commit yourself to a stranger for the rest of your life. The life you are about to embark on, though exciting, loving and adventurous, will be challenging and can be difficult at times.

Life generally is full of ups and downs. It has not changed and I do not think it ever will. So I invoke the promise of God on you as Moses told the people of Israel in Deuteronomy 11:10-15: -

"For the land which you go to possess is not like the land of Egypt from which you have come, where you sowed your seed and watered it by foot, as a vegetable garden; but the land which you cross over to possess is a land of hills and valleys, which drinks water from the rain of

---

[4]http://www.thefreedictionary.com/tolerate

heaven, a land for which the Lord your God cares; the eyes of the Lord your God are always on it, from the beginning of the year to the very end of the year. 'And it shall be that if you earnestly obey My commandments which I command you today, to love the Lord your God and serve Him with all your heart and with all your soul, then I will give you the rain for your land in its season, the early rain and the latter rain, that you may gather in your grain, your new wine, and your oil. And I will send grass in your fields for your livestock, that you may eat and be filled.'" NKJV

So in the married life you are about to enter, you will have a mountain top experience one day and a rock bottom valley experience another. But always remember that God is with you in all the experiences you will have. He has promised you in Deuteronomy 31:8 "And the Lord, He is the One who goes before you. He will be with you. He will not leave you nor forsake you; do not fear nor be dismayed." NKJV

Let me give some hints here and I am not making them a rule but these are things that I know that others have considered, used and have worked for them and who knows whether they may also work for you.

In considering who the prospective spouse will be some people have considered the attraction of their intended person. If they see them and they think Hum! It will be good to walk beside this person and be proud to introduce them as one's spouse, then that is a starter to the relationship.

However, this does not mean that the other person will necessarily feel the same but it will be worthwhile to pursue the start of the relationship and never feel afraid to get a NO for an answer. People have said that if one does not venture one cannot gain. One would never know who the right person will be until they are approached by whatever means.

I must say that physical attraction is important in relationship hence my disagreement with the popular saying 'it was love at first sight'. There is nothing like that but only attraction, likeness and infatuation at first sight. Love is a choice. It does not come naturally but one has to work at it and it is hard work too. So what I am saying is that love is an act of the will and people can love whoever they wish to love.

People often say that beauty is in the eyes of the beholder and it is very true. I believe that all people are beautiful in their own way because they are all created by God and in His image and all that He created is beautiful.

People also have had a picture of the person they would consider as their spouse which includes their physical build, height, looks, complexion, ethnicity and religious background. Nowadays when times are hard most people consider economic viability of the prospective spouse because with two incomes, people can do things better and quicker rather than to rely on one person working. For instance, two incomes will secure a mortgage quicker and easily than one income. They are also able to live more comfortably as a family. However, the only exception to this is if one is earning very well that they can meet all their financial obligations with one income.

I see nothing wrong in these criteria or standards as long as people don't set up too high a standard that they can't meet either. They should also be aware that others may be setting standards for them too.

If this is done one may find staying very late to marry if they ever will because of too high a standard they have set. My advice is that one looks at self and match the prospective spouse that they can grow and build things together. People say that Rome was not built in a day so also is marriage. People start humble and together achieve much with time. So what I am saying is that do not set too much and high a standard for self otherwise one may wait for a long time before they find the right person. Waiting for too long a time also has its ripple effects in child bearing and rearing. One may find that they will be using their pension to train their children instead of using for themselves.

Prayer is the key and there is nothing impossible with God, He will lead people to the right person. People should include God in their decision making process and allow Him to guide them to choose the right person and that person to accept their proposal. There is no point in gallivanting about from one person to the other like a butterfly on flowers. That is the reason why it is very important that people make such decision with God who to consider and approach to be their spouse.

I have always told people that if they see someone for the first time and they would not be proud to walk beside them and introduce them as the fiancé, that relationship is a nonstarter.

Young adults who are eligible to marry and are willing, have expressed fears and concerns about what is happening in their world today and it appears that they are in an uncertain and deceptive time. The uncertainty about knowing who will be trustworthy and genuinely interested in relationship is scarring them away from plunging into it. So no one is confident in entering into relationship anymore. But with God things will be easier and he will guide them and help them to make the right choice.

Young adults nowadays want others especially their ministers to give them prophecy to know who to marry. This is very dangerous and I will encourage people to rely on God and the Holy Spirit who lives in them rather than a prophet or pastor's prophecy. I am not saying the pastors and prophets are not hearing from God but whatever they hear about you must resonate with your spirit. The Holy Spirit must witness the trueness of the prophecy with you because the Holy Spirit lives in you as He lives in the pastors and prophets

I am saying this with all seriousness as a minister, father and a Christian. Any Christian has direct access to God without any human intermediary, Jesus has paved the way for us and anyone can speak to God about anything including the person they want to marry. God can speak directly into your spirit, into your ears and He can even show you things as in visions or dreams. Why not go to God directly instead of a prophet?

I learnt of a bitter experience when one prophet told one woman a particular man was her husband. She believed the prophet and took it seriously. But the prophesy never came true and it can happen so many times to different people. Please do not subject yourself to deceit and spiritual abuse and allow people to ruin your life. You too are a priest of God because you are a Christian and God is not a respecter of anyone. As He speaks to the pastors He can also speak to you. You only need to ask Him, listen and act in obedience and it will be well with you.

A young man visited the UK for a wedding and happened to meet us (my wife and I). he asked a very pertinent and good question. "How does one choose between 2 – 3 eligible women for a wife?"

The advice we gave him was that he should be praying and fasting about them because it is a life-long decision he is about to make and he should aim to get it right. We believe that God will answer him and will lead him to see who will be suitable and who will not. We encouraged him to adopt Abraham's servant method, who prayed to God "whoever I asked to give me water to drink and say yes and I will give to your carmels too, should be my master's son wife". We told him about Gideon's method too in Judges 6 to be quadruple sure that that person is the one God meant for him. We also told him all I have written above. What we have refrained to do is to make that decision for him because we are not going to live their lives for them. So, the decision must be totally his.

God's peace and joy are always present in what He has hand in and what He has ordained. I want to say to men that women are wonderful creature, when they say no at first, it may be a test for the men's persistence, endurance and longsuffering. So a bit of persuasion, insistence and importunity may help after which one should know whether there is willingness of the woman or not or vice versa.

Proverbs 19:14[5] "Fathers can give their sons an inheritance of houses and wealth, but only the LORD can give an understanding wife." (NLT)
So pray hard and obey God and He will give the spouse you desire in your heart.

I want to point out a dilemma here, my wish is that every Christian man and woman will find their spouse from the Church. But the reality is that there are more women than men in the Church and it cuts across all denominations and all over the world.

Tony Walter[6] , in "Why are Most Churchgoers Women? A Literature Review," Vox Evangelica 20 (1990):73-90 wrote:
"Throughout the modern world, more women than men go to church. In England, out of every 100 church attenders, 55 are women and 45 men (in England generally, women outnumber
men slightly, 51:49). The difference is most marked in liberal nonconformist churches, such as Methodist (60:40) and United Reformed (57:43), which tend to lack males aged 20-40.
Evangelical churches have a more even balance, with Baptists 57:43 and independent churches 53:47. The Church of England has a ratio of 55:45, and the Roman Catholics 54:46
(Nationwide Initiative in Evangelism 1980). The ratios in Wales (61:39) and Scotland (Protestant 63:37, Catholic

---

[5] Holy Bible; New Living Translation
[6] Tony Walter, "Why are Most Churchgoers Women? A Literature Review," Vox Evangelica 20 (1990): 73-90.

57:43) are more marked (Brierley & Evans 1983; Brierley & Macdonald 1985). The 1984 Mission England was particularly attractive to females, with a ratio of 63:37—nearly two to one—among those who went forward (Back 1985). In the USA, the patterns are somewhat different, with the more evangelical churches being particularly attractive to women (Pentecostals 2:1, Baptists 3:2)."

Paul wrote extensively on marriage with unbelievers in 1 Corinthians 7 and concluded whether the wife or husband know that they will save their spouse. Yes, you may argue that it is for those who are already married before they became Christians but the reality of the above statistics are still relevant today.

I was told of a story of an assistant pastor of a popular church who wanted to marry an unbeliever but all the other pastors were against him including the senior pastor. He was bent on going ahead with the marriage upon his conviction and the church would not marry them. They went to the Registry and got married there. Later the woman became a Christian and now God is using her powerfully in the same Church where she was not initially accepted. The senior minister since had changed his mind on this issue.

However, there may be many examples of such marriages that ends in disaster and that is the reason why I say that the decision is yours as to who to marry and when it is committed in God's hands He's more than capable to sort things out for you.

Whatever has made you think that she or he is the right person should be buried in your subconscious mind so that when the going is tough, you become tough by remembering the first day you saw her or him; or remember how God has ministered into your spirit and you will always remember that God is faithful. He never lies or changes his mind. He is the one that paired you together and He will be with you if you co-operate with Him. God is good all the time and all the time God is good. He will help you because you obey Him by choosing to marry.

Ethical Challenge.

While considering the question of how do you know that such and such a person is the right person to marry, alongside it is an ethical issue to resolve. The issue is a medical one and has to do with gene traits. All over the world there are some diseases that have serious consequences on marriage and relationships. For instance, Some Black communities from the Tropics have sickle cell, the countries around the Mediterranean have Sickle Thalassaemia and Cystic Fibrosis found predominantly among the whites but also among the blacks. All these are preventable conditions, which with proper education and the making of right choice the after effects resulting from these conditions can be eliminated. It is not sensible therefore, for example; that two people with sickle cell anaemia or trait marry each other, they are likely to produce sickler children. There is no need to subject yourselves to produce children that will spend considerable amount of their life in the Hospitals. The same goes with the other conditions like Cystic Fibrosis and Sickle Thalassaemia.[7] On this note I advise you to know your sickle and Cystic fibrosis status and marry by your head and your heart will follow.

On the other hand, if you are preparing for marriage, it may appear to be late to check all those things and you may be overwhelmed "where will I start from and with whom?"

You may be right, but today's disappointment may lead to tomorrow's joy and peace. Today's pain replaces tomorrow's more serious pain on the children you will have. Think about it and let God guide you.

Of course God answers prayers and with God all things are possible. It is only God who can prevent the abnormal HBs meeting; hence you could have normal children if both of you have A in your blood. But to ask God to change what He has already created to me is like testing God. You are asking Him to undo what He has done and it is like telling Him "You have made a mistake". It is also like asking God to change a girl into a boy for those who want a boy and they have girls and vice-versa.

Modes and Styles of Marriage

These varies from culture to culture, place to place and country to country. In other words, there is no right or wrong method, mode or style of marriage. As long as there is a covenant between the couple that is witnessed by people, then the couple have married. The covenant will include words of commitment accompanied by various gestures like signing a certificate, holding hands

[7] Please Seek medical advice from appropriate health authorities..

in unity, breaking kolanuts etc. in the presence of the witnesses.

Because of the varied modes and styles of marriage, we cannot make the assumption that marriage must always take place in a church, registry office or any such magnificent buildings, with an elaborate and flamboyant ceremony.

Marriage could take place, in any place and clergy may or may not be involved for the reason that not every wedding will be a religious wedding.

The important thing we must know is that whether Christian or non-Christian marriage, God blesses all. I believe this because God created marriage before any civil group, government or Church.

Marriage by traditional rites: for non- western people.

Cases where couples are formed of individuals from different cultures and even from different parts of the world, this raises numerous challenges. Therefore, of couples intending to marry; if one or both of you come from that part of the world where traditional marriage is very important and your relationship is not complete or formalised without this rite, and you are required to do it, please consider it. What I will object to is to bow down before the family gods or idols, that is no longer marriage. [The people I am thinking of, whom this affects are people from middle and far eastern Asia, Africans and south Americans and other culture that are into this kind of wedding].

Marriage is making a covenant between two people in front of people who are in authority (over those getting married) either in their family or community. The couple make a commitment to live the rest of their lives together until death separates them.

In a Nigerian setting the marriage ceremony is usually patterned in a way where the groom's family or representative go to the bride's family to ask for their daughter in marriage to their son. After the response, which usually is yes, the couple may be prayed for by both families, after the prayers other traditional exchange of vows are done, like breaking kolanuts or any other nuts, pouring wine as libation and other traditional rites. Then food is served and there is party and dancing and in the night, the bride retires into her new home where the husband lives. The description of marriage is culture specific and is not the only pattern for marriage that there is. We intonated that there are many more marriage patterns as there are traditions and cultures. What I would emphasise is that a marriage does not necessarily have to take place at the Registry, Church or any other place of worship.

In cultures where these type of marriages are practised, 'white weddings' as they are normally referred to, and carried out at the Church or Registry, such marriages are only but cultural. What is important is that couples must be married by traditions which stand by themselves and that are recognised in those cultures.

CHAPTER TWO

THE STRUCTURE FOR MARRIAGE

Digging a deep foundation

1. Building a Strong Foundation.

Considering marriage is synonymous with wanting to build a home, just as the physical structure of a building needs a carefully constructed, strong foundation, so too married relationships must be strongly founded and built up carefully on the pattern God has laid down. In physical building structure constructions some land may be sandy, some rocky and some clay. In entering marriage, the marriage home can be affected also by what we build on. Our upbringings, experiences and forms of education may constitute the type of ground we are building on our new home.

Technology has improved a lot nowadays so that there is almost nowhere you cannot build a house on. Unfortunately, technology cannot help couples build marriage relationships on unsuitable grounds. It takes God and the couple to build this marriage relationship to be strong.

Jesus illustrated what it takes to build a strong home in
Luke 6:46-49

> "But why do you call Me 'Lord, Lord,' and not do
> the things which I say? Whoever comes to Me,
> and hears My sayings and does them, I will show
> you whom he is like: He is like a man building a
> house, who dug deep and laid the foundation on
> the rock. And when the flood arose, the stream
> beat vehemently against that house, and could not
> shake it, for it was founded on the rock. But he
> who heard and did nothing is like a man who built
> a house on the earth without a foundation, against
> which the stream beat vehemently; and
> immediately it fell. And the ruin of that house was
> great." NKJV

The first main lesson Jesus was sharing in this passage
is 'digging deep'. Before you build a house, you need to
dig deep into the ground and lay a solid foundation to
build your home on. It is believed that the deeper the
foundation, the higher the house can go and the stronger
it can be. This means it will sustain more weight and can
go higher because its foundation is deep.
A shallow foundation will bear less weight and resist
outside (elements) forces less and so will support a
house weaker than the one with a strong foundation.

The same thing applies to marriage. Couples are
expected to dig deep into the word of God and obey what
is there, it helps in understanding your husband or wife to
be. In digging deep in tolerating one another and
enduring the challenges of the new relationship, you are
likely to enjoy your marriage and it is likely to be
successful.

Most Churches are aware of the need for a good marriage foundation so they offer couples pre-marriage discussions and try to guide them the right way. In the marriage ceremony, the importance of a good and solid foundation is reinforced in the word from the 'statement of purpose' to this effect:

"...In marriage, husband and wife
are called to a new way of life, created, ordered,
and blessed by God. this way of life must not be
entered into carelessly, or from selfish motives, but
responsibly, and prayerfully."

Or
"...Marriage is not therefore a thing to be rushed into, or undertaken or instituted lightly to satisfy our carnal lusts and appetites like brute beasts that have no understanding; But reverently, discretely, advisedly, soberly and in fear of God, carefully considering the causes for which matrimony was ordained ...[8]"

It is important to dig deep into understanding your motive for marrying and understanding your relationship with the person you wish to marry. Put God into the marriage as the main foundation and it will endure and be successful.

The second main point that Jesus makes is 'building the home on the rock'. Everyone knows that the rock is fairly permanently solid and hard. So building on it is safe. It brings peace of mind and stability and permanence. It is

---

[8] Gathering for worship -Christian worship

protected from the harsh elements of nature the likes of storms, floods and so on.

House built on the Rock

In marriage that rock has to be Christ Himself, the creator and sustainer of the universe. He is the one who promised to go ahead of you in your journey, and brings out water from the rock on your journey when there is desperation and thirst. He is the one who will bring manna and meat for you in times of need.

This summary of the preceding paragraph is taken from the Biblical texts of the story of the journey of the Israelites from Egypt the land of slavery into the Promised Land of Canaan, a land flowing with milk and honey. Although God had promised them good things, the Israelites met with challenges during their journey. At some point when they lacked water God provided water from a rock that previously had no water. At another time they craved for meat and God provided them with quails. He never let them be in need of bread [manna].

This same God called couples into marriage and is willing to go ahead of couples because He knows that there will be challenges ahead. As a couple you will need His help to live with each other successfully. You need Him to meet your needs from His riches in glory and to be your strength in the time of your weakness. So all you need is to hold on to Him and He will always be your present help in times of trouble (Psalms 46:1).

Jesus was the guest of honour at the wedding of Cana in Galilee (John 2:1-12). He was not only present but He also blessed the couple by providing a better wine than what they had served earlier and had ran out. With provision of wine and a better wine for that matter, Jesus saved the couple from social embarrassment.

After the honeymoon moments will come and go and the joy and excitement of the newly married may run out. But in allowing in their lives the presence of Christ by His Spirit, the married couple will always find Jesus brings new wine, which is joy from the Holy Spirit. Jesus' provisions never run out when he is present in a couple's lives. Just as Jesus honoured the invitation to the wedding at Cana in Galilee, He is prepared to honour your invitation and be present by the His Spirit; all you need to do is invite Him into your marriage.

Another key point in this passage of the wedding in Canna of Galilee is what Mary the mother of Jesus told the servants, "Do what He tells you". If only couples could obey Christ by doing what He tells them from His Word, He will always turn the couples' water into wine, and a better wine than before. Wine signifies joy; that is to say a couple will never be in want of the joy of the Lord in their lives if they obeyed Him.

Take the long view.

This means marriage is permanent. The phrases in the wedding vows say it all -

'for better for worse;
for richer, for poorer;
in sickness and in health'

Both parties should apply these vows literally.
I want to warn however, about a new wave of unwritten vows that say -
'for better to stay, for worse to go';
in health to stay, in sickness to go';
for richer to stay, for poorer to go
and until death do us part'.

Some people make excuses in marriage, "this is too much for me I just can't cope anymore". The responses of their spouses inadvertently are, "the door out is open, you can exit anytime". The question I am asking to whichever partner is leaving is: whom are you leaving for? Are you going back to your old family? This type of thought should not even cross a couple's mind. By entertaining this, a couple should know that Satan is in control, and the Bible tells us to, 'Resist the Devil and he will flee from you' [James 4:7 NKJV]. Couples should at all times remember the vows they made, `till death do us part`.

The objective of permanence for Christian marriages is always read out to the couple and the people present at the ceremony. The words of the above *vow*, or similar, are always pronounced.

This vow I believe is fashioned after the answer of Jesus to the Pharisees when they asked him a question about divorce in Matthew 19:3-10:

"The Pharisees also came to Him, testing Him, and saying to Him, "Is it lawful for a man to divorce his wife for just any reason?" And He answered and said to them, "Have you not read that He who made them at the beginning 'made them male and female,' and said, 'For this reason a man shall leave his father and mother and be joined to his wife, and the two shall become one flesh'? So then, they are no longer two but one flesh. Therefore, what God has joined together, let not man separate."

They said to Him, "Why then did Moses command to give a certificate of divorce, and to put her away?" He said to them, "Moses, because of the hardness of your hearts, permitted you to divorce your wives, but from the beginning it wasn't so. And I say to you, whoever divorces his wife, except for sexual immorality, and marry commits adultery; and whoever marries her who is divorced commits adultery."

His disciples said to Him, "If such is the case of the man with his wife, it is better not to marry." NKJV

From Jesus' statement in verses 8-9, clearly marriage is 'till death do us part'. This has to be resolved in couples' hearts before they commit to marriage. It is not fashionable and cool as it appears presently, to divorce. God did not create marriage so that people could abandon their vows for flimsy and often selfish reasons.

You may ask, why did Jesus teach divorce in Matthew 5:31-32? (Matt 19:9; Mark 10:11,12; Luke 16:18)

"Furthermore it has been said, 'whoever divorces his wife, let him give her a certificate of divorce.' But I say to you that whoever divorces his wife for any reason except sexual immorality causes her to commit adultery; and whoever marries a woman who is divorced commits adultery." NKJV

Adultery is always an easy way out marriage for most people who want a divorce. If they can establish the facts and evidence, it will be legitimate to cling on to this part of the scripture to back up their divorce. The law in most countries has provision for this and it can be abused to one's advantage. It is their choice if couples stick to their guns.

Despite the fact that this text on marriage in the Bible is clear, it remains a very tricky portion of the scripture. It is very true that once you marry you must not cheat on your husband or wife. No matter what the circumstances, love is what binds you and it must be adhered to. Conversely, scripture must be understood in its entirety. The same Jesus who made the statements in Matthew 5 and 19 as quoted above also made the statements in Matthew 12: 31 and Mark 3:28-30 about the 'Unpardonable Sin',

"Therefore I say to you, **every** sin and blasphemy will be forgiven men, but the blasphemy against the Spirit will not be forgiven men." NKJV

What I am saying with the underlined and bolded text, **"every"** is that, wherever there is love, we can forgive each other whatever the other `person has done. There is no sin that cannot be forgiven except blasphemy against the Holy Spirit. Couples should and must always be gracious to one another remembering that marriage is sacred and binding and the texts below sum this up.

Proverbs 10:12 "Hatred stirs up strife, but love covers all sins". NKJV

1 Peter 4:8 "And above all things have fervent love for one another, for "love will cover a multitude of sins." NKJV

Because we ourselves have received God's grace, we should and ought to dispense that same grace to those who offend us. We should forgive and expect those who offended us not to repeat their actions. This will of course win us respect and honour.
As Jesus told the woman caught in adultery in John 8:11 "... Neither do I condemn you; go and sin no more." NKJV we too should follow Jesus' way and tell each other to sin no more.

An exception

When people say that marriage is permanent and it is until death do us part, it is true that this is God`s intention that must be adhered to. But there is an exception, that is a situation of violence and the possibility of death in a relationship. God`s plan for you is to spend your full years and probably to die peacefully. Isaiah 65:20 prophesied this that "No longer will babies die when only a few days old. No longer will adults die before they have lived a full life. No longer will people be considered old at one hundred!"

So if your spouse is violent and abusive and your life is in danger, you must seek help. Seeking help is not a sign of weakness, it will help straightens things up in the relationship. It will reinforce to your spouse that it is not acceptable to be violent.

I remember a Christian couple where the husband was always violent and his wife was bearing it with the hope that he would change. Their Pastor was involved but to no avail. One morning after the man had gone to work, the wife was tidying the bed and she found a 12" kitchen knife under her husband's pillows. She just packed her belongings and left for safety. I did not blame the woman; it is better to be safe than to be sorry. Whatever excuse or explanation the husband had it was unacceptable because a knife is not meant for the bedroom and under the pillow! In my opinion, he had the intention to harm either himself or his wife or both. There was another case on the Television where a man was being abused and attacked by his girl-friend and he continued to cover her by lying. The truth never came out until she killed him.

It's not only men that can be violent, women too can be violent and when they do it they do it stealthily. My first experience in mediating between couples was a very serious one. The woman was violent. She would physically abuse her husband and then would fall on the floor rolling around claiming that her husband was the one who had struck her. I could not believe it until she was exposed to me on one occasion and she was unable to pull that trick on me anymore.

Couples need to be careful: violence is not part of the deal. It is totally out of the marriage covenant and should not be tolerated. Couples should develop zero tolerance to violence; it is a product of uncontrolled anger (rage). Anger is the mother (precursor) of murder. Allowing it once can lead to future attacks, so reject it straightaway. Just one attack is one too many.

Commitment to succeed on both sides

Some basic principles in marriage relationships are irrevocable. One of them is the principle of commitment to a successful relationship. Couples will do well to adopt such a commitment. The more couples are committed, the more likely they are to succeed in their marriage. Marriage is not to be entered into half-heartedly or with partial commitment. Couples need to give marriage 100% commitment that is unconditional because commitment with conditions never works and is never in the will of God. Couples need to plant firmly such commitment in their subconscious mind so that when they dream they dream commitment, when they wake up commitment comes to their minds. The same should be said in their trying periods the song they hear is commitment. It follows that as soon as Satan attempts painting a spouse as a monster, couples will still be committed to one another.

Nonetheless, in spite of the couples' best efforts, there are times when commitment will be tested, tried and challenged. For example, times of quarrels and other misunderstandings, and especially when a spouse cheats. Such a test is very hard and almost unthinkable and I pray it will not happen. If it should happen, couples should not rush to make decision, even though the scripture and the law are clear on this, couples should take time, pray and seek God`s face on the issue.

Couples should also consider what if the reverse was the case, in those situations where a spouse cheats? That is to ask the question, what if you who is cheated on was the one cheating? Would you like to be forgiven for any sins? If the answer is 'yes', then do the same to your partner. It is a step closer to being like Jesus. I am not advocating that you cheat on your spouse. That would be sin and unacceptable both to God and your spouse and you will be accountable for it even if you have been forgiven. Simply, do not do it. God always forgives all our sins, but He will never remove the consequence(s). Suppose adultery leads to the birth of a child, God will forgive the adulterer or the adulteress but will not kill the child to make the memory of the sin fade. The mistrust and suspicion will remain for a while and you must not think that by your partner forgiving you everything will be forgotten. No, it does not work like that unless the person has dementia (loss of memory). There will be flashbacks, but these can be contained by the help of the Holy Spirit. No one wants adultery and to be cheated on, no one wants his or her partner to be unfaithful and I pray that it will not happen, but if it does happen this maybe not the end of the world.

The story told in John 8:3-11 is my solution.

> "Then the scribes and Pharisees brought to Him a woman caught in adultery. And when they had set her in the midst, they said to Him, "Teacher, this woman was caught in adultery, in the very act. Now Moses, in the law, commanded us that such should be stoned. But what do You say?" This they said, testing Him, that they might have something of which to accuse Him. But Jesus stooped down and wrote on the ground with His finger, as though He did not hear.
>
> So when they continued asking Him, He raised Himself up and said to them, "He who is without sin among you, let him throw a stone at her first." And again He stooped down and wrote on the

ground. Then those who heard it, being convicted by their conscience, went out one by one, beginning with the oldest even to the last. And Jesus was left alone, and the woman standing in the midst. When Jesus had raised Himself up and saw no one but the woman, He said to her, "Woman, where are those accusers of yours? Has no one condemned you?" She said, "No one, Lord." And Jesus said to her, "Neither do I condemn you; go and sin no more." NKJV

This passage is interesting. This woman was caught in the act of adultery, but her accusers did not bring her co-perpetrator. Their accusation was one sided and partial. They concentrated on the woman`s sin but they failed to see their own sins. Even though their sins may not have been adultery, none of them was without sin. Jesus' reply that whoever is without sin should cast the first stone stunned and convicted them all, because none of them was without sin. Before cast the stone of condemnation and judgment the woman's accusers should also know that they too are living in glass houses. This supposition does not diminish the gravity of the sin of adultery. No, adultery is a serious sin and must be avoided at all cost. The apostles Paul's advice to the Colossians in 3:13; is up to the point for couples:

"..bearing with one another, and forgiving one another, if anyone has a complaint against another; even as Christ forgave you, so you also must do". NKJV

Commitment on each spouse's side of the marriage stipulated by God is absolutely crucial to making marriage work. Commitment must however be unconditional founded on your love for each other.

Submission in marriage

Let us look at Ephesians 5:17-33

"Therefore do not be unwise, but understand what the will of the Lord is. And do not be drunk with wine, in which is dissipation; but be filled with the Spirit, speaking to one another in psalms and hymns and spiritual songs, singing and making melody in your heart to the Lord, giving thanks always for all things to God the Father in the name of our Lord Jesus Christ, submitting to one another in the fear of God.

Wives, submit to your own husbands, as to the Lord. For the husband is head of the wife, as also Christ is head of the church; and He is the Saviour of the body. Therefore, just as the church is subject to Christ, so let the wives be to their own husbands in everything.

Husbands, love your wives, just as Christ also loved the church and gave Himself for her, that He might sanctify and cleanse her with the washing of water by the word, that He might present her to Himself a glorious church, not having spot or wrinkle or any such thing, but that she should be holy and without blemish. So husbands ought to love their own wives as their own bodies; he who loves his wife loves himself. For no one ever hated his own flesh, but nourishes and cherishes it, just as the Lord does the church. For we are members of His body, of His flesh and of His bones. "For this reason a man shall leave his father and mother and be joined to his wife, and the two shall become one flesh." This is a great mystery, but I speak concerning Christ and the church. Nevertheless, let each one of you in particular so love his own wife as himself, and let the wife see that she respects her husband". NKJV

From experience, this text has been widely misunderstood and misapplied to life and marriage. Some men think that loving their wives is dependent on wives submitting to them. Hence you hear 'how can I love her when she does not submit?' The same with some women, 'how can I submit when he does not love me? I am on my own'.

Loving your wife is not dependent on her submission or being good to you. You just love her as Christ loved you. He died for you when you were a sinner, unworthy and filthy. Love your wife even if she is unworthy and bad. Just love her as Jesus loves you and be prepared to die (literally) for her. Love covers a multitude of sins. If you love her, you tolerate her faults to show her love until she wants to change because she has been shown unconditional love.

Wives in a similar way, submitting to your husband is not dependent on him being good, loving, caring and providing for you. You should just submit because you want to obey the God who commands you to do so. Many women view submission as negative and think it will make husbands walk over them so they don't submit.

The foolishness of God is much wiser and better than human wisdom. Consider what the submission of Christ earned him. His name is exalted above any other name so that at the name of Jesus every knee must bow and every tongue confess that He is Lord. If you submit to your husband, I believe that God will honour you too as He has honoured Christ by exalting you in due course.

If anyone says to you that there will not be trouble or challenges in your marriage, this is not true and is also unscriptural. Some people believe that making positive confession or vows averts challenges or problems in their lives; so they write their own vows, full of positive words. But does that prevent a tide of trouble flowing and ebbing into their marriage? No. Jesus said in

> John 16:33 "These things I have spoken to you, that in Me you may have peace. In the world you will have tribulation; but be of good cheer, I have overcome the world." NKJV

With Jesus in the `boat` of your marriage, it will not sink. Just like Him at the centre of your wedding there will always be new wine that will be better than any you can produce.

CHAPTER THREE

COMMUNICATION

AN ESSENTIAL INGREDIENT FOR RELATIONSHIPS

What is communication?

The Wikipedia online dictionary[9] defines communication as "the activity of conveying information through the exchange of thoughts, messages, or information, as by speech, visuals, signals, writing, or behaviour. It is the meaningful exchange of information between two or more living creatures." Communication may be intentional or unintentional, may involve conventional or unconventional signals, may take linguistic or non-linguistic forms, and may occur through spoken or other modes."
Communication requires a sender, a message, and a recipient.

Nevertheless, the receiver doesn't have to be present or aware of the sender's intent to communicate at the time of communication. Consequently, communication can occur across vast distances in time and space. Communication requires that the communicating parties share an area of communicative commonality. The communication process is only complete once the receiver ___understands___ the sender's message[10].
If the sender has not understood your message, good communication has not been achieved. Therefore, efforts

---

[9] http://en.wikipedia.org/wiki/Communication
[10] Ditto

must be put on communication to your spouse so that they understand what you are saying.

Talking more effectively

A BT advert says, 'it's good to talk', and this is true and is what most of us do best. By talking we express what is inside of us. We let people look into the windows of our lives and enable them to know who we are and what we are capable of. But before you speak, think carefully and ask yourself, "Will what I am going to say bless and build up my spouse; will it add value to their life? Will it glorify God?" This in itself is a question applicable to all situations and all people.

Look at these quotes about words, what do you understand by each?

- Handle them carefully, for words have more power than atom bombs. --Pearl Strachan[11]
- Speech is the mirror of the soul; as a man speaks, so he is. --Publilius Syrus[12]
- Out of the abundance of the heart the mouth speaks. –Jesus Christ[13]
- Be careful of your thoughts; they may become words at any moment. --Ira Gassen[14]
- Words are eggs; once they fall you can't gather them. - Adedayo Ige[15]

Proverbs 16:24 (NKJV)

---

[11] http://www.goodreads.com/quotes/tag/power-of-words
[12] Ditto
[13] Ditto
[14] Ditto
[15] A Yoruba proverb

"Pleasant words are like a honeycomb, sweetness to the soul and health to the bones."
James 3:8 (NKJV)

"But no man can tame the tongue. It is an unruly evil, full of deadly poison. With it we bless our God and Father, and with it we curse men, who have been made in the similitude of God. Out of the same mouth proceed blessing and cursing. My brethren, these things ought not to be so. Does a spring send forth fresh water and bitter from the same opening? Can a fig tree, my brethren, bear olives, or a grapevine bear figs? Thus no spring yields both salt water and fresh."

James' conclusion does not mean that you should not talk, but rather, do think before you talk. If your thoughts are right your words will be right and you will act right too. You must weigh what you say and how you say it. For the reason that it is possible to say the right thing in the wrong way and at the wrong time. Your goal should be to say the right thing in the right way and the right time, since you must talk in order to be able to share your dreams and concerns together, it is the only way you will be able to grow together.

In talking however, raising one's voice sometimes is considered a sign of anger and aggression. It is a sign that you are losing control of yourself and the situation. Such a position usually meets with opposition, resentment and tends to drive the situation out of control. So couples are better warned to keep themselves in check. Talking positively on the contrary, always helps even when what the other person is doing is bad. Remaining calm even in the presence of anger is a great virtue to have and such a disposition is possible to achieve with the help of the Holy Spirit.

I remember one day when I took something from the kitchen and failed to put it back in its rightful place. My wife called me and asked in the softest tone that I have never heard in our years of marriage "darling, where did you pick this from?" I felt compelled to apologise and went straight away to put it back in its correct place. And I told her that if that was the way we are to relate to each other we will get the best out of each other and enjoy one another more. This example simply shows that there is always room for improvement. Each day is a new day and a day of improving our communication skills and consequently our relationships.

Most women want to talk but the moment they say, "let us talk", most men will ask "what's the problem?" Often there is no problem - she only wants to know what her spouse is thinking and planning. Whether she and the children [if they have children] are in his plan? It is a way she is asking of him to do things together with them. She wants him to share her desires, dreams and concerns. She wants to share with him what she heard at work and wants him to contribute to what is going on in her life and in the lives of their children (if children are in their lives).

This means whatever couples speak to one another, they need to ensure they speak clearly, unambiguously and in a way that spouses will understand. Actually there should be no secret between the two of spouses. Everything should and must be transparent. Husband or wife should know everything about their spouse; there should not be anything hidden. If there is, it will bring problems later. It will bring lack of trust. One of the ways we can interpret Genesis 2:25 'is to be transparent'. "And they were both naked, the man and his wife, and were not ashamed." NKJV.

Obviously, there will be moments when things may and will get rough and tough but, when they do, talking amicably and amiably is the best way to deal with problems. There must be no suspicion of the other person in a marriage relationship. You must always believe in each other no matter what happens. This means that trust must always be there. A relationship that lacks trust will not last.

Talk about the issue, not the person

In a relationship it is always advisable to talk about the issue and not the person. The way to do this is to say "what you said is bad" rather than "you are bad", "what you said is wrong" rather than "you are wrong" and "what you said is not true" rather than "you are lying". This last example is the worst thing to say. Never call your spouse a liar.

In our marriage of years, when I said something that surprised my wife and seemed unbelievable she would say "that's not true". That I interpreted literally and I would flare up in rage accusing her that she called me a liar. Whereas the environment she grew up shaped her the way she sees and understands things. She was not calling me a liar rather she was expressing the fact that my story surprised her. Couples always develop ways of relating and of sharing information, and no two sets of couples would communicate and act the same. Other features of relationship remain points of common sense. So for example, when you are going out, it's a matter of courtesy to tell your spouse where you are going, with whom and when you are likely to return. The reason for this is that if anything should happen, (God forbid) they will know where to look for you. If they know where you went, with whom and when you'll be back, they will be at peace. If you are going to be late then phone or text or use any other medium available to you and therefore allaying any fears. This is being responsible and accountable to each other. It is an act of caring not controlling.

Listening more effectively

The average person has selective hearing because they hear what they want to hear from whoever is speaking. Once a message is heard, it is processed to a state of understanding with the help of previous experience, knowledge and culture. This can inadvertently lead to misunderstandings and create unwelcome, unexpected and sometimes opposite responses. Therefore, in marriage relationships couples need to consciously and intentionally pay attention to what they hear, and if they do not understand it is better to seek clarification from the speaker. It is better to show your ignorance by saying you don't understand, than to go away with a wrong understanding. People always say that 'silence is golden' and I say that "listening is diamond". Listening is much more difficult than talking. We always want to talk but we find it difficult to listen. This aspect of communication James dealt with firmly in:

James 1:19-20 "So then, my beloved brethren, let every man be swift to hear, slow to speak, slow to wrath; for the wrath of man does not produce the righteousness of God". NKJV

God has shown us what is better by creating us with two eyes to see like the eagles, two ears to be able to hear twice as much and one mouth to speak only once. We have a big lesson to learn from God's wonderful creation. Several passages encourage us to listen rather than talk.

> Proverbs 17:28 "Even a fool is counted wise when he holds his peace; When he shuts his lips, he is considered perceptive." NKJV
> Job 13:5 "Oh that you would be silent, and it would be your wisdom! NKJV
> Proverbs 15:2 "The tongue of the wise uses knowledge rightly, but the mouth of fools pours forth foolishness. NKJV
> Ecclesiastes 5:3 "For a dream comes through much activity and a fool's voice is known by "**his many words.**" NKJV

I highlighted **"his many words"** in the text above because my experience with couples and in groups, is that the person who is always the more talkative, more often than not, they are always in the wrong when hard questions are asked. Such a one always want to use their skill of oratory to convince people otherwise. They do not allow the others to talk, even after they have had time to state their case. They always interrupt the other person appearing dominant and aggressive. Sometimes, realising that their tactics do not work, rather than listening to the other person they shut down and probably walk away.

These kind of tactics will not work in a loving relationship. Paul advised us to do better in,

> Philippians 2:3 "Let nothing be done through selfish ambition or conceit, but in lowliness of mind let each esteem others better than himself." NKJV

Clarifying misunderstandings

Many times we will not understand what the other person is saying. It is better to ask for clarification so that you can understand them better. The way you clarify communications matters a great deal and it is important. The tone of voice and body language say more about what a person's intentions are and usually gives the person away. Always say what you mean and mean what you say. Often, when these two conflict, there is suspicion, mistrust and problems. People often say that 'actions speak louder than words' and it's true.

A person's action, tone of voice and pitch in communications are important when talk to spouse. Shouting is not good it never gets the attention intended, instead the listener can shut off and not hear what is being said. It's like pouring water into a basket or on to the back of a duck: the water simply drains away having no effect. Understanding your spouse requires continuous clarification of issues in a relationship, and that removes putting strain on relationships and causing troubles.

CHAPTER FOUR

LOVE - THE SUPER GLUE OF MARRIAGE

Many times people say "when I first saw her; it was love at first sight." Really? It is commonly and universally accepted that there is a `love at first sight`, but the truth is that there is no such thing. I believe there can be an attraction or infatuation or a passion or chemistry at first sight. When one sees a beautiful girl or a handsome man they may be attracted to them from the start and wish them to be their spouse or friend.
Love is not the same as infatuation and attraction. It is something people have to work at and something they choose to do as it does not come naturally or cheap. It is hard work and often costly, this is because people have to spend time, energy, and money to love their spouse.

There are different terms for `love` in the Bible which have different meanings. The love we are exploring in this lesson is the `agape` love which means `unconditional love`. It does not come naturally like physical attraction. People have to work at it and it is hard work. It can be achieved if persons are committed; they will realise it and will be reflecting Jesus in their relationships. That is the reason the Bible lists love as first in the fruit of the Spirit in Galatians 5:22-23

> "But the fruit of the Spirit is love, joy, peace, longsuffering, kindness, goodness, faithfulness, gentleness, and self-control. Against such there is no law". NKJV

This is the kind of love that does not expose the faults of the other, rather it acknowledges and tries by example and prayer to influence Godly change. That means the wife should love her husband and the husband his wife, and the man must respect and submit to his wife as she does respects and submits to him according to Ephesians 5:21, "submitting to one another in the fear of God." NKJV. However, the submission and respect is emphasised more to the woman, and to the men to love their wives.

This love in my experience over the years can never be scaled 50/50 between the lovers at all times. Even though I can't put a figure on it, I have found out that sometimes the woman longs more for the man and at other time, the man longs more for the woman. It often seems as if God has made us in such a way that when the longing is waning in the man then it is growing in the woman and vice-versa.

This observation by experience is also typical of courtship in couples too. Either it is the man who wants to marry the woman or the woman wants to marry the man. The desire of one is always greater than the other. This does not mean that the other person is not willing; of course it takes two to tango - it takes the man and the woman to go to the altar and commit to live their lives together. But what I have experienced is that the desire to marry each other is never an equal 50/50 or 100/100.
If it's the man that wants to marry the woman, he will always go the extra mile in pleasing her and even put up with what he would naturally not tolerate or accept.

The same thing happens with the woman. If she is the one that really wants the man, she will do everything she can to please him and win him over. She will do things and tolerate things that some other time she may not be able to endure. The moment the dreams come true and they have what they wanted; it is as if a veil has been removed from their eyes. It is as if scales that once covered their eyes have been taken down. Unconsciously, if it is the woman, she will tell herself, "now you have won him you can be yourself now." This can also be said of the man, who will go to all trouble to get his woman and once that has been accomplished, he will also claim he can be himself because he has achieved what he set out to achieve, to marry this woman. This description depicts a sense of untruthfulness, that is not necessary nor healthy in building up a marriage relationship.

This is often the cause of the first conflict between newly-weds. The man who during courtship usually cooked and brings her tea before being married, but he is now telling her he can't do it and will even ask, "what's wrong with your hands and legs? Why can't you get up and do it yourself?" The woman is now perplexed and wonders, "Is this the same man that I have dated for so long, the same man who used to do this or that for me while we were dating?" It is the case that the same will be true of the woman. Things that she used to do for the man when she wanted him badly, now that she's got him, she dispenses with all that. She will argue that the man can do things for himself, she may even observe and question that, "do you think because you're married you've got a servant? No, you'd better get real. There's no servant in this house."

Moments like these are delicate and couples must understand that they may occur. Although they do not ensue often, they may, and couples should be aware of them. I call this period the period of realisation. Realisation in the sense that it is the time couples have realised their dreams and it's the time they now decide to be real to themselves. These moments call for no more hiding or pretence.

To avoid these awkward moments in marriage couples are encouraged to be real in their relationships from the start outlining whatever they would not naturally take on or accept. There is no need to bring surprises after they have made vows. I say it again that it is a shame that this happens. It shouldn't but it can. Couples must realise that after getting married, this is a period of realisation, nevertheless, with careful observation, understanding, patience and perseverance, things always work out. That said, it is better to be real from the start. We live in a fallen world and each of us is fallible but Jesus has cancelled our debt. He has forgiven us and we can also forgive one another.

Love in Action

Someone has said 'Don't tell me that you love me but show me'.

> 1 John 3:18 "My little children, let us not love in word or in tongue, but indeed and in truth." NKJV

It is easy to say "I love you" but to demonstrate the love is harder. Love is active and demonstrated in giving. `I love you, ` has become a socially desirable answer given to each other but to demonstrate it by our actions becomes difficult.

In Greek, which is the language of the New Testament, there are four words that are normally used to illustrate love.

The different kinds of love: –

1. *Agápe (ἀγάπη agápē)* means love in a "spiritual" sense. In the term 'agapo' (Σ'αγαπώ), which means "I love you" in Ancient Greek, it often refers to a general affection or deeper sense of "true unconditional love" rather than the attraction suggested by "eros." This love is selfless; it gives and expects nothing in return. Agape is used in the biblical passage known as the "love chapter," 1 Corinthians 13, and is described there and throughout the New Testament as sacrificial and spiritual love. Whether the love given is returned or not, the person continues to love (even without any self-benefit). Agape is also used in ancient texts to denote feelings for one's children and the feelings for a spouse, and it was also used to refer to a love feast. It can also be described as the feeling of being content or holding one in high regard. Agape is used by Christians to express the unconditional love of God.

2. *Éros (ἔρως érōs)* is "physical" passionate love, with sensual desire and longing. It is romantic, pure emotion without the balance of logic. "Love at first sight". The Modern Greek word "erotas" means "intimate love;" however, eros does not have to be sexual in nature. Eros can be interpreted as a love for someone whom you love more than the philia [love of friendship]. It can also apply to dating relationships as well as marriage. Although eros is initially felt for a person, with contemplation it becomes an appreciation of the beauty within that person, or even becomes an appreciation of beauty itself.

3. Philia/Phileo (φιλία philía) is "mental" love. In both ancient and modern Greek it means affectionate regard or friendship. This type of love is give and take. It is a dispassionate virtuous love, a concept developed by Aristotle. It includes loyalty to friends, family, and community, and requires virtue, equality and familiarity. In ancient texts, 'philos' denoted a general type of love, used for love between family, between friends, a desire or enjoyment of an activity, as well as between lovers.

4. Storge (στοργή storgē) means "affection" in ancient and modern Greek. It is natural affection, like that felt by parents for offspring. Rarely used in ancient works, and then almost exclusively as a description of relationships within the family. It is also known to express mere acceptance or putting up with situations, as in "loving" the tyrant[16].

All the four categories of Greek love should be present in every home. The unconditional love (agape) must dominate and permeate everyone, while allowing affectionate, sexual, brotherly and parental love to be present in every home.

Expressions of love:

How should you express love?

In Words:

---

[16] Henry George Liddell, Robert Scott, A Greek-English Lexicon, on Perseus in http://en.wikipedia.org/wiki/Greek_words_for_love

Words are powerful and can destroy or build relationships.

Proverbs 18:21 says "Death and life are in the power of the tongue and those who love it will eat its fruit." NKJV

From this text one can see how powerful words are and whichever way words are used you will eat their fruits. If you use words to build your spouse, you will eat the fruit of a solid and wonderful home and if you use them to destroy your spouse, you will eat the fruit of destruction. All of the wars ever fought in the human race start from words. Any peace that has ever been achieved was through words as well. Words form the core value of communication.

The Bible encourages us to let our words be seasoned in:

Colossians 4:6 "Let your speech always be with grace, seasoned with salt, that you may know how you ought to answer each one. NKJV

Paul encouraged his readers to let their speech or words always be with grace which is an unmerited favour. In other words, let your words administer favour to the other person even if they do not deserve it. I remember a conversation with a fellow minister about a misunderstanding. I said to him that I was sorry that I didn't understand what he had said and to my surprise, he replied, "Adedayo, it was I, that was clumsy with words and did not explain myself clearly". That is humility and love and this I believe is the way forward for couples in dealing graciously with each other.

Paul the apostle believed that our words should be seasoned with salt. In order to understand this better, let us look at some of the uses and the qualities of salt and how we can apply this into our relationships. Salt in one way is used as a preservative agent. That means it is used to preserve some other foods from going bad. So Paul is advising us to use our words to preserve our relationships. While this is applicable to a couple it is also applicable to any relationship, at work, in the Church and anywhere. You can use your words to preserve the dignity and integrity of the person you are in relationship with therefore strengthening and preserving that relationship in the home and outside of the home.

Salt is also used for seasoning food. Too much of it is unsafe and harmful, but a right amount makes food tasty. So used wisely, words are seasoning element to the life of your spouse, build them up with your words and do not tear them down. Conversely, do not patronise your spouse instead say what you mean and mean what you say in the nicest possible and genuine way. Let him/her feel good about the words you speak to them. Telling your spouse, you love him/her is powerful and triggers positive emotion and romance and he/she will want to hear it more often.

But don't say what you don't mean. Whatever you want to say, first ensure that it will bless and build him/her, add value to his/her life and will honour and glorify God. Let your words tickle your spouse` ears. If you practice this on a daily basis, you will enjoy each other's relationship. Proverbs 18:21 says:

> "You are snared by the words of your mouth; you are taken by the words of your mouth." Proverbs 6:2 NKJV
> "Death and life are in the power of the tongue and those who love it will eat its fruit" NKJV

The above scripture is the opposite of what I have just encouraged you to practice. Don't behave like the above examples and trap your spouse and yourself into unnecessary hardships and trouble with careless and unthoughtful words. Harsh words will always attract harsh words in return.

Remember that your words are the windows into your heart. Words reveals who you really are and what you are capable of. So be careful of what you think because it soon becomes words, and be careful of what you say it may soon become an action, and be careful of what you do it'll soon become a habit and the habit will lead to a destination. Your word will exonerate or convicts you.

In Actions:

You have heard that actions speak louder than words. Practise this in your marriage. Yes, I have advised couples to tell their spouses that they love them and I am now encouraging as well as to move a step further. Let their words be translated into actions. What actions ought you to take in showing your spouse that you love them?

> 1 Corinthians 13:4-13 sums it up and I would not add more.
> "Love suffers long and is kind;
> love does not envy;
> love does not parade itself,
> is not puffed up;
> does not behave rudely,
> does not seek its own,
> is not provoked,
> thinks no evil;

> does not rejoice in iniquity,
> but rejoices in the truth;
> bears all things,
> believes all things,
> hopes all things,
> endures all things.
> Love never fails... "

What love does is clear and unambiguous. There is no need of much explanation and I encourage couples to do what this passage says. You can't fail if you both stick by love, because love never fails. Every other thing in life can and will fail but not Love.

In Time:

R.T Kendall in his 'In pursuit of His glory'[17] says children and women understand love the same way, and this is the way - T-I-M-E. Most men think that bringing huge amount of money home will satisfy their wives and children but they often make a mistake. An average woman will want to have quality time with her husband. She would prefer him to be there so that she can talk and share her experiences at her place of work with him. She would like to tell him what somebody told her that she finds strange and she wants to get his opinion about what her colleague said. Not only that, she wants to share from his own experience at work as well. She wants him to know what's going on in the family and if they have got children, she wants to tell him what the teacher said

---

[17] R.T. Kendall 'In pursuit of His glory' 2002, Hodder & Stoughton, London.

about their daughter or son. Money is essential but it is not everything, listen to this.

My experience as a school governor for about 7 years brought me an experience that really made me to appreciate children more and changed my attitude towards my own children, even though they are now grown.

In one of the parents' evenings, a father came to see his daughter's work. One of the pictures she drew was of her family, which showed only her mother, brother and herself. The father asked her, where he was in the family picture she drew. She responded, "You are never there". We found out that the man was working so hard for the family to be comfortable. He truly was delivering that, they never lacked anything. They had the latest gadgets and toys in town. They ate out whenever they wanted to without problems. But to the girl, it wasn't all about money; it was about being there at home with them. It was about him being there so she can play with him. That's food for thought, isn't it? That single meeting changed my attitude to my family and I pray it will do the same to you.

Being there for your wife and children is important and I encourage husbands and fathers to do their very best for their families. Obviously, there may be situations where your best does not seem to be enough. You may have done your best and you wonder, "What else can I do, how else could I have done it for her to be satisfied?" I will encourage you to examine yourself and see if you have done your best and if you have and your conscience is true and free you will always enjoy God's peace. So you would not be disappointed and get frustrated. But if you find out that you have not done enough, improve the situation and God will help you. R.T Kendall made the following anecdote in his retirement, if he could wind the clock back, he would devote more time to his family[18] (wife and children). I am reiterating this to men, spend time with your wife and children. You will never get the time back and you can't buy back it.

In Presents/Gifts:

I have said that love is giving and is active. You can't say you love someone if your wallet is tight for them. On their birthdays, your anniversary, on occasions like Christmas, Easter, Mothers' Day and Fathers' Day your love should be shown through the gifts you give. It is not how much you spend that matters but the thought and gesture behind it. You should not get into debt because you want to give gifts. Unless you are able to manage your credit card well without incurring interests I would discourage you from the habit of using it. It is essential to know the size of your spouse's shoes, blouse, shirt, chest and waist, trouser length, his or her choice of colours and other biometric data because these will help you buy an appropriate gift. Here is a trick. If you see something you really appreciate in the market or shop or owned by other people, if you can afford it get it for them too.

A friend of mine saw some very nice shoes the other day and bought them for his wife. Because he knows her foot size and her taste in shoes, it was a perfect gift. She

---

[18]R.T. Kendall 'In pursuit of His glory' 2002, Hodder & Stoughton, London. pg 265-7

cherished those shoes so much that she only wears them to big occasions. On most of the occasions she wears those shoes people always compliment her and some want to know where she bought them. Of course, with pride and a beaming smile she will say "My husband bought them for me." How do you think the husband would feel on hearing that? My advice to you is to do likewise for your loved one.

In Touch: Tactile Communication

Touch is the first sense we acquire and the secret weapon in many a successful relationship. Here's how to regain fluency in your first language. In 'the power of touch' by Rick Chillot, published on March 11, 2013 - last reviewed on March 15, 2013[19], we are introduced to the fluency of first language of love. The idea that people can impart and interpret emotional content by a nonverbal modality—touch—seemed iffy even to researchers such as psychologist Matthew Herterhen of DePauw University. Herterhen studied tactile communications in 2009 and demonstrated that we have an innate ability to decode emotions via touch alone in a series of studies.[20]

In my life I have experienced the power of tactile communication in my own relationship. My wife loves travelling but she is aeroplane phobic, so whenever we travel together (and most often we do) she always holds my hand for comfort, assurance and support that she is not alone and I am with her. Whenever we travel in our car, from time to time she will hold my idle hand (which is

---

[19] http://www.psychologytoday.com/articles/201302/the-power-touch
[20] Ditto

always the left one in the UK as we have an automatic car) to give me a boost and encouragement and to keep me awake.

On most occasions, sitting down together holding each other's hands and cuddling each other sends a powerful message of love to each other. So make it a habit and practice it. This is especially to the men; your wife will always have something to do at home, sorting out this and that, tidying this room and that cupboard. You have to consciously create a time for her to stop and let you have time together. Hold each other, talk about things, dreams and laugh together because laughing is therapeutic. When you touch your spouse you pass important and emotional messages to them and it is likely to attract a positive response unless your gesture is misunderstood or your spouse is going through some rough patch for which they want to be left alone for that moment. The touch I am talking about is not only about making love (sex). It is for assurance, confidence, comforting, consoling and all sorts of other emotional feelings. It is good to touch because touching passes stronger emotional messages than words alone can. Touch can heal, comfort, console, show solidarity and reconciliation.

CHAPTER FIVE

MAKING LOVE (SEX).

Gone are the days when the issue of sex was a secret and not spoken of in public. It has now come really into the open and in fact, things have gone to the opposite extreme so that now nothing sells without sex. Whilst making love is extremely important and indeed crucial to marriage, marriage is much more than making love.
God created sex, and everything He has created is very good. So, sex is very good, exciting, enjoyable and sweet. Genesis 1:31

> "Then God saw everything that He had made, and indeed it was very good. So the evening and the morning were the sixth day." NKJV

Why did God create sex?
We can draw out two purposes from the Bible.

1. God created sex for procreation.

The scripture states the first reason for sex in Genesis 1:22.

> "And God blessed them, saying, "Be fruitful and multiply, and fill the waters in the seas, and let birds multiply on the earth." NKJV

It was not beyond God to create the entire population of the world all at once. Nonetheless, in His Wisdom He decided that procreation was the way forward to replenish humanity with many generations living together. So every married couple wanting to have children is doing God's will and He will always bless them. But God is also happy with those who can't or choose not to have children.

Until recently the only way to have children was through having sexual intercourse with the opposite sex. However, nowadays with medical advances that include artificial insemination, IVF and other techniques have made having children possible without sex. So if you want to have children and multiply your family and generations, and there are no contradictory conditions, making love is the way forward. God has created the woman to receive the man's sperm to fertilise the egg in her womb, and for the woman to nurture the embryo to term and then to deliver the baby.

For me this is one of the most wonderful miracles apart from the salvation of our souls through faith in Jesus Christ that God is performing daily for His creation. God did not limit procreation to human beings, He created it for every creature He made so it should be celebrated and enjoyed.

2. God created sex for our enjoyment.

Making love is intimate, exciting and sweet and should be enjoyed by both parties. Proverbs 5:18-19 and 1 Corinthians 7:1-5 confirm this and there are other references as in the Song of Solomon and you are encouraged to read it.
Solomon advised people in Proverbs 5:18-19:
> "Let your fountain be blessed, and rejoice with the wife of your youth. As a loving deer and a graceful doe, let her breasts satisfy you at all times; and always be enraptured with her love." NKJV

Solomon knew what making love was about and it was from his experience he wrote the text above. So enjoy each other to the full and make love with each other anytime that is convenient for both. The Corinthian Church wrote to Paul asking him questions about sex and expected answers. Paul, an unmarried man, moved by the Holy Spirit gave the answer quoted below.

> "Now concerning the things of which you wrote to me:
> It is good for a man not to touch a woman. Nevertheless, because of sexual immorality, let each man have his own wife, and let each woman have her own husband. Let the husband render to his wife the affection due her, and likewise also the wife to her husband. The wife does not have authority over her own body, but the husband does. And likewise the husband does not have authority over his own body, but the wife does. Do not deprive one another except with consent for a time that you may give yourselves to fasting and prayer; and come together again so that Satan does not tempt you because of your lack of self-control". NKJV

In this passage, making love is firmly put at the centre of marriage. There is no limit to how many times or how long you can do it. Paul says that a woman is not in control over her body but her husband is. This in my understanding is that when the man wants sex, the woman should consent. The same goes for the woman, if she wants sex, her husband should consent and not refuse.

Having said this, couples must be sensitive to know that there may be times when the other person will not be in the mood of having sex. There may be many reasons for this and therefore care must be taken to understand why it is not possible to have sex whenever you want it. By understanding this, you will attend to each other's needs by not forcing it on them. Even when the other person is in the mood, there must be negotiations, and nudging each other and therefore setting each other up for the great sex. In this way couples maximise the time and enjoy sex fully.

Denying each other sex is neither healthy nor helpful. It drifts couples apart and strains relationships. This is not to say that the man or woman has to be autocratic about making love and uses his wife or her husband as a machine. There must be some understanding, negotiation and consensus about making love. Genuinely one of you may be tired that making love is the last thing you want. At such times, the other person must understand and show empathy by putting himself/herself in the spouse's situation. On such occasions physical intimacy without full intercourse may serve both parties' needs. I am sure as couples move along in their relationships; they will work things out better than I have put in this book.

In the Bible, it is clear that, when you want to address something important in prayer this may involve fasting. Should this be the case, then couples in agreement could abstain from sex. Paul warned this should not be prolonged so that Satan can capitalise on it to tempt one or both to sin. In my opinion it is better for couples to observe fasting and prayer together; this way agreeing together will not be difficult. But if it is only one person who wants to fast, he/she must tell the spouse and get agreement to do so. It should not be a unilateral decision because the agreement of two is powerful and effectual and God will honour it. Matthew 18:18-20 says:

"Assuredly, I say to you, whatever you bind on earth will be bound in heaven, and whatever you loose on earth will be loosed in heaven. "Again I say to you that if two of you agree on earth concerning anything that they ask, it will be done for them by My Father in heaven. For where two or three are gathered together in My name, I am there in the midst of them." NKJV

Both of you agreeing to fast and pray is powerful and will bring unprecedented results.

Making love is not a punishment or reward exercise

Making love or having sex must neither be used as **a punishment nor as a reward.** It should be an obligation and commitment that couples in the relationship must perform. Each person in the relationship must willingly and gladly seek to satisfy the other sexually. I am thinking in this regard particularly of women whom from experience, I have found out that more often than not see and treat making love as a reward when their husbands do well and satisfy them in other areas; or use sex as a punishment when they are unhappy with their husbands for whatever reason. It appears women understand that they have the power to accept sex or deny it and they know that majority of men like and enjoy having sex, so they exploit that situation to the maximum to punish their husbands.

This is wrong, and for the men that are weak in that aspect of life, their wives refusing them sex, can become a perfect reason to go for sex outside the married relationship. Although a wife's denial of sex should not be used as an excuse for men to go for sex elsewhere. They should talk things through lovingly so the issue can be resolved. Two wrongs can never make a right. Men are not animals without control, denial by their wives should be a motivation to learn how to control themselves in this regards.

Whether their husbands do well or not, in good times or bad, women should not deny them sex. The couples have read the scripture above where God has made the guidelines clear and that making a covenant in their marriage vows that "with my body I honour you; I will know no other man/woman etc.". This is a serious business and God will hold both accountable for whatever choice they make regarding this vow. Making love is one of the most important reasons why people and especially men, marry. If that is the case, refusing what is legitimately his or hers without good reasons is a sin and a breach to the marriage vows and it is very serious. Couples can't allow their emotions to drive a wedge between them and to ruin the relationship that God has given them to enjoy. Unfortunately, denying husbands sex forms a significant part of the mediations I have done between couples over the years and it is not only limited to how long they have been married. It happens with newly married and to old married couples as well. Most of the times, it is when the woman is not happy with her husband.

I can hear someone say "it's only when I am happy that I can make love". This may be true, if that is your view it makes your view of marriage conditional and it shows that you have not taken your vows seriously. It is no more "for better, for worse; for richer, for poorer; in sickness and in health". Think about it.

Having said that, women must not be seen and treated as sex objects. They are not robots or dummies, so men must not just expect them to respond automatically whenever they want to have sex. There must be negotiation, preparation, dropping the hints, paving the way, and stimulating her towards agreeing to the proposal. Therefore, women must be respected, loved, cuddled and cherished.

In no way am I saying that only women use sex as a punishment or a reward; men also use it and that is not right either. I remember a woman who in one of our telephone conversations told me that it was about 15 months since her husband had slept with her. That was a very difficult thing to say and especially for a woman, and it shows how much she had missed the intimacy, love and enjoyment that comes from making love. Denial leads to feelings of being un-wanted, rejection, being despised and filthy. Do not allow your marriage to be like that; allow each other the request. Making love is sweet, enjoyable and romantic. Sex is therapeutic as it heals the wounds of quarrels, it also heals the pains in the heart, and it makes you feel wanted, appreciated and loved. It is also a tension manager. This life is stressful enough and the world is treacherous. When you are stressed at work or outside and the wind of treachery blows at you, home is a place you find stress relievers, and sex is one of them.

Keep up your physical attraction

Something that will keep your desire for each other going stronger is your physical appearances. Before you marry, both of you take great care especially the women to look good, to look sharp and stunning. Physical attraction is one of the reasons why people marry. After marriage and children, nothing should take that physical attraction away. Take time to look good to your spouse. You may argue but Apostle Peter advised us differently by saying:

"Do not let your adornment be merely outward - arraigning the hair, wearing gold, or putting on fine apparel - rather let it be the hidden person of the heart, with the incorruptible beauty of a gentle and quiet spirit, which is very precious in the sight of God." 1 Peter 3:3-4 NKJV

I want to clarify the issue and the key word to look for is `merely` which means `only, just, purely, simply, solely, entirely`. My understanding of this passage is that; Peter admonishes women not to concentrate on making themselves beautiful on the outside alone but also on the inside. Their character must be beautiful; their hearts must be pure, Peter is not in any way discouraging them from being physically attractive.

It is unfortunate that some Christians have mis-interpreted this passage and do not use make-ups anymore. If the Holy Spirit convinces you not to use make-up anymore that is fair enough and good for you too. But if your husband's resentment and complaint is borne out of you not looking good any more than you used to, then that is something you have to think seriously about and address to prevent calamity. You are to please your spouse and not any other human being. The Scripture is clear and most women in the scripture were so beautiful even in appearance as well as inside and that is what God is calling wives -women to do but not to overdo the outward beauty over the inner beauty.

Who initiates sex?

Since men are mostly the main initiators of sex, women must not see them as sex machines or think that they must be promiscuous or that this is how they behave to and with other women. This would be a great error. He loves you and wants you to himself all the time. Marrying you is a permission for him to gratify his sexual desire in a legitimate way and that is pleasing to God and enables both of you to truly become one flesh. Rejecting him means he's not wanted, not valued and it is disrespectful to him. Men can be very emotionally upset about this, so please bear that in mind.

Times have changed, however and nowadays women too propose sex to their husbands and there is nothing wrong in that. It should be welcome. After all, they are created with sexual appetite and there is nothing wrong in seeking to satisfy that appetite in a legitimate way. If a woman complains of sexual starvation, it is a sign of gross neglect on the part of the man and it should never happen. If a woman makes observations to this effect *"I don't even know the type of sleep, he sleeps"* or *"Why are you always tired?"* These are warning signs and very serious ones too. It is an indirect way of complaining that her husband is neglecting her. Instead of allowing such complaints to arise, men must ensure that they fulfil their obligations to satisfy their wives sexually. When men deprive their wives the intimacy of love (sex) it could be due to one or several of reasons.

For example, if the man is unhappy with the woman for whatever reason, he may feel emotionally detached from her and the urge for sex may not be there forcing him keep away. This is a dangerous state to be in, where men become vulnerable to be tempted sexually. Satan is good at this and that is when he may set up another woman at work who is unusually caring and goes the extra mile in doing things. You must not yield to that temptation because yielding is sinful and may break your wife`s heart. You must not do that on any account. Whether you are happy with her or not, whether she is good to you or not, making love with her is not an option but an obligation at a mutually acceptable time.

It may also be that she is not so appealing to the man anymore through neglect of her body. Whilst they were courting, she always looked stunning, but now that she is married she pays less attention to looking good. Maybe, for some religious reason she does not use make-up anymore, so she is not as attractive as she used to be. I have discussed this earlier, I encourage women to look into this and make the decision and effort to continually look the best they can.

From experience as a married man, a pastor and a person experienced in relationship mediation, during the years of procreation, when couples (and especially the woman wants children), making love is easy. Even when the man does not want sex she will motivate and arouse him and do everything womanly to lead him to it.

But when the desire to have children is gone, either because they have had the number of children they want or by nature children are not coming anymore then making love becomes an issue with some women creating tension in relationships. This should not be so. Couples must always see themselves as they saw each other when they were young. Even though strength may be diminishing, make love as far as your strength allows.

I am not saying this to portray women as being bad and unreasonable. Nevertheless, what I have said is often true and I believe that it may be due to their hormonal changes, especially in their late forties when they start getting to menopause.

Menopause is simply a circle of life advanced by hormonal changes in a woman's body and therefore affects women's attitude and behaviour as the article below states:

> "The loss of oestrogen and testosterone following menopause can lead to changes in a woman's sexual drive and functioning. Menopausal and postmenopausal women may notice that they are not as easily aroused, and may be less sensitive to touching and stroking -- which can result in decreased interest in sex".[21]

If it comes to this, men should be understanding and bear with women. However, come what may, even at those periods (which are challenging) there is always a way round to keep making love alive and at the centre of your relationship and to satisfy each other sexually. As you journey together in your marriage, you will discover new

---

[21] http://www.webmd.com/menopause/guide/sex-menopause

ways of making love and stick to the ones that you both love and enjoy.

Besides menopause, it may also be that the woman does not want sex, due to the fact that her attention shifts from her husbands to their children. Whatever reasons are advanced, I want to say to women that you knew your husband before the children came and it's him you will be left with after the children have left home. The two of you started the home and you should plan to finish it together, so let nothing put a wedge between your romantic lives.

Do not wear him out

I must let women know that a lot of energy is required by men and women to have sexual intercourse. Men are different from women because without erection of the male organ the man cannot perform sexual intercourse. If he has spent considerable energy in persuading the woman and expressing his interest and the woman is reluctant for most of the time and only to agree to it later, the couple are unlikely to enjoy the sex. The man is likely to have premature ejaculation and that is likely to frustrate the woman who may not to have sex next time. It also frustrates the man because he too will not enjoy it.
Because of prolonged persuasion the man is likely to lose the turgidity of the male organ so that only a remnant of it is left and that is often what leads to premature ejaculation.

This is my suggestion for couples if they found themselves in this situation. If the woman does not want sex at a point in time, she should explain it to the man with empathy and persuasion in a loving manner and probably arrange it for another time. But please keep the promise. The man will always look forward to the promise and another denial can be devastating and cause him to be very unhappy. So since sex is one of the major reason why the couples marry, it is good and right for them to realise and accept that when the man wants it the woman should not wear his energy out only to agree when he is tired.

Sex during pregnancy

Sex during pregnancy is normal and nothing is wrong with having sex during this time provided it is convenient for the woman. What is important is the convenience of the woman and at this time the man must be understanding. I am sure couples will always work things out during this period to ensure that no one is neglected. Couples may want to improvise different sexual positions easier for them in the later stages of pregnancy.

Sex during menstruation

Sex during the monthly period is in my own opinion messy and unhealthy and even the Scripture prohibits it Leviticus 20:13. It may cause the woman to bleed more so making love is not good at this time.

Other ways of sexual intercourse

Let me say something about modern derivatives of sexual intercourse, like penetrative oral sex and particularly penile-anal sex. Non-penetrative sex acts, such as non-penetrative forms of cunnilingus or mutual masturbation, have been termed outer-course. I consider all these as aberration in sexual intercourse. And as Christians I think we should not engage in them.

CHAPTER SIX

CONFLICT - A TOOL TO GROW OR TO SPLIT?

Marriage is a life-long journey and it takes love, grace, endurance, perseverance and forgiveness to carry on. Just as I have quoted in chapter 1 the scripture below,
> Deuteronomy 11:11 "but the land which you cross over to possess is a land of hills and valleys, which drinks water from the rain of heaven", NKJV

Marriage life will have its ups (hills) and downs (valleys). I compare marriage to two stones at the source of a river. They are sharp and rough at the edges. But as they are driven along the river bed they rub each other along the way the smoother and less sharp they become. Their beauty begins to show through to their destination at the sea shore where you pick them up rounded, shining and beautiful and they find themselves in your home as ornaments and decoration. See the pictures below.

Rough and sharp edged stones   Smooth, rounded and beautiful stones

Before you pick them up, a lot of work has been put into them. In the same way couples will need to put in a lot of work to deal with the rough and sharp edges of their marriage. These rough and sharp edges that causes conflict are inevitable occurrences in any new relationship.

The online Oxford English Dictionary defines conflict as *"a serious incompatibility between two or more opinions, principles, or interests."*[22]

Even though there are many more definitions of conflict, I prefer this one because it is impersonal and that is the key message I want to pass on in this chapter. Whenever there is disagreement of opinions, the approach should be to talk about the issue and not the other person.

TWO VIEWS OF CONFLICT

1. Conflict is destructive, so avoid it.

Some people consider conflict a bad thing that should not happen because it is a sign that people are not getting on. People avoid conflict by piling things up, sweeping things under the carpet or bottling things up inside. When things reach the climax, however, such people suddenly explode and become unmanageable and unhealthy and will probably ruin the relationship. If you see conflict as an unhealthy thing and you try to avoid it instead of confronting it, you are unlikely to develop well emotionally. You will always want things your way, (which you are unlikely to get) so you abandon the present relationship and go from one relationship to another. When will it stop?

---

[22] http://www.oxforddictionaries.com/definition/english/conflict

Such people are unable to hold down their jobs, they are unable to settle in a relationship and they are always running away. The question is 'How long are you going to act this way?' It's like when you put some wood on the fire to cook your meal. You realise that one of the pieces of wood is smoking so you pull it out. Soon you realise the second, the third, fourth and the rest are making smoke and then when you remove every piece of wood that creates smoke there would be nothing left to cook your meal. In a nutshell, what I am saying is that we all 'make smoke' and if we run away from each other there will be no one left to befriend and live with. I would not think you will be able to live with yourself either. I want you to stop and think about this.

2. Conflict makes us grow. Manage it well.

Others see conflict as a means to grow (if managed well). You will grow, develop and you will be maturing. Conflict is not necessarily bad but the way it is managed, is of the utmost importance and will determine the outcome. Because people see, say and do things differently, we are bound to be in conflict with their opinions. Therefore, responses to correction or criticism depends on how we see it. There is nothing wrong in being corrected or criticized if the reasons, motives and the gestures behind it are right. If people say to you "this is not good", they should be able to offer a better alternative; if not, then that correction or criticism is both ineffective and not useful. This is also applicable to you. It would be wrong to condemn or criticize something if you do not have a better alternative. If you have no better alternative, hold your peace and work at it until you find a solution you can put forward to work with.

This is how I try to handle correction or criticisms. I believe that everyone has good intentions for me and I see their correction and criticism as genuine and that it may be for my growth. I would like to take criticism with better alternatives if it resonates with my spirit. That is, if the Holy Spirit who lives in me witnesses to what they are saying I'll take it; if not, I discard it. However, if they criticise me and are unable to offer a better alternative, I ask them to hold their peace until they provide me with what an improvement would be. We must love correction and accept criticism readily unless it is unhelpful. The Word of God says it better than I can, and this is what it says in,

Proverbs 12:1 "Whoever loves instruction loves knowledge, but he who hates correction is stupid." NKJV

There are bound to be differences in opinion and how couples talk and express themselves. This is so because a marriage relationship brings together people different from each other. Couples will have been born and raised in different homes, towns and probably countries, there are bound to be differences that are likely to result into tension. So, conflict is unavoidable in marriage just as it is in life generally. Couples have to accept this fact and find ways of resolving it to promote growth.

Proverbs 15:1 states "A gentle answer turns away wrath, but harsh words stir up anger."

This is the most profound statement about conflict by the wisest person who ever lived King Solomon. I too have found that speaking softly and lovingly gets the attention of the other person much better than shouting, being confrontational and aggressive, these tend to put the other person into a defensive position. Take for example in my house; I went to the kitchen to prepare some food for both of us (my wife and I) and I forgot to put a can opener back in the place I took it from. Listen to what I heard – "Daddy, where did you take this from?" The voice was so soft and the gesture did not suggest force but a willingness to help put it back. You can guess what my reaction was. I commended her for the way she had spoken. It was so powerful and it compelled me to do the right thing and put the article back in the right place. It was never my intention not to put it back but I just forgot. Your spouse will just forget to do and say things; it's not the end of the world. We all humans are full of imperfections, but when we communicate in a less threatening, gentle and loving way things get sorted out. And for couples, you will realise that after talking about a serious matter; it will always end in hugging, kissing and even making love.

It seems the cause of the first set of conflicts for newly married couples is when one or both of them take off their masks. As I said in lesson four of this book, the desire to marry each other is never 50/50. If it's the woman who wants to marry the man she will do, give and tolerate what she would not normally do to get the man she wants and longs for. And if it's the man that wants to marry the woman, he will do and tolerate things he would not ordinarily do or tolerate because he wants the woman badly. Therefore, he will leave no stone unturned to get her. But the moment the familiar statement at the wedding 'with this ring, I do wed thee' is over; the mask they have worn even for years unconsciously will be removed. That is when Satan will come and tell you, "You have now got what you wanted; there is no need to pretend anymore so be real and come out of your shell now."

This of course will be a total surprise and shock to the other person in this relationship. Then Grace (not real name) will be asking herself "How is it that Tom has changed the way he used to act and behave before we got married? Or, Tom (not real name) will be asking himself - and if he is courageous he will ask Grace – how come you have changed, you don't act and behave any more the way you used to before we got married? During this phase each spouse sees the other person as unreasonable because they are expected to continue to do the things which they did before marriage.

This is the time couples should stop to examine themselves. In what way have they been faking relationship, it is better that masks are removed. Let your fiancé know who you are, say what you mean and mean what you say. Be who you really are and there is no need to wear any mask.

When couples remove the masks, this is the moment of realisation. The relationship will still work if they start all over again to get to know each other and adjust to one another. I would not think that wearing the mask was deliberate or done with a bad intention. However, because we generally do not want NO for an answer, especially from the one we would like to marry, we will go all the way to get a good and positive response from them.

Some of the other things that causes conflict could be so minute as the way a tooth-paste tube is squeezed, how the bath towel is hung and all those small things that we have magnified to be huge issues. The sky will not fall if things are not done in our way. You are not losing anything if the toothpaste is squeezed from the bottom or in the middle. It's all down the way you perceive and process it.

RESOLVING THE CONFLICTS

1. Accepting your differences:

The first thing you have to do in resolving your conflict is to accept your differences. You are different from your spouse. You have to accept that you are two different people from different backgrounds, cultures, and experiences. Even though God says you will no longer be two but one flesh, you have to work at becoming the one flesh God intends for you. One flesh is God's goal and intention for you. It is where He is taking you both to and it will take a while and much effort to get there. Your commitment and co-operation with each other will help you resolve conflict quickly.

Accepting each other's differences is not a licence for bad behaviour. Your differences need to be brought into focus and discussed amicably in an atmosphere of respect to each other as you iron them out. Remember, children don't marry but only the grown-ups, so I urge you to grow up in the way you think, say and do things. Ephesians 4:14-15 states:

> "that we should no longer be children, tossed to and fro and carried about with every wind of

doctrine, by the trickery of men, in the cunning craftiness of deceitful plotting but speaking the truth in love, may grow up in all things into Him who is the head - Christ." NKJV

Even though the above passage is about our faith in Jesus Christ, I believe we can apply it into relationship between spouses, friends and the church. We should grow up and matures in dealing with our differences.

2. You can't change your spouse:

The second thing you must do is to accept that you cannot change your spouse. Nobody can change the other person. It is only God and your spouse that can effect any change in themselves. To think that you can change your spouse is a fruitless exercise and not worth embarking on. This is not to say that you should not correct each other when you notice an error or mistake. In fact, correction in a relationship is love, that is true, when you correct your spouse in love and tell the truth in love. This shows that you love them and you want them to grow and be made better. This is in line with scripture.

And when your spouse tries to correct you, don't see it as if they are discrediting you or putting you down. Rather, see it as a way of improving you and making your life better. This is the time when we rub off each other's rough and sharp edges as I said about the stones from the source of the river. The more you correct and encourage each other in love, the better both of you are becoming and the more attractive you are in character. This will radiate out to the people around you. In fact, spouse is your mirror. If your spouse can't tell you the truth no one else will. If you can't accept the truth from your spouse, neither will you accept truth from elsewhere.

And you know what, the truth is the truth, either said by your friend or your foe. If it by your friends, you may acknowledge him and say, 'friend you are telling the truth.' But if it is said by your foe or the person you don't agree with, after he had left and you don't catch a glimpse of him then you concur and say 'stupid person but he's telling the truth'.

So I encourage you to take criticism from your spouse it is intended for your good and not harm you.

Something I have experienced is that people do not value the advice or correction from their spouses because they don't value them. They are too close, too familiar and that of course, brings contempt. However, when they hear it from outside, they take it and make it as if it is something new. They will always forget that their spouse already told them the same thing. Should you find yourself in this position, I advise you never to say to your spouse "haven't I told you that before?" Instead, you may say "Really!" if you must say something and let them save face.

3. Focus only on the issue and not the person:

The third thing to do in resolving conflict is to focus on the issue and not the person. If your spouse says or does something you consider bad, you may say 'what you have said or done is bad' instead of saying 'you are bad'. You may say 'that is a wicked statement' instead of saying 'you are wicked'; you can say that 'this is a selfish attitude' instead of saying that 'you are selfish'. You can say that 'that is not true or correct' rather than saying 'you're lying or a liar'. Talk about the issue and do not label the person. The difference between the two types of statement is that one deals with the issue and the other labels the person.

When you attack or label the person and not the issue, there is a tendency for the person to want to defend him/herself. They will usually not allow you to talk, become aggressive towards you; if not become defensive by giving excuses and rationalising their behaviour. This is usually counter-productive and unhelpful. Nonetheless if you let them see the issue, they will be more at ease and are likely to listen and adjust their behaviour or change their language. Take the example I gave above when my wife asked me about the item in the kitchen. If she had said in an aggressive manner 'you never put things back from where you take them'. I could have responded back with a high tone or a defensive manner, 'I have not finished and please get off my back'. This of course would have upset her and the quarrel escalated.

4. A win-win situation:

The fourth feature of conflict I want you to see and practice is to see it as a win-win situation.
Most people take conflict whether at home, work and anywhere else as a win-lose situation. A state developed from childhood when siblings rival each other. It is reinforced at school where they compete with each other and as adults at work where people are constantly proving themselves to be better than the other person. It

is hard to switch off from this socialised habit into something new and neutral.

This attitude of a win-lose situation is what some people take into marriage. Every time there is a conflict, they flex their muscles, argue at the top of their voices, not giving a chance to the other person to talk or explain themselves out. They behave ferociously as one who wants to devour their spouse. Human beings have more sense than other animals. Therefore, whenever you are in conflict, you must apply decency, calmness and sensibility to what you say and do. Respect deserves respect, if you give it you get it back.

Seeing and treating conflict as a 'win-lose' situation pulls relationships apart, creates more tension and discord. Instead of helping it makes the situation worse. People who treat conflict as win-lose situation intend on satisfying their ego, power appetite and sense of superiority. They think and feel, "I've won, he's lost" "I'm superior they are inferior" "They are less and I'm much more worth". They may win the conflict but they lose the relationship, respect and love that make the relationship work better. It is as if they are in the court of justice where a verdict has to be pronounced.

It is important to know that in a marriage relationship, you are not on a battlefield where one person has to be a winner and the other a loser. There is no point in one of you being happy and the other unhappy. What you must seek is the happiness for all.

Your view of conflict must be that of a 'win-win' situation where both of you gain and no-one loses. See conflict as a corrective and not a punitive measure and consider the advice I shared in the communication chapter. You must always think - "Will what I am going to say or do bless and build my spouse up, add value to (improve) their life, and will it honour and glorify God?" If you adopt these measures, there are chances that your conflicts will be resolved amicably and it will be a win-win situation for all of you. The following verses from the scripture say what should be taken into consideration when resolving conflicts.

Proverbs 10:12 "Hatred stirs up strife, but love covers all sins." NKJV.

Talking about your differences in love with your spouse prevents strife. Treat people as you would want to be treated.

Proverbs 17:9 "He who covers a transgression seeks love, but he who repeats a matter separates friends." NKJV

James 5:20 "Let him know that he who turns a sinner from the error of his way will save a soul from death and cover a multitude of sins." NKJV

1 Peter 4:8 "And above all things have fervent love for one another, for "love will cover a multitude of sins." NKJV

Also listen to what Paul said about conflict 1 Corinthians 6:7-8

"Now therefore, it is already an utter failure for you that you go to law against one another. Why do you not rather accept wrong? Why do you not rather let yourselves be cheated? No: you yourselves do wrong and cheat and you do these things to your brethren."

You may think it is weakness to accept wrong when you are right. But that is not true. Instead it shows you are gracious, kind and strong. Allow yourself to be cheated rather than cheating others, forgo your rights for peace and relationship. That is when God blesses you and makes you fruitful. So, you are not in competition, and do not see your conflict resolution as a win-lose situation but rather you win and they win too.

5. The Power of Forgiveness:

The fifth feature and most important in resolving conflict is the *power of forgiveness* which brings healing and restoration. Under the section about taking a long view, I discussed the fact that marriage is for life. I quoted Jesus as saying that every sin and blasphemy will be forgiven except blasphemy against the Holy Spirit. I said that my understanding of that passage is that even the sin of adultery (though very serious, unthinkable and unpleasant) can still be forgiven. If that can be forgiven, then every sin and misconduct can and should be forgiven. The 'forgiver' displays grace and mercy and they are the giver. The 'forgiven' receives grace and mercy and they are the recipient. *Life is give and take but you must learn what it takes to give*. So I encourage couples to always be forgiving to one another.

You will always step on each other's toes, learn to forgive when you are stepped on. Be a giver of forgiveness and you will always be forgiven as Jesus has commanded in:

> Matthew 6:14-15 "For if you forgive men their trespasses, your heavenly Father will also forgive you. But if you do not forgive men their trespasses,

neither will your Father forgive your trespasses". NKJV

Ephesians 4:32 "And be kind to one another, tender-hearted, forgiving one another, even as God in Christ forgave you." NKJV

Colossians 3:12-14 "Therefore, as the elect of God, holy and beloved, put on tender mercies, kindness, humility, meekness, longsuffering; bearing with one another, and forgiving one another, if anyone has a complaint against another; even as Christ forgave you, so you also must do. But above all these things put on love, which is the bond of perfection." NKJV

Forgiveness is not something you do just once or think 'how many times should I forgive?' Listen to this:

Matthew 18:21-22 "Then Peter came to Him and said, "Lord, how often shall my brother sin against me, and I forgive him? Up to seven times?" Jesus said to him, "I do not say to you, up to seven times, but up to seventy times seven." NKJV

The text above speaks about how important forgiving one another is. And where love cements a relationship, you never re-visit the past that has been dealt with; you should always talk about the present situation. If you re-visit the past it is unlikely to help especially if you have to turn the situation around. Suppose God decides to re-visit your past mistakes and sins. Would you like it? I am sure your answer will be 'no', so don't re-visit your spouse's past mistakes. Keep on forgiving no matter how many times you are offended. Forgive those who offend you until they have no choice than to change. Embarrass them with your forgiveness that they will realise that there is no other choice than to change.

People often say "Forgive and forget." I agree with the forgiveness but not with forgetting. It is impossible to forget unless you have a memory problem. It is only God that can choose not to remember (Isaiah 4:25). The natural thing is when you are offended is that you resent it and want to fight or flee. There is tension and anger inside you and you want to boycott your offender at all costs if you choose not to fight. But when you choose to forgive, you put behind what the other person has done to you, you don't allow it to hurt you anymore and you move on with life. When you remember what has been done to you and you are not angry or upset anymore, when it does not hurt you anymore, then you have truly forgiven that person. This is the level you want to be at the earliest moments you deal with the issues in your marriage relationship.

6. Resolve conflict quickly:

> Ephesians 4:26-27 says "Be angry, and do not sin, do not let the sun go down on your wrath, nor give place to the devil."

The more you prolong conflict, the more complex and difficult it becomes to resolve. The passage above should be understood literally. Practice it conscientiously and you will see that life will be easier and lighter for both of you. Sort out each day's conflict within that day. It is the best thing to do and you would not carry the baggage of one day into the other. However, there may be situations when resolving conflict immediately may not be the best option. Please give allowance to the person who is aggrieved and deal with them gently, sensitively and compassionately too. Wait for the right opportunity to come and I am sure God will always bring something quickly too. The rule I will advise is admit it when you are wrong and say sorry, but when you are right, then keep your mouth shut.

7. Praying together:

The 7th feature and very important thing to do is to be praying and studying the Bible together. When you study the word of God together as a couple and open yourselves to its teachings you will get closer and more likely to stay together. Someone has said "the family that prays together stays together" and I also say that "the couple that prays together stays together." Share each other's joys and blessings, and share your challenges too.

Paul in 2 Timothy 3:16-17 says "All Scripture is given by inspiration of God, and is profitable for doctrine, for reproof, for correction, for instruction in righteousness, that the man of God may be complete, thoroughly equipped for every good work." NKJV

Since the word of God is profitable for reproof, correction, instruction and encouragement too, be willing to accept you are wrong and apologise. More importantly, it is always good to cultivate the habit of letting your spouse save face. What do I mean by this?

When you do not say a word after you know that you are right and you do not say 'didn't I tell you?' or 'I have told you before', then you are letting them save face. The reason why you should let them save face is that the moment things go wrong, the first thing they will remember is 'that's what you said would happen'. They will regret not listening to you and wish they had done it right. Then they may think of how they would defend themselves when confronted with this. But if the confrontation does not come, you can imagine how much trouble and unpleasantness will be averted. Also because they got it wrong, they are already feeling bad, so if you are now saying "that's what I told you", you will be rubbing salt into their injuries.

We always tend to see the faults of others and never our own. But the moment we confront ourselves with our own faults, then we see less of our spouse's

8.   Make conscious efforts to change.

When people tell you that what you have said or done is wrong, most often they mean it for good. R.T. Kendall[23] in 'Total Forgiveness' has said that when two or more people are saying the same thing about you, it is probably true and it will be wise to consider what they are saying.' Most criticisms are genuine and are meant to help you. However, there is some criticism that may be malicious and unhelpful. This is my test: if they say to me that what I said is wrong and they cannot tell me how to say it right, then it is malicious. But when they offer me a better alternative to what they have criticised in me it is probably with genuine intention for good. There is also a possibility that what they consider better is not all that better, I would thank them and weigh my options.

[23] R.T. Kendall 'Total Forgiveness'

9. Engage outside help (if need be)

Some situations may be difficult for couples to handle and on their own, if you feel that it will be better to get external help there is nothing wrong in that, as long as both of you agree to and respect the person who will do the mediation work. I strongly believe that people who are experienced and are mature in their faith are always in the best position to help in mediation. The number one person on the list is your pastor or your elder (it is their responsibility to do this with and for you). It may be from your church or if you prefer, they may be from outside. To seek outside help is not a sign of weakness. Rather it is a sign of humility, but both of you must resolve to sort out your challenges between the two of you. That is more dignifying, growth promoting and satisfying and it is best if both of you can sort things out with each other. God will help you

9. Engage outside help (if need be)

CHAPTER SEVEN

THE INTERESTED PARTIES

1. Parents and Parents in-laws:

All over the world, if allowed (and they should be rightly so) parents want to be involved in the wedding of their children. I think they should be involved. But after the wedding day, they should give the newlywed couple space to enjoy themselves, to navigate their own paths of getting to know and understand each other and to understand where God is taking them. It is often the case that if the woman is very close to either of her parents and often takes advice from them, there is a tendency for her to want to go to them when something happens in her marriage. The same can be true of the man. It is as if they want to clone their parents but this will not always work, since parents are different from you. A woman's husband can never be her father nor can a man's wife be his mother. Couples should not expect spouses to be copies of their parents. A conscious effort and decision must be made **not** to go back to one's parents. 'A man will leave his father and mother and be united with his wife' should be understood literally as it will help both of you to trust one another and grow together.

Pay them occasional visits and buy them gifts on their birthdays, anniversaries and at festival periods. It is good and wise to ask your spouse how their parents want you to address them and to make conscious efforts to take that on board. This is particularly important if you marry from a different culture.   I also will encourage you not to forget your parents on both sides. They have brought you up, they have invested heavily in you and you have now grown up and are married. This is the time to pay back some of the things they have done for you. The Lord requires of you to look after your parents. Every now and then you can give them a call to see how they are doing and tell them that you are well too. If there is anything that both of you have agreed to share with them, you may and should. They want to share your joys as well as hearing of your challenges. It's their right to enjoy the fruit of their labour and all that I have suggested above. Apart from the fact that this is their right, it makes them happy and they will be proud of you. But if they begin to ask probing questions that will give away that there is a problem between you and your spouse, you have to be wise in how you answer them. If they could be helpful in resolving any issues without necessarily being seen to take sides, that will be great but, I will encourage you to consult a neutral person, your Pastor or an elder for example, or a person both of you respect and know may be helpful.

If either of you perceive that your parents are saying or doing something that your spouse may not like, it's better to put a stop to it immediately because this can ruin your relationship.

I heard a story of a couple that were newly-wed. The grandmother to the groom would ask questions about what his wife had bought for him on his birthday or festive period and she would go and buy for the man a better (an upgraded version) of the same product. This of course created tension with the man to either take his wife's gift or his grand-mother's one. The story goes further - this grandmother had ruined the marriage of her own son who is father of the groom, with the same behaviour and now she was starting on her grand-son. This type of behaviour should be stopped straight away. However, it needs wisdom, courage and prayer to be able to achieve that effectively.

I remember another story of when the mother of a man came to help her daughter-in-law at the birth of their first child. The woman cooked and set the table for her junior brother-in-law and called him that the food was ready. Before the brother-in-law came out, his mother came to the table and spitefully looked at the food as if to ask, "What is this she has given my son?"

Fortunately, the husband of the woman, the father of the new child and senior brother of the one called to the table saw what their mother was doing. Telling no- one, he went to his mother and asked her to get ready to go back home and that her husband needed her more than they did. He ensured that she never came back for whatever reason. This man has saved a lot of hassle and problems in order to preserve his marriage by sacrificing his mother's visits. As much as parents are blessings to you, you should be vigilant and be wise about how much you allow them to interfere in your affairs, if at all. You should be as gentle as a dove but as wise as a serpent.

Past baggage

By past baggage I mean previous relationships. Once you have been friends there is always the possibility that you will be friends again. So care must be taken not to allow a previous relationship or friendship to affect this wonderful new relationship which God has brought about. The previous relationships are distractions from this new one and must be ignored and discarded. This is very important especially if one or both of you have had previous relationships. It is helpful to bring this into the open and make decisions together about how both of you will deal with those relationships. Once you have left a past relationship, you have said 'goodbye'. Please let it sleep, never to wake up again. Never compare your spouse with your previous boy-friend or girl-friend. It is the most dangerous thing and its unhelpful. Be open with each another and if there must be communication with someone from a previous relationship, it must be transparent and involve your spouse.

Also 'past baggage' is not only about previous lovers; it's about previous friends, colleagues and even family members. Some people have been closely attached to these groups of people and had sought counsel and help from them and in turn gave them counsel and help. It has been a two-way thing. If these past relationships are not brought into the open and an agreement made how to deal with them, these relationships may create some uneasiness for your spouse. Care must be taken not to allow your spouse to become suspicious – give them no ground. I discussed about releasing yourselves from your parental control while dealing with them appropriately and graciously. I am now encouraging you also to release yourself from your other previous relationships.

What about previous habits? Some people carry dolls or pets and allow them to be their companions in bed. How will you deal with that when you are married? I was watching a television advertisement the other day in which this young man marries a girl with a pet dog. She treated the dog as a friend and allowed it to sleep in the same bed. It put a strain on the new relationship with the dog getting in the way when they want to be intimate. To be honest, I am not a fan of pets but I believe that an animal is an animal and must not be given equal rights and space with your spouse.

Siblings and friends: no over-crowding in the relationship

Your friends, siblings and significant others can and may constitute a crowd in your marriage if you allow them. Treat your siblings as siblings but not at the expense of your spouse. Your friends and siblings should not have preferential treatment over your spouse. Your spouse is the first of all the people in your life and every other person (no matter how close they have been to you) must come after your spouse. Your spouse is the closest person to you and your next of kin. Nonetheless, you must be careful if your spouse is trying to drive all your loved ones away by his/her behaviours and attitude. You must draw a boundary and work out what and how much space, time and money will be given to your siblings and family members

CHAPTER EIGHT:

FAMILY FINANCES

Dealing with family income and expenditure

Money is very important to sustain life. It is not everything, but certainly it is important to enable couples to live comfortably. Couples must work hard to obtain it and to manage it. Or, if only one person is working, enough must be earned to sustain the family. This is how important money is according to the scripture.

> Ecclesiastes 7:12 says "For wisdom is a defence as money is a defence, but the excellence of knowledge is that wisdom gives life to those who have it." NKJV

If you have money, you have a kind of security that assures your provision. You may not have to worry about getting things, although other anxieties and worries will emerge. Human needs are insatiable - as soon as you meet one need, another emerges and it goes on and on. It never ends.

> Solomon in Ecclesiastes 10:19 says "A feast is made for laughter, and wine makes merry; but money answers everything". NKJV

This is very close to the first text I quoted but this one has a different meaning. Even though Solomon says that money answers everything, craving for and making money a small god enslaves us and makes us sin against God. Money may buy us sleeping pills, but it cannot give us rest. It may help us buy anxiety calming medicine but it can never buy us the peace which only comes from God. Making money a god is idolatry.

> Paul in 1 Timothy 6:10 says "For the love of money is a root of all kinds of evil, for which some have strayed from the faith in their greediness, and pierced themselves through with many sorrows." NKJV

Times are changing. Some time ago, women were home-makers, producing and nurturing children. But now that family lifestyles are changing, things are different, hence one income is often not enough to meet the family's financial commitments so the woman has to work. With two incomes, things can be somehow easier and this allows the woman to contribute finances towards the family upkeep. This makes the woman view herself as an essential part to the family wellbeing, allowing a sense of 'we contributing' and not his duty or her duty to provide for the family.

In terms of spending, the rent or the mortgage will be the highest family expense followed by utility bills, i.e. electricity, gas, water and council tax. The other important expenses are food and drink. These three categories are important and they are a must. Everything else apart from these can be waived or attended to as you need them, if a couple is blessed with children then their needs become a priority.

It is believed that there are two groups of people: the spenders and the savers. In a marriage relationship, it will be advisable for the savers to be in charge of the finances. Care must be taken not to starve and deprive the family of essential needs because you want to save. You will not take money outside this world; it is meant to be spent on earth and to meet needs. However, reckless spending and lack of savings puts the family at risk because there will be a shortage at the time of need. Hence it is important to have savings to buy a house (if it is possible and they want it) and to do other things. For the spenders, even though it is good to treat the family or your spouse, you must be sensible not to spend the money that is meant for important things on items that are not important.

It is better to evaluate each other and let the better person do what they are good at.

I learnt of a family whose boiler packed up. The husband said he has no money but the wife struggled to find the money, gave it to her husband to replace the boiler. Instead, he spent the money without replacing the boiler. This is gross irresponsibility on the part who supposed to be providing for the family now becomes a squanderer.

How to deal with family income and expenditure

I have two suggestions to make in dealing with family's financial income and expenditure but you are at liberty to devise your own method.

1. Joint accounts – everything together.

When a couple's incomes are pooled together, life is much easier. It creates trust, dependence on one another and confidence in the ability of each other. The advantages of a joint account are transparency, openness, co-operation, accountability and respect for each other and joint participation in doing things. The disadvantage of this is that one person may feel that too much money is being spent on the other person`s family. Another disadvantage is a lack of freedom in wanting to do what you really want especially when the other person is not interested. Notwithstanding, all the family income is put into one pot and all the expenditure of the house in another pot and the expenditure is met from the pot with the joint income. The left-over, if any, may be put into savings or as determined by the agreement of both of you.

It is important that you don't spend all of your money, no matter how little you earn. There will always be something you can do without and not everything is a need or important. You are to attend to the needs first; then if you have savings left you may look at your wants.

The only golden rule to affluence is to spend less and save more. No matter how much you are earning, if you spend all your earnings there will be no reserve for you on a rainy day. Therefore, you must balance this because there is no need to starve yourselves to malnutrition in order to have savings. Enjoy whatever you can, but remember that things may not always be the same and you will always need some savings for the future and the rainy day. I have seen people who were made redundant and although they couldn't get another job for two years, they were still able to pay their mortgage and bills. This was possible because whilst they were working, they spent less and saved more so that when the difficult times came and they could not work, they were able to dig into their savings to meet their needs. I envy them in a positive way and I am trying to emulate that type of habit.

The extended family needs to be considered and a suitable plan worked out to meet their needs. This is important especially if you come from cultures where this custom is prevalent such as Africa, Asia and Latin America. If you have junior siblings or aged parents, you will have a responsibility and will be expected to contribute to their upkeep or help with their education or the cost of when they get married and so on.

2. Separate accounts – proportionate expenditure

There is nothing wrong in having separate accounts as long as both of you agree that the expenses are not too heavy on one side of the family. In the western world a joint account is no big deal but in other parts of the world it is still a challenge.

In some parts of the world they follow the old tradition that men are the bread winners and the women need not contribute anything except to manage the home. This will work if the man is earning enough to sustain that tradition. But in modern life, I think that type of belief is dying out even in places where it has been deeply rooted such as Africa.

Now women are educated, some more highly than the men, and they feel unfulfilled if they do not use the education and skills that they have acquired over several years and probably at huge expense. So, most of them work, and since they work I think it's just and fair that they contribute too. My suggestion is to contribute to the common purse in proportion to your earnings. For this purpose, I am just going to use an arbitrary figure. Suppose the husband earns 1,500 and the woman 1,200

per month making their family income to be 2,700, and they have outgoings or expenditure of 2,000; they have a surplus of 700.
This is my suggested formula for sharing the expenses.

Man's income: 1,500/2,700 x100 =56%

Woman's income: 1,200/2,700 x 100 = 44%

So the man will contribute 56/100 x 2,000 = 1,120

The woman will contribute 44/100 x 2,000 = 880

Total: 1,120 + 880 = 2,000.

So the husband has 380 left for himself out of which he can save and the wife has 320 left which could be her savings too. I want to remind you that this is only a suggestion; I believe that God may give a better idea to both of you how to work things out in a better way if you keep separate accounts.

When husband and wife are both working, to expect one person to pay the rent, the bills and probably food and still expect them to have savings is unrealistic. Many people have got themselves into trouble because they believe they are expected to meet all family financial obligations. They perceive this is what is expected of them although they do not have the financial capacity to absorb all those expenses. Instead of coming out and saying "Darling, I am struggling here", they go for a credit card and are encouraged to pay the minimum repayment (previously it was 5%, I do not know how much it is now) to keep the credit line on. Before they realise it, a hundred pounds becomes one hundred and twenty and after a year you will be seeing the deficit as £1,200 if not more.

I have seen on the television programme and read in the papers that people are in debt up to £75,000 or more on their credit cards. They did not buy a house or anything tangible but with this amount they spent the money on those gadgets that are out today but in 6 months' time a new version is out and the old one becomes obsolete and out of fashion. They may also spend the money from their credit card on clothes that are in fashion just for 3 months and by the time the next season comes those items are generally thrown into the bin or if they're lucky, they're in the charity shops. You must be sensible, disciplined and shrewd. It is only the savers of money who will be rich but not the ones that squander money.

Despite the fact that you keep separate accounts, you can and should still help each other in times of need. One can bail the other person out if the situation demands but with agreement that the other person will not put the rescuer in that situation again. Do not exploit each other because you keep separate accounts. Do not use the other person to enrich yourself by making them poor. Do not put them into debt for you to be in credit.

At the end of the day, what profit is there when one of you has savings in the bank and the other is drowning in debt? One rich man in the midst of 1,000 poor people is also poor. Leaving your spouse to their debt has many ramifications that will affect all the people living at your address especially in the developed world. All of you may become credit unworthy, your house will be blacklisted and there may even be a re-possession order on the house for as little as five thousand pounds' debt. So be wise, co-operate with each other and it will be well for both of you. Help one another and you will be helped by the Almighty God.

> Proverbs 11:25 says that "The generous soul will be made rich, and he who waters will also be watered himself." NKJV.

When couples are generous to each other, they honour God and build each other up. There is no need to be selfish with each other's resources.

Proverbs 11:28 also says that "He who trusts in his riches will fall, but the righteous will flourish like foliage." NKJV

Not long ago the world market collapsed and billions of pounds in shares and stocks value were wiped off in just a moment. That is the world of uncertainty we live in and if you think it will not happen again, you are misguided. In fact, another crash is round the corner unless we change our attitude to money and refrain from greed.
A billionaire can become a pauper in a moment and there is nothing anybody can do about it. Since the world thinks that greed is good then falling from grace to grass must be expected.

I have seen and heard of people whose accounts are fully in credit while their spouses are drowning in debts even though they have not been reckless. These are people with huge sums in bank accounts but, they are never happy, always looking miserable and are touchy and edgy even though they have money. If money can buy happiness, such people should be happy. But they are miserable because they have neglected the more important thing to do – helping their spouses, standing with them in times of difficulties. They do not realise that happiness and joy is infectious. If your spouse is happy it will radiate on you and their sorrow can affect you badly. A note of warning here! Some people are reckless with money and they take unnecessary gambles. I am not saying you should encourage and help such people if they are not ready to change their behaviour. Confront them with their financial mismanagement but in a loving manner that shows that you want a genuine change in behaviour. Probably it will be better to help them manage their money and when they are better off they can take control of it back.

I am not ashamed to let you know that I used to be a financial wreck but thanks to God and my wife, I have been bailed out on occasions and she has helped me out of my debt. My debts were not due to gambling or recklessness but the inability to be realistic about my income and expenditure. But I do not encourage you to go into debt thinking that your wife will bail you out; she may not be in a position to do so.

Expenses outside the immediate family
(for parents, siblings and significant others)

You should jointly decide how much you are going to spend on siblings, parents, friends and other significant people who may need your help or whom you want to help and bless. It's your wallet that should determine that. There is no need to borrow money to help people – you cannot give away what you haven't got! It does not matter if you are unable to give as much to those who have given to you before and there is also nothing bad if you can give more than what people have given you in the past. My encouragement is to give according the need of the other person and within what you can afford.

3. Hidden Expenses:

There is always what I call hidden expenses that is incurred by one of you and not known or acknowledged by the spouse. The example I have in mind is this: if there is one car in the family owned or registered in the name of one of the spouses, there is always the hidden cost of insurance, road tax, parking permits, petrol, MOT and repairs which may be an average annual cost of about £1,500 (arbitrary figure for explanation purposes only). This hidden expenses should not be ignored or taken for granted.

Now suppose that you and your spouse are intending to travel to a wedding and to give a gift to the couple. I expect that the two of you to share the cost of running the car for that purpose and the gift you intend to give to the new couple either equally or in proportions depending on what you both decide. However, I want to point out that you should add the hidden expenses of petrol and parking (if parking is not free) to the amount of gift you want to give otherwise the person who covers them may be out of pocket. For instance, you plan to give £25 to your friend who is getting married and you will need £15 worth of petrol. It is sensible to budget for £40 because the one driving has put in extra effort in driving, they should not be made to buy £15 worth of petrol and still contribute about £10-15 to the gift. This is something to think about.

CHAPTER NINE:

SOCIALISATION OF MEN AND WOMEN

A FUNDAMENTAL SECRET TO KNOW

Men and women are created by God in His image, meaning they are spiritual beings as God is spirit. Although God created the man first and from him He created the woman, men and women are different in their physical and emotional constitutions. Also, after birth men and women are socialised differently in the way they are made and raised. Their societies, families, cultures and education all influence the way they are expected to act and behave. I believe that their different hormonal constitutions too contribute to the differences between men and women. I call this the socialisation of men and women. This socialisation shapes their thoughts and influences their behaviours according to the societal expectations.

Understanding the Socialisation of men and women is important for building marriage relationships. [For ministers leading this course the couple is to be seen separately for 45 minutes each.] Conversely, since you have this book in your hands it is a big advantage to know the make-up of women and men as defined by the society in their upbringing. The way the society perceives and raises boys and girls play a major role in how they behave and how they want to be treated.

If this book is used by a minister to prepare people for marriage, the next section can be divided into two. The first part 'socialisation of man' is to be discussed with the woman in the absence of the man, and the second part of this chapter 'socialisation of women' to be discussed with the man only.

This is necessary so that the couples understand the other person is made and shaped by the society in which they function. I believe that if they understand this, it will help them deal with their spouse appropriately and will enhance their relationship in a positive way.

This section is for the woman only.

The socialisation of men:

No matter how small or poor a man is, he does not want to be dominated by his wife. He will want his wife to respect him and know that he is the head. Paul in 1 Corinthians 11:3 says that:
> "But I want you to know that the head of every man is Christ, the head of woman is man, and the head of Christ is God." NKJV

There is no school of sociology that teaches this principle or ideology, but I believe it to be inherent in all cultures and in every nation. If a man is 4ft tall and his wife 6ft he will still want to be respected and accepted as the head. The moment that his authority is threatened, he instinctively will fight. That is when you hear statement like "I won't have any woman speak to me like that even if she is the one that feeds me". Once a woman hears that type of statement she should know that she has crossed the line and the earlier she retracts what she said or did the better, and peace will come.

Thinking through this innate behaviour of men, I feel that it is so important to them that they guard their ego jealously and they will do all they can to do so. I sense this behaviour may have originated from our creator, God Himself, based on this text below [see also the text quoted above], Genesis 2:21-24 states that:
> "And the Lord God caused a deep sleep to fall on Adam, and he slept; and He took one of his ribs, and closed up the flesh in its place. Then the rib which the Lord God had taken from man He made into a woman, and He brought her to the man. And

Adam said: "This is now bone of my bones and flesh of my flesh; she shall be called Woman, because she was taken out of Man." Therefore, a man shall leave his father and mother and be joined to his wife, and they shall become one flesh". NKJV

I think it is inherently and unconsciously planted in the man that the woman was made out of him as a helper and so she should not dominate him. Whether this is true or not is a matter of debate that I don't want to get into now. I am just trying to explain how in my understanding the reason a man does not want a woman to dominate him.

Again Genesis 3:16 states that "To the woman He said: "I will greatly multiply your sorrow and your conception. In pain you shall bring forth children; **Your desire shall be for your husband, and he shall rule over you."** NKJV

The above bold text is very clear and unambiguous in its meaning and interpretation. God said to the woman her desire will be for her husband and the husband will rule over her. If God says it then it has become a command which is irrevocable.

Jesus in Matthew 24:35 says that "Heaven and earth will pass away, but My words will by no means pass away." NKJV

The understanding or misunderstanding of Ephesians 5:22-24 and of Colossians 3:18-19 plays a major role in this belief.

Ephesians 3:18-19 says that "Wives, submit to your own husbands, as to the Lord. For the husband is head of the wife, as also Christ is head of the church; and He is the Saviour of the body. Therefore, just as the church is subject to Christ, so let the wives be to their own husbands in everything." NKJV

And Colossians 3:18-19 says that "Wives, submit to your own husbands, as is fitting in the Lord.

I do not think it is a matter of superiority or inferiority; it is an inborn tendency that men want to be in charge of women, I think this is wrong, because verse 21 of Ephesians 5 states "submitting to one another in the fear of God". NKJV

My general understanding of these texts is that all of us, male and female, should submit to one another. However, because of the need for orderliness and the prevention of chaos in the home, God commanded that women should submit to their husbands who on their part are loving. This is not in any way suggesting that men are superior to women or women are subservient to their husbands. Both are made in the image of God and equally joint heirs of God through Christ. However, for the purposes of administration and orderliness, there has to be a leader wherever there is more than one person.

It is important that the woman recognises that her husband has this innate understanding of himself. Because men are very egotistical in nature and want to be recognised as always in charge, her husband will derive gratification and satisfaction from this. If she is prepared to let him be in charge she will enjoy him very much. Just as the Church submits to Christ so wives should submit to their own husbands.

One thing I always say to women is to understand the meaning of submission, and Jesus' submission is the best example to use as an illustration to women when discussing submission in marriage. In Philippians 2:5-11 we find 'The Humbled and Exalted Christ',

> "Let this mind be in you which was also in Christ Jesus who, being in the form of God, did not consider it robbery to be equal with God, but made Himself of no reputation, taking the form of a bondservant, and coming in the likeness of men. And being found in appearance as a man, He humbled Himself and became obedient to the point of death, even the death of the cross. Therefore, God also has highly exalted Him and given Him the name which is above every name, that at the name of Jesus every knee should bow, of those in heaven, and of those on earth, and of those under the earth, and that every tongue should confess that Jesus Christ is Lord, to the glory of God the Father." NKJV

This passage says that Jesus is God and equal to the Father but He chose not to compete with the Father; he submitted to the Father's will even unto his death on a cross. Because Jesus did this, God has now exalted this Jesus and has given Him a name that is above every name that at the name of JESUS, every knee must bow in heaven and on earth and every tongue confess that He is Lord.

Paul asked the wives to emulate this example of Jesus' submission, and God will exalt them too because they have obeyed Him and submitted to their husbands even though they are equal with them. Peter was also inspired to write about God's will for the family and each other's roles in this mystic relationship marriage that is likened to that of Christ and the Church. Peter admonished women to see that submitting to their own husband as submitting to Christ Himself. Therefore, not submitting to one's own husband is not submitting to Christ. In 1 Peter 3:1-6 it is expressed that women',

> "..., likewise, be submissive to your own husbands, that even if some do not obey the word, they, without a word, may be won by the conduct of their wives, when they observe your chaste conduct accompanied by fear. Do not let your adornment be merely outward — arranging the hair, wearing gold, or putting on fine apparel - rather let it be the hidden person of the heart, with the incorruptible beauty of a gentle and quiet spirit, which is very precious in the sight of God. For in this manner, in former times, the holy women who trusted in God also adorned themselves, being submissive to their own husbands, as Sarah obeyed Abraham, calling him lord, whose daughters you are if you do good and are not afraid with any terror." NKJV

Here Peter emphasised something that Paul did not: 'that even if some do not obey the word, they without a word may be won by the conduct of their wives, when they observe their chaste conduct accompanied by fear (reverent fear)'.

This I understand in two ways. First, if the husband is not even a believer he may be convinced, convicted and converted by the behaviour of his wife, that is, his wife's inner beauty and outward submission. The second way I understand this is that if the husband is a believer but not obeying God, completing his part of the deal of loving his wife as Christ loves the Church, his wife should and must still submit and be like Sarah and by his wife's chaste behaviour and attitude the husband may change being won over by his wife.

I also want to encourage wives to see their husbands as the head. Since it is God's command they need not argue or find excuses not to obey God. If they find excuses, they will miss the blessing that comes with obedience and most importantly the peace and joy of the Lord.

I have something for women here. If their husbands are the heads which is rightly so according to the Bible, the wives are the necks and if the neck does not turn, the head is going nowhere. (This is a secret. please keep it and do not let men know!). The moment women get this loving and submission challenge right, there will be peace at home and in their minds and of course Joy will follow. Wherever there is the peace of Christ, His joy is always present. Wives can't find the peace and not the joy, but they can have both by submitting to their own husband

How can this be done?

1. Wives should internalise in their spirit the fact that, because God commanded it and they are committed to obeying Him, He will help them fulfil His purpose in their lives. Wives should pray that God will always help them to submit to their husbands.
2. The wife must not entertain Satan's argument that her husband will trample over her or walk over her. Satan will always argue that wife is equal to her husband (and this much is true). But what he will obscure in her eyes and mind is the fact that God commanded her to

submit to her own husband. Satan will paint the word "submission" as very negative and unbeneficial. Satan will be silent about the loving husband and therefore the benefits of submission, and will only capitalise on the idea of your husband walking over her. James 4:7 talks about the humility that cures worldliness. "Therefore submit to God. Resist the devil and he will flee from you." NKJV

3. The wife should practise what she now believes. Just as an illustration, when her husband is at home she may say to him "darling (if that is the language she uses or the name or pet name she calls him) I am so blessed to have you as my husband. What would I do without you? God is so good to me for giving me you." Things like "you are such a handsome man, turn to your right, left or around" (I guarantee you he will) and before he knows that she is commanding him, he's done what she wants him to do.

It may be difficult initially but people say 'practice makes perfect'. Even if she does not mean it initially, because she is saying it and doing it, it begins to travel from her head to her heart. The moment it gets to her heart it is consolidated and becomes part of her and her character. It's only what gets into people's heart that they can draw from. However, the longest journey in people's life is the journey of knowledge and information from their head (the seat of knowledge) to their heart (the seat of faith). We do what we believe in and we believe what we know and want to believe. God helping us we are winning.

This section is for the man only

The socialisation of women:

Women are emotional and that is how God created them.
1 Peter 3:7 (NKJV)

> "Husbands, likewise, dwell with them with understanding, giving honour to the wife, as to the weaker vessel, and as being heirs together of the grace of life, that your prayers may not be hindered."

This text does not suggest in any way that women are to be dominated and controlled. Instead it says: live with them with understanding, i.e. endeavour to study them and know them. When the men know them, they will know when and how to deal with them. Their hormonal components are different from men's; so they behave differently from men. They naturally look up to their husbands for leadership despite the fact that they want to be in control. They look to the husband to be in the driving seat, but the moment that they see that their husband is taking them in the wrong direction, then women will lose their confidence and trust. They will respond depending on how men handle the failure or disappointment. If men are transparently honest and apologise for it, it's in their nature to forgive and move on and give men another chance believing that they are going to change.

I have noticed this in women; they are responders to whatever men throw at them, but when they respond, they do it in full measure and with full commitment pressed down, shaken together and likely to overflow. I would not see them as retaliating but as responding to what men have given to them in their words and actions. If men want to enjoy women, please study and know them, their good and bad times and when their monthly hormonal changes affect their behaviour.

The text further says 'giving honour to the wife.' The online Oxford dictionary[24] defines honour as "High respect; great esteem." In other words, God commands that men should give their wives great respect or high esteem. If they are to be treated as slaves, subservient and to be controlled would God ask men to give high respect or high esteem to them? Of course men's answer can't be anything other than NO. Therefore, wives are not to be controlled, gagged or intimidated. They are never to be spoken to harshly, derogatorily or unkindly. Please do not injure their emotions.

Why should the man honour his wife? Because she is like the weaker vessel. In other words, she is marked "'FRAGILE', HANDLE WITH CARE". None of the men would handle glass as they handle a stone or wood; they would not handle glass roughly but rather with great care. There is no-one too, who will squeeze a fresh egg as it will break and mess their hand, even if it did not injure them. Therefore, the man should handle his wife with great care - she is fragile.

The other thing this text tells us is that she is an heir with the man in the grace of God through Christ. If she is a joint heir, then she is equal with the man. And if she is equal with him and chooses to submit to him, as Christ is

---

[24] http://www.oxforddictionaries.com/definition/english/honour

equal with God and chose to submit to Him even unto death, why would the man not choose to love her unconditionally just as Christ chose to love the Church and even died for her. In the same way, men should love their wives unconditionally and be prepared to die for them in a literal sense.

Why must the man do these things for her? So that his prayers will not be hindered. All men want their prayers answered, but when they don't love their wives, when a man doesn't treat his woman with great honour and care, his prayers are likely to be hindered according to God's word.
Genesis 3:16 says
"To the woman He said: "... your desire shall be for your husband, and he shall rule over you." NKJV

This passage is not contradicting my discussion thus far. Your wife's desire will always be for you; she will be looking up to you for provision, protection, comfort and succour and naturally will expect you to lead; so you need not ask her to recognise that you are the leader - she knows it already. Just do what God has asked you to do and the submission will come automatically. If it does not, check yourself: do you really love her unconditionally? If your answer is 'no', then work it out better and the situation will improve. If not, be patient, continue to do what God has commanded and in due time God will meet her and help her submit.
Paul in Colossians 3:18-19 says:
".... Husbands, love your wives and do not be bitter toward them." NKJV

No matter how educated, famous and wealthy a woman is, she longs for her husband. She wants things from her husband and she loves to say 'my husband did this and that for me.' They derive joy and pride in this kind of things. This does not mean they want money or gifts all of the time, they will appreciate spending time with them. Tell her, I just want you to sit by me. Let her sit under your arm holding her to yourself and ask her how her day has been and about anything that is of interest to her. She will love it.

She longs to be in your arms, to be by your side. She needs your cuddle and caressing. She would like you to come home straight after work if possible or, if this isn't possible, at least to be kept informed of what is happening. She wants to go out with you and do stuff together. As long as you keep these things in the relationship, you will enjoy them.

Stability, reliability and love are important to them in the relationship because of their emotions, and those are the things God has commanded you to provide. The moment the man realises that his wife is an emotional being and she says that a particular thing is important to her, no matter how ridiculous you think that thing is, please treat it as important. Then you will have peace. Failing to do this will likely result in trouble.

Women want to be appreciated; they always want to hear the words 'I love you'. The more the men say this to them the better for the men because they will receive women's approval. The man telling a woman how beautiful she is and how blessed he is to have her as his wife means a lot to her. So go on, tell her she is an exceptional gift from God to you, and that you will never be complete without her. Tell her how you long to be with her always, and whenever she is away you feel her absence so much. These sort of words are important to women and especially when they are backed up with actions - you will always be their hero. Her initial reaction may be "hum! You're only saying this because I am your wife; what else could you have said?" Do not be discouraged by that. You've said exactly what she enjoys hearing you say, and when you just touch her, she may say "hey, hey, leave me alone" but with big smiles and enjoyment.

Women want men to desire them. Sometimes they set up a situation that will make you chase after them, and all they are testing is your longsuffering, endurance and perseverance. They want to know that when things are difficult, whether through their own making or yours, you still will long for them. They want to see whether you are still committed to the vows 'for better, for worse' which you made with them.
At this time, especially when you want to make love, they may resist initially, but with a bit of gentle insistence and persuasion, they give in.

A woman will want to test the trustworthiness and honesty of her husband. She may ask for a fiver (£5). If you say you don't have it, even though you only have five pounds left, she may not be happy and her trust may be shaken. But if you say "darling, I would love to give you the fiver but that is all I have in my wallet" and you show her your wallet and you say "let me give you two pounds and I'll keep the last three". She probably may not take that fiver from you, especially if she doesn't really need it and besides, no woman would like her husband out of pocket.

Because they are more emotional, women's reactions to things may and will be different. I learnt something from an Africa illustration of emotional difference between men and women. In some parts of Africa men and women tie wrappers round their waists. The women tie theirs to the left side and the men tie theirs in front.

If for example a fire or other horrible thing occur, what the woman will do is to unwrap herself not caring if people see her underwear (which in normal circumstances they will hide, protect and guard jealously), whereas the man acts differently and in complete opposition in response to the same event. Instead of unwrapping himself, he re-tightens his wrapper; he makes it tighter and goes into action to arrest or remedy the situation.

What lesson can we learn from this analogy? When bad situations occur in the family, the woman may react in such a way that what is supposed to be a family secret can be exposed. At that moment they don't care if other people around know that secret. The consequence of their action is not in their thoughts at that moment. They never intended such a consequence but when their emotion takes over, they give in to it easily.

Please note that it is not every woman that does this, there are also men who are more feminine in nature and they do this as well. Men's reaction to the same incident is totally opposite. By re-tightening their wrapper, their attitude and belief is saying "no it's going to be OK, the secret will not be leaked and we can work at it. Our secret will stay intact and we will hold things together". The men tend to want things to hold together, maintain the family secret and not allow outsiders into the situation. However, not all men behave this way too. There are some who are more emotional than women and they may behave even worse by falling apart emotionally.

So whenever there is a situation like this, do not be surprised at your wife's behaviour. It's not her fault. I think her hormones play some part in it. Accommodate her and attend to her emotions and all will be well. You have to make women's emotions important to you; then you are able to gain their confidence and trust and lead them out of their emotions which may at times be irrational.

For the two of them (man and woman):

If the man continues to build the emotions of his wife, and if she continues to build his ego, they will grow together, loving each other more, Meeting each other's needs graciously, they will move closer to each other in behaviour and character, understanding each more and will reflect Christ. Remember that whatever you want to say and do to your spouse must meet the criteria which I mentioned to you in the section under communication: Will it bless my spouse? Will it add value to their life? Will it build them up? Will it honour and glorify God? If these criteria are met, go ahead, do and say it. God will be honoured.

CHAPTER TEN

MARRYING A PERSON WITH CHILD(REN)

Marrying to someone with one or more children carries enormous challenge. It is good to know what one is entering into right from the start. This is why I advocate complete openness and transparency in the communication chapter. There is no need to hide anything because sooner or later the truth will come out. Starting a marriage relationship with a hidden agenda is not good and if discovered later it will shake and strain the relationship and to restore trust could be very difficult.

I heard a story about a woman who had a child and entered into a relationship with a man and did not tell the man about her child. Even when he suspected that the child was hers, she denied it and said he was her nephew. The truth came into the open after the wedding that the child was actually hers, no amount of begging could stop the dissolution of the marriage. This is a true story and I tell the story to let couples in this situation know what lack of openness can result into.

People have found themselves in broken relationship for whatever reason. But life does not and should not end there. They can pick themselves up again and find a loving relationship that will work. Some people whilst they were young found themselves pregnant and the man did not accept responsibility for the mother and child leaving them to be single mothers. In some situations, the man takes responsibility for the child but not the mother. Some men walked out of their relationship leaving the woman with one or more children to fend for themselves. These situations are hard enough but that is not the end of the world. God is a God of new beginning and He can make all things new. Part of making things new is by providing a new person who would be interested in marrying the abandoned man or woman (single parent). It is good that one lets the intended person know what they are letting themselves into.

Whoever will be marrying the person who has had children before must know and understand that, my definition of marriage is very much at the heart of the new relationship they are about to enter.

Step son or daughter and step father or mother is definitely a baggage. Therefore, one must know that there will be extra challenges to the relationship for several reasons:

1. The children may not initially be warm to the step father or mother so it will take extra grace, tolerance and patient to go through this.
2. The step father or mother may not be warm to the step son or daughter hence may not be as tolerant as they ought if they are their own children.
3. The step father or mother may be seen as a threat to the existing family relationship between the biological children and the biological parents. The step father or mother may be seen as rivals as children realise that they will share their father or mother's love, resources and attention with another person. So efforts to eliminate the threat may have to be pursued and that may be very challenging.
4. Comparing step children with own children, step mother or father with own mother or father may put strain into the relationship.

So before anyone enters into such a relationship, they should spend time looking at those issues I have discussed and make a clear plan of action agreed by all parties, i.e. the man, woman and the children. All the parties to this agreement must recognise that this type of relationship is more complex and therefore need extra tolerance, endurance and understanding.

Because this relationship comes with extra dimension of step children, step father or mother added to it, I have some suggestions that may be useful in helping go through the challenges smoothly and in loving ways.

1. The adults involved must accept the children as their own and love them unconditionally as they would love their own children.

2. The adults must realise that those children involved are special and important to their spouse or the person they are about to marry hence making those children special and important to selves too will greatly enhance their relationship and will make their spouse happy.

3. The adults must treat the step children as their own and not drawing differences especially when they get to have their own biological children. I must stress this point because the tendency to think that one's children will not behave in an unacceptable, upsetting, rude or unruly or cantankerous way is a fallacy. Thinking or feeling this way could be the greatest mistake one can make. One's children could behave even worse and what would one do? No matter how badly a child behaves the parents would not cast them away. Couples should not have two standards of treatments, one for their own children and another for their step children. If this happens it is unhelpful

and damaging. It is a recipe for internal family warfare and unrest.

4. The couple should agree between themselves who will be responsible for discipline, giving out allowances for the children and the rest of family affairs that involves the children. This agreement should be communicated to the children in a clear and unambiguous language ensuring that children understand and both parents must be united and adhere to it as well.

5. The couple must know that children nowadays are clever than their age and they will exploit the seemingly weaker parent of the two. There must be agreement between the couple about what they will permit and what they will not permit but with reasons. So it is important that the couple stick to the plan and not give in to the temper-tantrum of the children. If the children know that they can't get away with their exploitation, they will respect both parents and will fall in line with the decorum of the home.

The couple would do themselves injustice if one of them refuses the children something and his or her spouse allows it. The way the children will see that is that the one who refuses them is horrible and not good, but the one who gives the children what they want is good and cool. The children will always go to the one they believe, see and know will attend to their request even the most ridiculous one.

The couple should know that children are generally open and have no boundaries between each other and the parents should exploit this aspect of theirs to bring strong relationship and bond between them.

The couple must trust each other that their spouse will act in the best interest of their children and that trust must be sustained leaving no room for suspicion.

The question the couple must ask themselves is, 'what is the best they would do for their child?' I encourage the couple to do whatever their answer will be. By doing this the couple will have no problem and their spouse will trust them.

I was listening to a woman in a step-parent situation talking about her husband. She said 'whatever he does for his child he does for mine and in fact he does things first for mine'. This is an impressive comment from a woman about her husband and that is what I suggest for every couple in similar situation.

On the contrary I heard a comment from another woman in a similar situation. She said, 'if he does not accept him as his child and treat him as such and I have to choose between my relationship with him and my child, I will choose my child.' This is pretty serious and resolute statement and very dangerous for the relationship. Jesus' statement in Matthew 7:12 is the golden text for the couples regarding this issue. "Therefore, whatever you want men to do to you, do also to them, for this is the Law and the Prophets." NKJV

To end this section, I want to remind couples or people who are about to enter into this type of relationship to understand the complexity of their situation and take time to discuss, and sort things out before they enter into any serious relationship. It has worked for people in the past, it is still working now and I believe that it will work in future with love, understanding and tolerance.

CHAPTER ELEVEN:

MAKING A FAMILY

To have children or not?

Psalms 127:3 says "Behold, children are a heritage from the Lord, the fruit of the womb is a reward." NKJV
"Children are a gift from the LORD; they are a reward from him" (NLT)[25]
We must appreciate that children are gifts from God and He gives them to those He wishes. It is not a right but a privilege. I would not want you to think that those who are unable to have children have done anything wrong. No, I just think that it is for those who have them to thank and glorify God. So if we are blessed with them we must thank God.

However, there are some people who may not have this blessing. Jesus mentioned this in Matthew 19:11-12 and this is what He said.
"But He said to them, "All cannot accept this saying, but only those to whom it has been given: For there are eunuchs who were born thus from their mother's womb, and there are eunuchs who were made eunuchs by men, and there are eunuchs who have made themselves eunuchs for the kingdom of heaven's sake. He who is able to accept it, let him accept it." NKJV

---

[25] The New Living Translation Bible

A eunuch is a castrated person who is unable to produce children especially in historical times. They were often found in royal Palaces. The king would castrate them so that they will not be sleeping with his wives and concubines. Jesus is saying through these passages that there are three categories of people who will never be able to produce children.

The first group are born that way; they will never be able to produce despite any amount of intervention. The second group were made by people and those are the one I explained above that live and look after kings' wives in the palace. The last group made themselves eunuchs because of the gospel. These are like the Catholic priests or any other Christians who choose to live celibate lives to honour Christ.

I write this as a background for the reader to appreciate children as gifts from God and as a privilege, not necessarily as a right.
Couples must decide whether they want children or not and how many and at what intervals if God permits. But I must encourage them here to remember that it all depends on God.

They may wish to have children at a particular interval but God may have a different plan. Even without family planning there may be a gap between them. Some people decide not to have children for the first few years of their marriage because of whatever reason. The most common of those reasons is for them to enjoy themselves before entering into the business of producing children. I do not see anything wrong in this but I want to intimate to those people that they are not in control of things but

God. When they are ready and the child does not come what are they going to do but regret not to have started sooner. I am not saying that people have problems when they start but it could happen.

Medical science believes that the younger the couple especially the woman the more likely they are fertile for procreation. The longer women leave child bearing the more difficult it can be. I know this because I am a nurse. If the delay of having children happens, the waiting for one could be long, painful and frustrating.

This period of waiting is always a trying period for a couple. It is characterised by anxiety and fear, and if care is not taken there may be quarrels between the couple. Satan will be glad about this and will want to exploit the situation by magnifying the problem to more than it is. He will play it on a couple's emotion first and then shift results in a physical effect on the man because it may lead to secondary impotence. This is when the man loses erection easily or has no erection at all because he is anxious and unhappy. He may be wondering 'what is going on?' He may start losing confidence in himself which may lead to more anxiety and complicating the matter more.

This is the time the couple needs 'the peace of God that passes all understanding' more than anything else. Remaining calm and resting in the everlasting arms of God is the best option. There is probably nothing wrong with the man except for anxiety. A Clinical Nurse Specialist in sexual health in one of London's hospital once told me that about 95% cases of secondary impotence are a problem of the mind. This is the time therefore, when the wife must understand and be helpful by not getting frustrated. She must be ready to help arouse him by the various methods and tactics she knows. It is a very difficult time for the man. She must re-assure him and let him know that she is there for him and they are going through it together. This will boost the confidence of the man and enables him to recover quickly and things may become normal before you know it. Support from the wife is crucial at this moment.

I am not saying that every man will experience this, but if it happens, the couple should not be alarmed. The man will catch the fire again and things will work out well. There is help medically and otherwise. If the man can forget about himself and the situation, putting himself above the need for children he is likely to be restored without help. The couple should adopt the mind of enjoying their sexual life together without expecting children resulting from it. That will make them relax and whilst they are enjoying their sexual life they may find that what they have been waiting for may arrive unexpectedly. We have experienced it and not only once but three times. God is good.

Most women will do calculations about their ovulation periods and that is the time they will want to make love with their husbands because that is their fertile period. Generally, this may work, but sometimes it may not. From experience, what works better and most effective is for the couple just to enjoy their sex lives without condition, especially when they are looking to have children. The children will come at the time God wants them and those times are always the best for the couple too when they look back.

God has a sense of humour. Our first child is four years older than the second and the second is eight years older than the third. At the time God was planning our family for us, it was not a pleasant time for us as human beings. We found it trying but we thank God that He pulled us through those years. However, little did we know that He was acting in our best interest. The year our first child entered University was the year the students' bursary was abolished and school fees introduced. At that time, we were not strong financially. There was no way we could have had two children at university without obtaining a loan. But God was on our side and he pulled us through it all. He sees the end before the beginning and has promised never to leave us nor forsake us. He is always faithful. He will always act for your good and blessing too.

Our first child graduated in June and the second entered university in September of the same year. What an awesome God we have. Of course there was a breathing space between the second and third child and by the time the third was ready to go to university, we had had a break and had accumulated some savings. It has not been difficult to see her through, even though the fees and living expenses have doubled. God saw us through it without any hardship.

I pray that couples will find favour from God and they will be able to give their own testimonies in due course too. Once the couple have their desired number of children, the next decision is to plan their family. Couples should not be naïve and unwise otherwise they may find themselves having more children than they bargained for. I do not believe contraception to be wrong although others may disagree. But the decision is for the couple to make and they can do whatever both of them believe and agree.

From my experience, a child is a 25 years' project. At least in the UK today education has been structured according to age, which I think is good. A child will enter university at eighteen and, depending on the course they do, they will graduate at twenty-one if it's a three-year course or twenty-four if it's a six year course such as medicine. If it is medicine, they will do a house job before becoming a medical practitioner. This analysis is the basis of my theory that a child is a twenty-five-year project. The couple need to consider the cost of supporting their children for this sort of duration.

So the couple need to use wisdom in planning their family. The earlier they start their family the earlier they will finish. But it is up to them if they choose to start late. They should bear it in their minds that they may find themselves still paying school fees with their pension if they follow this delay course.

Teaching and training children

> Proverbs 22:6 says "Train up a child in the way he should go, and when he is old he will not depart from it." NKJV

While children are growing up, they will need the guidance of their parents and as examples. The parents are the best teachers for the children example. The parents are the children's role models consciously or unconsciously. What they see their parents do is what they are likely to do because they will believe it is the right thing. Parents should speak to them always in a gentle and polite manner; making them to know the reasons why they must behave in certain way and why they must speak and do things in certain ways. This method will go a long way to influence their behaviour to make them good citizen in the future.

Both parents are responsible for teaching the children, even though there is a special bond between father and daughter and between mother and son. There are things that the mother should handle with the daughter and things that the father should handle with the son.

If parents ask their children to lie for them, the children will always lie to them as well. I telephoned a house years ago and asked for a woman. Her daughter picked up the phone and she told me to hold on. After a few seconds she came back and said "mum says she's not home". Think of that statement from the little girl. The parents must remember that their children are watching them and that they, the parents are accountable to God for how they train their children. Shouting parents are likely to influence their children to shout, all things being equal. We know that there is also peer pressure which influences the children greatly, but with prayer and guidance from the word of God, good examples from the parents and good advice from experienced people things will be well.

Discipline:

Children will always be children. Sometimes they will be naughty and will do or say something that is wrong and will need correction or discipline. Please do not hesitate to correct or discipline them, no matter how young they are. The earlier they know what is acceptable or not the better for them and the parents. If parents start training them early, the children will listen early and they will give the parents rest.

The law never prohibits parents from disciplining their children. The only thing it prohibits is to hurt them in such a way that marks are left on the children' bodies. Smacking and flogging are often counter productive. There are other means of discipline that are more effective than smacking. Source them from good books, good internet web sites and other means and I am sure parents will find an appropriate one for their children.

There are other means of discipline and correction like withdrawing reward, sitting in a naughty corner or withdrawing privileges like going out with friends etc. It is the parents' responsibility to discipline and correct their children. If parents love their children, they will discipline them.

CHAPTER TWELVE:

PREPARING FOR THE WEDDING DAY

Do you want a small or big wedding?

Everyone has an idea of how their wedding should be but it does not matter whether small or big, your wallet and aspiration should determine how big. If both of you have money and have enough to deposit to buy your house, you may choose a big one. But if not why do you want to lavish 25 or 30 thousand pound on a wedding when that could form a big chunk to deposit for a house? You may choose to have a quieter wedding, that is great. It is not the size of the wedding that makes marriage a success. In fact, wedding need not and should not be expensive and we should not be dancing to the tune of the society by believing that weddings should be expensive.

You may have a big and expensive wedding and the marriage may not be successful (I pray not) and you may have the modest wedding and your marriage be successful. It is the understanding, the efforts and putting into practice what I have highlighted in this book that may make your marriage succeed. All what the law requires is that apart from the Authorised person (if from a place of worship) or the Registrar if from the local authority and the officer or minister conducting the marriage, only two people are needed to witness a marriage of a couple. That makes a total number of 6 in the minimum. Whatever you wear is totally your choice and no one can query and if anyone dares to do so you have the right to answer or not and no one will take you to court about the way you want to conduct your wedding.

Thank God that I have participated in various forms of weddings from the minimum number to a large number but what gladdens my heart is that they all are doing well even with their challenges. So my friends, it does not matter what the size of your wedding is, the success is what you should put efforts in. *And please make sure you are not in debt, not even a penny, because of wanting to marry.* As I have said before it is a bad start and do everything possible to avert it.

The woman and the man will have a picture (like an unprinted photograph – Negative or blue print) of what they want the day to look like. It's a blueprint of their big day. It is good to verbalise the picture and write it down. How does she want her dress, shoes, veil and other things to look like? What colour and style will the groom's suit be? Write down who will be the bridesmaids and the groom's men, the page boys and flower girls and the ring bearer. What kind of decorations, catering and the kind of music you will want? At what church or other venue will the wedding take place? What sort of reception hall - what is the capacity and how many people will you be expecting? For some Africans, what colour combination of dress would you want your guests to wear? You must document all of these things. Your memory can fail because of pressure and anxiety. What about the wedding car? Who is the photo and videographer? Who will be your event organiser if you can afford one? The earlier you start your preparation the better. Good planning leads to a good outcome. From time to time or at a regular agreed time you can check all these things to keep on top of the plan and these are the points to check:

How much preparation have you made?

Look at how much preparation you have made, what has been done and by whom. Make sure you tick what has been done.

How much preparation remains?

Check what things remain to be done. Who will do them and when? How much are they going to cost? Have you got the money? If not, when and where is it coming and from whom? All these things need to be discussed. As soon as each item is completed, you tick it and move on to the next item.

How much money have you got now and how much can you save by the end of two months before the wedding?

It has been said money says, "Without me don't make a plan". Weddings are very expensive nowadays but I want to caution you that it's not the amount of money spent that makes your marriage successful. The wedding could be fantastic but the marriage may not if you do not work at it. It is advisable not to plan on the basis of promises and the help you are going to get from other people. It is not because they will want to disappoint you but because something may happen that will make them unable to help and fulfil their promise. If you're relying on them, what will you do then?

I remember sharing this with a friend who wanted to get married two years after our own marriage and he asked for counsel. I told him not to rely on anyone for financial help because a situation could prevent them from fulfilling their promises. Another person told him to ignore my advice, saying how it was impossible that her senior sister would disappoint him. When he told me about this second opinion, I asked him to make a choice about which advice to follow. A week before the wedding he told me that his very senior sister could not meet her promise. If he had not allocated money for what his sister had promised, he would have had to find money at the last minute which would have been difficult and even plunged him into debt. Generally, I would discourage going into debt particularly over the cost of a wedding.

I advise you to plan financially only on the basis of the savings for your wedding which you have already made and the amount that you can save up to two months before your wedding. If the budget is more than what you already have or will have two months before, prune it down. The salary for the last two months before the wedding should be kept intact. Do not touch it because you are likely to be broke after the wedding. What you will rely on then will be the salary that you put aside for the 'after the wedding' shortage of cash. I call it the bail-out salary.

Who is helping and who is doing what?

A wedding is a huge occasion and it is advisable to involve others to help you. It is not a sign of weakness to ask for help in organising your wedding. It is a sign of friendship and anyone you ask for their help will consider it an honour and privilege. They will not want to disappoint you. Put names against the tasks you want them to do for you and put a time limit on it. Tell them that the success of that task depends on them and they can't afford to fail. Involve people. Get as much help as possible and delegate responsibility for various things such as the hall, music, catering, church and reception, ushers and waiters (if the caterer will not provide these) etc. The hairdresser, make-up artist and other associated services.

Nowadays, couples book hotels where they are going to stay with the bride maids and the groom's me. It has been shown that the earlier you book the hotels and the halls for the reception the cheaper and chances of getting a good and desired venues.

It's your parents' day as well.

Most importantly it is your day but remember that it is also your parents' joy that their son or daughter is getting married. Ensure you give them their rightful place. Put them on the high table and ensure that you acknowledge the care they have given to you and how much you appreciate them. They will love that public recognition. Focus on the picture you have in your mind, stay calm. Speak to your ministers and mentors all the time about issues which are unclear to you.

Above all, keep praying together and involve your ministers and elders. It will be well with you.

CHAPTER THIRTEEN

MAINTAINING YOUR MARRIGE

When you buy a new car, for most of the first few years it does not need any maintenance except that you buy petrol. There is always the manufacturer's warranty covering it for the first few years. The warranty is based on experience and research that nothing can go wrong with some elements on the car within the first few years. Most of the time and in a majority of occasions, nothing goes wrong in those first few years otherwise the manufacturers will be in trouble and probably bankrupt.

It is not so with the newly married because we are human beings whose behaviours are always unpredictable. Right from the start, you have to work hard on how the relationship will be improved and made better day by day, month by month and year by year. Nothing should be taken for granted. The fire of love must be kept burning, the fan of affection should be blowing at every time, and the door of tolerance and forgiveness must be widely open at all times. It is often said that 'it's only a foolish person that says his patience is too much. Patience has no limit.

The rate at which marriages are dissolved is greater than the rate at which they are contracted and most breakups are for flimsy reasons like "we always argue", "he doesn't appreciate me enough", "we are not compatible" and some cannot even give any reason for their decision. What I think is the problem is that couples do not understand the vows they have made and do not know how to live in the light of them. Therefore, I am reiterating to you that marriage is for life and you must take a long view of it. It is not a job career that you can change at will as you like. Neither is it a game that when one person is not performing well, you substitute him or her. Through thick and thin of life you must stick together. In the rain and in the sun you must remain by each other. When it is good and when it is bad you must be there for each other. In health and in sickness you must support and be together.

In relationships and especially in marriages, there will always be challenges and testing times. No one can escape such times but the way you see and handle challenging times will determine the outcome of your marriage. There will always be sweet and sour times in marriage, there will always be easy and difficult times, there will always be hills and valleys and ups and downs. In the bible texts, Job in his calamity said "Shall we indeed accept good from God, and shall we not accept adversity?" Job 2:10 NKJV. Job is not suggesting that God causes evil to happen because that will not be His nature. God is good at all times. However, He allows Satan to inflict assault and injury on people but He will always uphold, sustain and strengthen them to overcome the evil one, and they will come out purified and more beautiful and be mature in their lives together.

Husbands must always attend to their wives' emotions and wives must always attend to their husbands' ego. This I have discussed in the Socialisation chapter. Always make sure that you give befitting cards and messages on your spouse's birthday, your anniversary, Easter, Christmas and other significant days and occasions in your lives. You must always seek each other's good no matter what the other person does. I want to even encourage you to raise the bar of your commitment and love for one another. Always look for something exiting to share with one another, doing stuff together and travelling together if you can afford it.

One of the things I believe that can help sustain couples is to develop interest in each other's interests and hobbies. For example, if the husband loves football, it will be worthwhile for the wife to develop some interest in it as well so that they both can enjoy and comment on the game together. And if the wife is interested in a soap opera, it will be wise that the husband has some interest in it and learn about some of its characters as well so that you will always have something in common to talk about. Just like you would renew and check the MOT (Road worthiness) of your car in order that it can drive on the road safely, so you need to do the MOT of your relationship from time to time. Small issues are sorted out quickly before they become big. What is working should be endorsed and encouraged to continue and what is not working well should be visited, analysed and modified to make it work and, if need be, abandoned completely.

The things that you need to maintain your marriage.

Just as you need to be filling your car with petrol or diesel to keep it moving, and engine oil in the engine, gear oil in the gear box, coolant to keep the engine from over-heating, brake fluid to enable the brake to function well and keeping all the lights functioning well so marriages need all the equivalents of those illustrations. We need to keep them in shape so as to be at the optimum functioning level and they are listed below.

1.   LOVING ONE ANOTHER:

Love is the cement of your relationship. Every other thing depends on it. Keep on loving one another irrespective of what the other person does and say. The unconditional love is the winner. It cannot fail; it prevails over every evil and maintains relationship. Ephesians 5:2 says that "And walk in love, as Christ also has loved us and given Himself for us, an offering and a sacrifice to God for a sweet-smelling aroma." NKJV Just as Christ loves us, we too must love one another. 1 John 4:11 states that "Beloved, if God so loved us, we also ought to love one another." NKJV

Do not just say you love him/her but demonstrate your love by your actions by doing those things discussed in the love chapter and even as the Holy Spirit would lead you. This is the fuel (petrol or diesel) that keeps the marriage going without this the relationship is not going anywhere.

If you have a piece of string or rope and you have been warned not to allow it to cut because you would not get another. If you ignore the warning and you allow the rope to cut, then in order to use it again you have to tie it together, it will have a knot and will not be smooth again. The same with your marriage, it is better to prevent it from breaking than wanting to fix after it has broken, it will have a knot. If the rope of trust breaks, it will take a while before it can be restored. Doubts may creep in and Satan is good at capitalising on broken trust. Breaking trust is preventable by keeping on loving one another and remaining transparent at all times regardless of the circumstances and consequences. 1 Corinthians 13:8 Paul says "Love never fails" if you apply it, because it never fails you won't fail either.

Colossians 3:14 says that "But above all these things put on love, which is the bond of perfection." NKJV Love binds people together and enables them to trust one another and keep the relationship better, sweeter and stronger. This is achievable and doable only if we observe what has been put down for us in the Scripture.

The only thing that works better than prayer is obedience. 1 Samuel 15:22 says that "So Samuel said: "Has the Lord as great delight in burnt offerings and sacrifices, As in obeying the voice of the Lord? Behold, to obey is better than sacrifice, and to heed than the fat of rams." NKJV

If you want to obey God concerning your marriage, even a thought in your heart resounds like thunder before God and He will grant your heart desire. If you obey God, you need not strain yourself in praying. But if you choose not to obey and you are praying and even fasting, your prayer and fasting is not lifting up at all. But if you obey God, He delights in you and is attentive to your prayers and makes your thought to become realities.

2. RESOLVING CONFLICT

There is no way you will not offend each other or step on each other's toes. When this happens, know that the other person did not do it intentionally. Believe that it is a mistake on the part of the other.

> Ephesians 4:26 says "Be angry, and do not sin": do not let the sun go down on your wrath" NKJV

This is part of the Scripture to be translated and understood literally. When your spouse upsets you, yes it is right to be angry but do not sin. Do not let your anger take the best out of you leaving you with the worst. Talk about it immediately if it is appropriate and convenient and let it go, but if it is not appropriate and convenient at that time, as soon as it is, please resolve it and never refer to it again. When I say appropriate and convenient, I mean when your anger has subsided and you are calmer, you will get the best out of the situation than when you are angry and boiling. It is wise and appropriate most of the times, that you let your anger subside before you try to resolve problems otherwise you might make matters worse which is not wise and godly. As you want people to do to you, do likewise to them.

Remember that s/he loves you and love does not intentionally hurt the other person, hence it is an error on his/her part. Consider that if it was you, would you like to be forgiven? Would you like him/her to forget it? Whatever your answer will be that I advise you to do also.

3.   FORGIVING EACH OTHER WHATEVER

Forgiveness is the lubricant that makes the relationship moves smoothly and keeps it from stiffening or drying up. Keep on forgiving one another. There is no limit to forgiveness, forgive as many times as your spouse offends you and you do not go back to the past events that has been sorted out.

Paul in Colossians 3:13 states "bearing with one another, and forgiving one another, if anyone has a complaint against another; even as Christ forgave you, so you also must do." NKJV

We must be honest with our forgiveness. It is easy to say 'I forgive you.' But when we see the person that offended us and or remember what they have done and become upset or unhappy either about the person or the situation, then we have not fully forgiven. Not until the pain, hurt and ill-feeling disappear when we see the person or remember what they have done, have we forgiven. When you feel at ease, comfortable and relaxed when you see that person or remember the thing they have done, then you have truly forgiven.

Above all, keep praying together and the relationship will work and be fruitful and beneficial to all that are in it. Psalms 118:24 says that:

"This is the day the Lord has made; we will rejoice and be glad in it." NKJV

This song of David is a profound message that encourages us to rejoice and be glad in any day God has made. When you look at this, you will know that every day is the day that the Lord has made. We should be rejoicing and be glad every day. As long as it is today, it is the day that the Lord has made. This rejoicing and gladness was not dependent on David's circumstances, it was about who God is, what He had done for David and what He was doing and what He was going to do. I want you to look at this text the same way. The joy and gladness God commanded is not dependent on your circumstances, neither does it depends on how you feel or think. It is about who God is, what He has done, is doing and what He's going to do in your lives.

CONCLUSION

One thing I would like couples to understand is this, if they allow what their spouse says and does to them, it will pain them beyond the level they bargained for. This situation will always be exploited by Satan and if they allow him, he will do it beyond what they negotiated for. When that happens there will be no time to enjoy the day and themselves. On the other hand, if they choose to ignore the small things that do not matter and tell Satan to get behind them, then those things that do not really matter will not hold them back. If they decide to enjoy each day and each other they will really enjoy the day, themselves and each other. The more they enjoy, the more they want and the more they can get from each other. Couples must decide to enjoy every day and each other. They should practice what the Bible says in Psalms 118:24 "This is the day the Lord has made; we will rejoice and be glad in it." NKJV

Challenges will always be there, but if couples wait for the challenges to go before they enjoy the day and each other, they may have to wait for quite a while. Worry and anxiety are joy stealers and Satan is an expert in orchestrating this and magnifying beyond its size and limit. So I encourage couples to use Jesus' advise in Matthew 6: 34

> "Therefore do not worry about tomorrow, for tomorrow will worry about its own things. Sufficient for the day is its own trouble." NKJV. And Paul's advice in Philippians 4:6-7 "Be anxious for nothing, but in everything by prayer and supplication, with thanksgiving, let your requests be made known to God; and the peace of God, which surpasses all

understanding, will guard your hearts and minds through Christ Jesus." NKJV.

People too could steal the couple's joy if allowed to crowd the marriage. If couples do not resolve matters between themselves and decide to involve outsiders no matter how close, those outsiders can bring more conflicts than the one on their hands. Couples should learn to resolve their problems quickly and preferably between themselves. I will strongly advise couples to only involve trustworthy people in their conflict if it is absolutely necessary and only if they cannot do it between themselves. Such people may include their Pastors and elders.

The last note to couples is that they should know that there is no perfect family on earth. There is no couple without their own issues. No matter how old they are there is always one thing or the other. But "THE ABILITY TO TOLERATE THE INADEQUACIES OF THEIR SPOUSE (HUSBAND OR WIFE) in marriage, that is what can keep them going. I encourage couples to look at the first picture of rough, sharp and un-even edged pebbles at the source of a river. As the river propels them along its bed making them to rub on each other they become the second picture, rounded, smooth and beautiful. By the time they get to their destination, they look beautiful and that is when people want them.

Rough and sharp edged stones   Smooth, rounded and beautiful stones

The same is true for all relationships. Whilst they first start to know and live with each other, couples are like the rough, sharp and un-even edged stones with chips on their shoulders, needing to be rounded and smoothened. Then after they start rubbing on each other, offending and forgiving each other, seeking each other's good, they start becoming roundish, smoother and more beautiful as the pebbles on the right picture. But I must tell couples that it is hard work and only when they can put the hard work into their relationship, only then can they reap the reward of the smoothness, roundness and beauty.
Marriage is good and enjoyable if they choose to enjoy it.

MAY GOD BLESS AND PROSPER YOUR MARRIAGE, AS YOUR SOULS PROSPER AND I WISH YOU BOTH BEST WISHES.

Adedayo Ige
Minister,
Harringay United Church-Baptist
London N8 0RG
June 2016.

REFERENCES

1. http://www.oxforddictionaries.com/definition/englis h/marriage
2. Gathering for worship p190, 2005, edited by C.J. Ellis and M. Blyth, Canterbury Press, Norwich
3. The Holy Bible, New Kings James Version
4. http://www.thefreedictionary.com/tolerate
5. http://en.wikipedia.org/wiki/Communication
6. Ditto
7. Henry George Liddell, Robert Scott, A Greek-English Lexicon, on Perseus in http://en.wikipedia.org/wiki/Greek_words_for_love
8. In Pursuit of His glory, R.T Kendall, 2014, Hodder & Stoughton, London. pg 265-7
9. http://www.psychologytoday.com/articles/201302/t he-power-touch
10. Ditto
11. http://www.webmd.com/menopause/guide/sex-menopause
12. http://www.oxforddictionaries.com/definition/englis h/conflict
13. Total Forgiveness, R.T Kendall, 2001, Hodder & Stoughton, London
14. http://www.oxforddictionaries.com/definition/englis h/honour
15. In Pursuit of His glory, R.T Kendall, 2014, Hodder & Stoughton, London.
16. HOLY BIBLE, NEW LIVING TRANSLATION ®Copyright © 1996, 2004, Tyndale Charitable Trust.

LIFE ON THE
VICTORIAN STAGE

LIFE ON THE VICTORIAN STAGE

Theatrical Gossip

Nell Darby

PEN & SWORD
HISTORY

Cover Image: 'A Variety Actress and the Dudes' from Illustrated Police News, 10 June 1899, p.12. (Newspaper Image © The British Library Board. All rights reserved. With thanks to The British Newspaper Archive, www.BritishNewspaperArchive.co.uk)

First published in Great Britain in 2017 by
PEN & SWORD HISTORY
an imprint of
Pen & Sword Books Ltd
47 Church Street
Barnsley
South Yorkshire
S70 2AS

Copyright © Nell Darby 2017

ISBN 978 1 47388 2 430

Printed and bound by
Gutenberg Press Ltd., Malta

Pen & Sword Books Ltd incorporates the imprints of Pen & Sword Archaeology, Atlas, Aviation, Battleground, Discovery, Family History, History, Maritime, Military, Naval, Politics, Railways, Select, Social History, Transport, True Crime and Claymore Press, Frontline Books, Leo Cooper, Praetorian Press, Remember When, Seaforth Publishing and Wharncliffe.

For a complete list of Pen & Sword titles please contact
PEN & SWORD BOOKS LIMITED
47 Church Street, (Barnsley: South Yorkshire, S70 2AS, England
E-mail: enquiries@pen-and-sword.co.uk
Website: www.pen-and-sword.co.uk

Contents

For Aunty Liz – acting was in her genes.

Foreword

This book originated with my own family history. Having found out that my great-grandfather's three sisters were all on the stage and that two died young – at 18 and 26 respectively – I originally researched their life stories and found a complex tale of life on the Victorian stage. One sister, Alice Harper, eloped with the actor Fred Solomon – brother of the noted composer Edward – in Edinburgh, whilst touring the provinces with him; her sister Edith and Edith's husband, fellow performer Lytton Grey, attended the unofficial 'wedding' in a private house. The night Alice died, in the City of Dublin Hospital, of typhoid fever a month later, she was all alone – her husband, sister and brother-in-law were all due to perform on stage at the Gaiety Theatre at 8 pm that night and did so. The show must go on, after all.

Their stories, like many of those involved in the Victorian theatrical world, were never recorded in the press. If you were a minor figure, your only hopes of getting a mention were to advertise your services in the classifieds, to get a review – bad or good – or to be the instigator or victim of an offence or scandal. Through trying to find my own theatrical family in the pages of the newspapers, I found many more like them, trying to make a living against all the odds. Some of their stories are given here, as well as some linked to my ancestors; Lytton Grey's divorce from his second wife – an actress who fled to America with a colleague she had an affair with – featured in the press, as well as Fred Solomon's brother's bigamous marriage to an American star. This book is not about the plays they appeared in, or the development of the theatre over the nineteenth century – for those subjects, there are other books around that take a more intellectual look, perhaps, at the Victorian theatre. This book instead concentrates on the professional, personal and criminal lives of individual performers over the course of the era – focusing on the gossip that was integral to the nineteenth-century press and public alike.

A note about sources. I have referenced all non-newspaper sources, but to acknowledge every single newspaper and article I have used would make this book far too unwieldy. However, the newspapers looked at include, obviously, *The Era*, but also a range of regional and national papers from England, Scotland, Wales and Ireland. Newspapers in America, Australia and New Zealand have also been consulted. The majority of the cases here are concerned with provincial or London-based theatres, such as the former patent theatres; however, some music halls are also mentioned – for the purposes of this book, 'theatrical' covers both Victorian theatres and music halls. The Theatre Royal, Drury Lane, is commonly recorded here as 'the Drury Lane theatre', as the press similarly referred to it by this name. Similarly, the former Theatre Royal, Covent Garden, is also referred to as 'the Covent Garden theatre', as it was in the press, it reducing confusion between the two.

I would like to thank the Society of Authors for granting me a Michael Meyer award to help with research for this book. Thanks too to the staff at The National Archives

(TNA), London Metropolitan Archives (LMA), Dublin City Archives and the New York Public Library for their help and also to Janet Zimmermann. Lucy Bailey, Lucy Williams and Andrew Chapman have given me lots of support, encouragement and the occasional historical debate and I could not have written this book without the support of my family – my husband John and children Jake and Eva – and so the biggest thanks go to them.

'Authentic anecdotes of eminent persons connected with the stage have ever been most welcome to the public, who generally find in them amusement while they gratify their curiosity'.

The Era, 28 September 1856

Introduction

Celebrity gossip is nothing new. Throughout the centuries, certain people in society have been singled out for attention and even adulation, their actions and speech, their clothes and hair, commented on and copied. In the eighteenth century, individual actors, actresses and even stage managers became the focus of such attention and the burgeoning newspaper industry duly covered their productions. Actresses were seen as rather risqué characters and were the focus of royal attention. Dorothea Jordan, for example, an actress said to have the most beautiful legs ever seen on stage, became the lover of the Duke of Clarence – later King William IV – in 1791. She was with him for two decades, giving birth to ten children. This was in addition to the other illegitimate children she had previously had by a police magistrate and a theatre manager.

The nineteenth century was a period that saw great change both in the world of the theatre and that of the press. In 1843, the monopoly of the patent theatres ended and this saw new theatres open that could undercut the prices of the old theatres such as Drury Lane and Covent Garden. The established Theatres Royal, such as the one in Cardiff, fought to prevent other theatres opening in their towns and taking trade away from them, but this was ultimately futile.

Cheaper tickets in the new theatres meant the working classes could increasingly enjoy the theatre – but alongside this, the development of the music hall put greater pressure on the theatre managers and owners, giving them greater competition and leading to theatres' fortunes declining. They reacted to this in perhaps a surprising way in the later part of the century. Rather than by trying to get the working classes back to the theatres and away from the music halls and penny gaffs, they instead focused on the middle-class audience, making efforts to attract them in a variety of ways, including a clampdown on violence and disorder.[1]

The development of the music hall in England went in tandem with the growth of theatrical reporting and gossip in the press. They had originated in taverns where, by the 1830s, music rooms were being established where singers performed while the audience drank. By the 1850s, purpose-built venues were sprouting up and by 1875, there were nearly 400 music halls in Greater London alone.[2] Alongside this, there was a 'profound revolution' taking place in the world of the newspapers, where there was an increasing number of readers and an increasing number of publications. The sheer number of daily, evening and Sunday editions of the newspapers needed items to fill their pages – not just hard news and breaking stories, but advertisements and gossip too. Filling pages meant an increasing reliance on soft news – theatre news, sports and gossip. Technological advances in terms of transport and telegraphy meant that news could travel both around the UK and around the world quicker than ever before; it also meant a wider world of gossip and scandal could be plundered for copy. The introduction of images – both illustrations and photographs – also changed the nature of the press. There was a recognition that readers liked them and they also gave individual publications a USP. The likes of the *Illustrated London News* and the *Illustrated Police News* gave their readers news and gossip that was presented in an attractive, dramatic way; the news was no longer focused on serious world events in dry, complex language or tone, but in shorter soundbites, with the focus on speech, description and drama. The rise in literacy rates in the Victorian era meant that the working classes were increasingly able to read these newspapers themselves and the cheaper newspapers were an affordable form of enjoyment for workers. Children, too, were able to read publications designed for them, that focused on gripping tales of adventure and crime that were worlds away from their own hard lives – and although the authorities worried about the effect these papers had on individuals, they were a reflection of the need for escapism and the desire to read about those with more exciting lives.[3]

It was the press that cultivated the theatrical celebrity, then, obsessing about the exploits of those working in the theatre. For example, Sarah Bernhardt, who became famous in the 1870s, was known as the 'most famous actress the world has ever known' and 'the divine Sarah', working with the press by lying about her origins to create a more exotic 'back story'. Her affair with a nobleman, a rumoured lesbian affair and speculation that she had also been romantically involved with the future Edward VII, only added to her attraction for the press and public alike.

But it was not just those at the top of the acting tree who were written about; this was the age of the provincial theatre and the local and national press eagerly covered not only regional productions, but the off-stage antics of those who acted in them. These lesser actors and actresses provided a constant stream of stories for the increasingly gossip-driven press – the London weekly newspaper *The Era*, established in 1838 by Frederick Bond, just a year after Victoria became queen, became renowned for its theatrical coverage, even being known as 'The Great Theatrical Journal' and having a regular column entitled 'Theatrical Gossip', from which this book gets its subtitle. Its early editions were fairly limited in terms of their theatrical coverage; in the late 1830s, it was not dissimilar from other publications, with a blend of foreign and national news, political comment and letters – but even at this early stage, there was a hint of things to come, with cases drawn from coroners' inquests, sheriffs' and debtors' courts and the London police courts, and gossip based on the latest dances and fashions. This gossip, as time went on, became increasingly focused on the theatrical profession.[4]

Taking their cue from the nature of American newspapers, these Victorian publications were 'cheap, visual and by the standards of their time, often sensational'.[5] Their readers wanted to read about what their favourite actors and artistes were doing, both in their public and private lives, and the actors and their managers wanted to publicise their shows to ensure good crowds and good takings in an increasingly competitive market. But this competitiveness and pressure led to problems for actors, actresses, managers and agents and the press were keen to report these, too. This did not just apply to the national press – the regional newspapers eagerly reported events not just locally, but those involving actors and actresses both in London and overseas. The railways enabled the rapid distribution of the London newspapers to the regions (and vice versa). In addition, the development of the telegraph over the nineteenth century led to speedier communications and with the establishment of the transatlantic telegraph in the 1850s, telegraphy to Australia in the 1870s and the increasing popularity of telephones in the 1890s, gossip from around the world could be transmitted to the British press and on to their readers quicker than ever before.

Debts, unemployment, personal problems – all were leapt on by the gossipy Victorian newspapers. Some actors resorted to holding their ex-girlfriends up with guns to extort money from them; others killed themselves. Travel was integral to the lives of many actors – in 1895, for example, it was noted that Queenie Leighton, who at that time was performing in the pantomime *Sinbad the Sailor* in Middlesbrough, had had 'tempting offers recently to play in foreign parts – South Africa and South America'. Some actors took advantage of performing around the world to leave their partners, or to marry new ones whilst failing to remember that they already had a spouse back in England. They were involved in civil and criminal cases, they seduced or were seduced; they married, divorced, died – in sometimes tragic or difficult circumstances. Their complex, erratic, peripatetic lives led to a wealth of stories that the Victorian press, with their increasing focus on gossip and theatrical gossip in particular, were only too eager to exploit.

This was all set within the context of continuing political debate over the morality of the theatre and those involved with it. It has been suggested that 'moral prejudices against actors and more particularly against actresses, were stronger in the provinces than in London and only started to decline late in the century'.[6] Actresses were viewed in one of two ways, though. Some felt threatened, as the Victorian stage offered opportunities to women that they were not able to gain elsewhere, particularly in economic terms.[7] These were independent women, making their own money and having the freedom to travel for work.

Yet they were also viewed by some as innocents who needed protecting, for fear that they could be seduced by immoral actors. Critic Clement Scott had criticised men who allowed their wives to become actresses if they failed to accompany them on tour; such a husband must be 'either a fool or a knave'.[8] This was also applicable to children; when the age at which children should be allowed to take on paid theatrical work was debated in the House of Commons in 1889, the Cirencester MP Arthur Winterbotham had to apologise for earlier comments he had made about the morality of actresses (he had implied that when actresses came to the end of their careers, they became prostitutes). However, he added, 'I do not desire to withdraw my grave protest against this door being specially opened to little girls to enter a profession full of danger to their purity and morality.'[9] At around the same time, in 1896, the Chief Justice of Victoria, Australia, Sir John Madden, discoursed on the theatrical profession during a divorce case, where an actress on tour was charged with having had affairs with three itinerant actors. Although she didn't deny the facts, her husband was refused a divorce, the Chief Justice stating that he had 'contributed to the domestic catastrophe by permitting his wife to go on tour for a prolonged period without adequate safeguards'. He noted that the wife 'had to travel about and constantly associate by night as well as by day, with a class of men often attractive and not unfrequently lax in their views of sexual morality. Of course, there are many actors and actresses of the highest principles and circumspection, but notoriously, there are many who are otherwise.'

In the same year, Lord Russell, the English Lord Chief Justice, stated that he was 'thankful' that he had nothing to do with the stage in a professional capacity, because there were 'thorny questions' relating to it 'as to whether the drama ought to be attractive or repulsive, according to nature or according to imagination, or whether certain plays are to be forbidden or not forbidden'. He added that some said actors did not 'live always as they ought to have lived and so forth. Well, I leave these things to moralists.'[10]

This association of the theatre with sex and perceived immorality was perhaps part of the attraction both for the press and for its readers – and newspapers including, but by no means restricted to, *The Era*, duly filled columns with a range of theatrical gossip. And here, for the modern reader, is just a sample of that theatrical gossip, which shows, above all, how the Victorians were as much driven by celebrity culture as we are today.

PART 1:
BUSINESS LIVES

CHAPTER 1

Licensing the Theatre

Theatres were not, despite what some newspaper writers and readers thought, places of simple enjoyment and fantasy. They were businesses – and ones that were difficult to make money from. Everyone involved in the theatrical way of life, from managers, lessees and agents to actors, actresses and chorus girls, hoped to make money – but more often found themselves mired in financial complications, or even penury. It was only a small percentage of actors who became stars of the day and were able to enjoy a certain lifestyle; and fortunes could be as rapidly lost as gained. Dickens, in *Nicholas Nickleby,* gave a more prosaic view of the theatre when he wrote that in a touring company, 'the actors depend in the most direct way on the patronage of their audience – for their benefit nights, they have to go round selling tickets'. He also stressed the gap between the actor's public persona and 'the sometimes dingy realities of his life'.[1]

Actors' lives were, as they are still today, precarious. This is why they had to work hard to get engagements and to promote themselves. *The Era*, throughout much of the Victorian age, was full of advertisements placed by theatres, managers, agents and the actors themselves, publicizing their latest productions and the availability of individuals for roles. Actors' adverts were a 'valuable channel of self-publicity', stressing their successes so far.[2] Yet they also had an element of pathos, as can be seen in repeated ads placed by actors who were 'unengaged' or who highlighted minor roles in provincial plays as evidence of their achievements. Nobody wanted even a brief break; they were constantly seeking work and had to diversify in order to make a living. In 1860, for example, *The Era* included an advert placed by the Misses Maskall – as the singing sisters Elizabeth Wadd Maskall and Mary Malkin Sherwood Maskall were known – wishing to notify readers that they would 'make their last appearance at Scarborough this season, on Monday evening, Sept 17th, when, having completed their Summer Tour in the North of England, they will return to their town residence, 11 Norland Square, Notting Hill, where all communication respecting concerts, public or private pupils, &c, must be addressed'. It was sent to the paper from Tynemouth in Northumberland, with four days left of their northern provincial tour.[3] Actress Mrs Moreton Brookes advertised in the same edition. She put her 'provincial and metropolitan theatre' experience at the top, but then added that she was 'prepared to receive pupils for the stage and qualify them for the profession according to the best received rules'. These women shared what we would call the classified ads pages with a host of others all about to be 'unengaged', from Henry Cooke and his circus troupe of dogs and monkeys, to Herr Christoff, the tightrope walker and Monsieur Oriel, the French clown and chair performer. There was not just a performer for every occasion – there were too many performers, all scrabbling to get regular – or semi-regular – work and having to diversify in order to support themselves when roles could not be found.

It is interesting that, in the 'wanted' section of *The Era*, were lots of positions for practically-minded people – scene painters, props men, watchmen and fencing teachers (to teach swordfighting to actors). Acting roles were fewer, although one can imagine thespians leaping on the odd advert for 'an entire theatrical company'. Henry Butler's Dramatic Agency, which was located at 21 Bow Street, Covent Garden, placed a large advert in *The Era*, stating, 'artistes in every line and of every kind, required for London and Provincial Theatres of standing. Wanted, first-class English and Italian Vocalists for a Metropolitan Theatre; Principal Singing Comedy and Burlesque Ladies; Leading Actors and Actresses; Heavy Men; Juvenile and Walking Gentlemen; and Pantomimists of every description.' There were certainly a huge variety of performers that the Victorians wanted to watch; but there were also a huge number of performers who would only get a rare chance to perform at a London or provincial theatre, regardless of their skills. Then, as now, it was a competitive and precarious occupation.

Those who were the lessees of theatres could also face an uncertain career. The complexity of theatre licensing meant that a production could be refused a licence, or have it withdrawn, as a result of complaints or concerns about morality and behaviour – not just within the theatre, but outside, too, as moralists expressed concern about the impact of theatres on their neighbouring communities. The history of the licensing of theatres and other establishments in London is a long one. The Disorderly Houses Act of 1751 meant that places of entertainment either within the City of London or Westminster, or within 20 miles of them, had to get a licence from a magistrate in order to carry on staging entertainment for audiences. These licences were not a foregone conclusion – they could be issued or renewed, but they could also be refused. Where theatres got into trouble, reneging on the terms of their licences, their proprietors could find themselves hauled before the magistrate at the General Sessions. These were known as Quarter Sessions outside of London as they met four times a year – however, in London and Middlesex they met more frequently due to the higher number of cases needing to be processed.[4]

In 1737, the Licensing Act (10 Geo II c28) was passed and this set out to control travelling actors considered to be rogues and vagabonds, thus putting actors under the remit of the various eighteenth-century Vagrancy Acts as well. The Act stipulated that anyone acting in a play, or involved in its performance, who did not have either a letter patent or Lord Chamberlain's licence, or who did not have a legal settlement in the place of performance (likely for itinerant provincial actors) could be convicted as a vagabond. The Act also set out that a copy of all new plays had to be submitted to the Lord Chamberlain's Office at least two weeks before the first performance was scheduled. Therefore, the Lord Chamberlain was a censor of plays; he could ban all or part of a play and refuse to grant a licence. His jurisdiction did not just apply to Westminster, but also to royal residences and public houses. By 1800, as Jacky Bratton has commented, there were only two theatres – Covent Garden and Drury Lane – catering for an expanding population in the winter, with the Haymarket Theatre covering the summer season. A few small theatres were allowed to perform plays with music and others opened outside the Lord Chamberlain's geographical remit, such as on the South Bank, operating under the jurisdiction of local magistrates.[5]

The Licensing Act was repealed in 1843, when the Theatres Regulation Act (6 & 7 Vict c68) was passed. However, this had a similar function and under its remit, the Lord

Chamberlain and Justices of the Peace had responsibility for the licensing of theatre managers (in 1788, JPs had already been given some responsibility for licensing within their areas of jurisdiction, under 28 Geo III c30). All London and Westminster theatres could apply to the Lord Chamberlain's Office for a licence to perform drama, as could the boroughs of Finsbury, Marylebone, Tower Hamlets, Lambeth and Southwark. New plays had to be submitted for approval – for a fee – at least seven days before a first performance and licences could be withdrawn for inappropriate behaviour. However, matters were not simple. Small saloon theatres (including public houses) could apply for either a magistrate's licence that enabled their customers to drink on the premises but not watch dramatic performances, or a Lord Chamberlain's licence, that enabled an establishment to put on dramas, but not allow drinking in the auditorium. This situation resulted in theatres and music halls developing separately, catering to those who wanted 'serious' drama and those who wanted more varied entertainment.

These attempts to regulate theatres and other places of entertainment hint at what the authorities *really* didn't want people doing – entering into prostitution, or using prostitutes. As Frederick Burwick has noted of the 1788 Theatrical Representations Act, 'moral supervision was the rationale' behind it and subsequent legislation.[6] From the attitude that female actresses were little more than prostitutes or loose women developed the Victorian conceit that theatres, and their environs, were hotbeds of iniquity, where prostitutes gathered. The newspapers and archives are full of cases involving theatres having their licences refused or rescinded. For example, in 1866, the *Oxford Times* recorded that Charles Moralli had his application for a theatre licence refused, after the mayor had spoken out to say that 'he did not think that theatres were beneficial to the interests of the young men of the town and therefore he could not be a party to such things'. A majority of Oxford magistrates consequently decided to refuse the licence. The licensing of theatres, music halls and dance halls was a popular issue; when Middlesex magistrates gathered to hear applications in October 1850, it was noted that 'the court was crowded with parties interested in and connected with, the musical and theatrical professions and places of public entertainment'. Although many establishments had their licences approved or renewed without objection, the Catherine Wheel in Great Windmill Street was not so lucky. The churchwardens and overseers of St James, Westminster, petitioned the court, asking for the licence not to be renewed. It emerged that they had decided to oppose every music or dancing licence submitted by an establishment within the parish, as it thought 'the granting of such licence[s] had a demoralising effect upon young people'. In this case, the magistrates approved the licence anyway, after hearing that there had been no complaints about how the Catherine Wheel had been run over the previous year. A perusal of the cases that came up in this period suggests that complaints made by individuals about how a licenced establishment had previously been run affected the decision to renew that licence far more than a vague argument about the moral effect of granting licences. However, the Middlesex magistrates were still accused of inconsistency in how they dealt with licences – approving one whilst refusing another that looked identical and making their minds up about individual applications before they had even walked into court. The chair of the Middlesex magistrates in 1850 was stung by such accusations, saying, 'He was supposed to be against music and dancing and for the curtailment of enjoyments of the people, but he had done a great deal to promote those enjoyments.'

Competition was also taken into account when deciding licence applications. In 1887, the Cardiff magistrates met at the city's police court to hear Harry Day's application for a dramatic licence for a newly-built music hall adjoining the Grand Hotel on Westgate Street. Harry, originally from Birmingham and running the Days' Concert Hall there, intended to provide drama to a 2,000-strong audience in the new hall. His barrister argued that the population of Cardiff, which was around 100,000, needed more than one theatre – there already existing the Theatre Royal. However, Louis Reece, who spoke on behalf of the Theatre Royal's lessee, Edward Fletcher, argued that not only were two theatres not needed, but it would be detrimental to the Cardiff Theatre if a second was granted. He argued that the new build was called a music hall and therefore, only music should be allowed to be performed there – not theatrical productions. In addition, competition was not healthy – 'all competition in regard to theatres in small towns [*sic*] was the reverse of healthy'; Mr Fletcher had spent a lot of money on his theatre and his expenses were large. Cardiff had declined in 'social importance' and fewer people now wanted to visit the theatre there – 'attendance was anything but satisfactory'. However, it then turned out that Harry didn't want to put on dramas; he wanted to use the building as a music hall and really needed a music licence, but the magistrates weren't due to hear music licence applications at that time. As he had already booked a number of acts, he had tried to apply for a drama licence instead, as that would cover the other acts he had booked and it was the only type of licence up for discussion. The magistrates felt that Harry had been rather rash to book acts prior to being granted a licence and therefore refused him one – almost as if to teach him a lesson.

The moral effect of theatregoing, and of music halls, was regularly used as a reason to refuse a licence. In 1865, a case in Paisley involved a statement from one Robert Kerr regretting the fact that magistrates were advising that a licence be granted to 'permit every sort of immorality' (in reality, it was an application for a licence to put on theatre productions at the Exchange Rooms Concert Hall in Paisley). He saw the stage as having gone downhill since the mid-eighteenth century, it now 'abounding' in immorality – 'How would any man like to see his children going to such places, where they heard indecent talk which, to a great extent, inflamed their passions? And yet they heard a magistrate speak of the wants of the public in this matter . . . The town was very much degraded already by drunkenness, without increasing the means of promoting its immorality.' Another man who wanted the licence refused stated that, 'Another ground was the religious element. He was quite sure if the religious people had known of this application, there would have been a great many petitions sent in against it.' These people were fighting what seems to have been a losing battle; in this case, the licence was granted and it was similarly in many other towns where moral objections were raised.

Yet this was not always the case and, on occasion, such moral objections resulted in action being taken against allegedly offending theatres. In 1894, the London County Council (LCC) took action against the Empire Theatre of Varieties in Leicester Square, due to its alleged links with prostitution. The Empire had a somewhat chequered history in terms of licensing; in 1886, the Middlesex magistrates had refused to grant it a licence. The *St Stephen's Review* then published a piece stating that the magistrates had then told the Empire that if they paid £1,000, they could have the licence. It was later determined that this was a libel, but the *Review* then published another piece stating that 'the matter was a joke' and apologizing for the original article. However, it was published so late that an action for libel was still formally brought before the Queen's Bench. Mr Justice Stephen commented, 'It was said it was a joke. He failed to see where the joke lay. It was a serious imputation the attributing to magistrates what, if true, would be a national disgrace.' It was decided that the defendants should plead guilty and enter into recognizances of £500 each. This case shows that there was some bad feeling towards the licensing of theatres, with some believing – even if couched as a 'joke' – that magistrates were using the licensing laws to line their own pockets.

The Empire had duly opened in 1887, presumably without the payment of a bung to gain its licence, and its licence was duly renewed regularly until 1894. The late chair of the LCC Licensing Committee had gone on record that he did not intend to 'interfere in any way with existing licences or the conditions on which such licences were granted'. In 1893, the Empire spent £2,000 on a new entrance to the theatre and its directors were confident in its continued success, noting that, 'the entertainment at all times has been entirely free from double entendre or vulgarity. Large sums of money have recently been spent, both on the stage and front of the house, to meet the requirements of the County Council.'

But then, when they applied for their licence to be renewed in 1894, their application was rejected by the Licensing Committee, who linked the Empire with prostitution and advised on several alterations they wanted to the fabric of the theatre, to eradicate this perceived problem. They requested that the theatre promenades be demolished, 'and the space now occupied by them be disposed of to the satisfaction of the Council' and that no 'intoxicating drinks' should be sold in the auditorium.

The theatre directors were appalled – 'the alterations proposed would necessitate the removing of the roof and other important structural alterations'. It was commented that the minority of people who had suggested these changes were not the 'only champions of virtue in the Metropolis' – there were numerous Vigilance Societies who might have been expected to complain if the Empire really was a hotbed of iniquity – but they had not found anything to complain about in the past seven years. Instead, the licensing Committee members were 'extreme in their views and intolerant of the views of others. They visited the Empire expecting and intending to see solicitation in the promenade and of course they saw it. Imagination went a long way in this matter.' One woman who had instigated the concerns, Laura Ormiston Chant, as a member of the National Vigilance Society, went as far as to declare that 'the promenade of the Empire was an open market for vice' and was a 'moral dustbin' that threatened to 'spread its contents through the streets of London'. However, one MP, John Burns, had said 'he had been to the promenade of the Empire five times. What surprised him about the women there was not their gaiety but their dismal melancholy. He thought they should try to get rid, not of these women, but of those men who went to the Empire and who had nothing to do but play with vice night and day.'

The Empire's directors issued a statement warning that 647 people employed by the theatre would lose their jobs if the LCC Licensing Committee recommendations were put into effect. In total, some 3,000 people were directly or indirectly reliant on the

Empire for their economic survival – 'principally persons of the lower classes'. If the Committee's recommendations were approved by the full council, 'the Empire will be compelled to close its doors. This would entail a loss of capital to the shareholders of some £200,000, as well as a very heavy sum to the freeholder.' It was also noted that the building had been converted into a variety theatre previously, under plans passed by the council's predecessors and that 'owing to entrances, exits and structural difficulties', it would be impossible to carry out the Committee's recommendations for changes. The Church and Stage Guild passed a resolution regretting the action of the committee. On 8 November 1894, the matter was discussed at the Queen's Bench, with Justices Charles and Wright dismissing the Empire Theatre's allegations of bias. Justice Charles said there was no doubt that the county council had 'discharged a judicial function in deciding the question of the licence'.[7]

As a result of the Empire's problems, a new association – the Public Amusement Protection Association – was set up, aiming to 'support the continuance of existing places of entertainment and refreshment, uncontrolled by the opinions of persons to whom such places afforded no amusement; to bring about an alteration of the existing licensing laws and to promote the movement for the opening of museums and other places, where rational enjoyment might be obtained by the masses and to support any such movements.' This new organization joined forces with the Theatrical and Music Hall Operatives' Union for a protest meeting against the Licensing Committee's actions, held at the Prince of Wales Theatre that weekend.

The Empire did put into effect the alterations ordered in 1894; but the following autumn, it successfully gained a renewal of its licence that was 'unhampered' by the previous conditions, after arguing that the alterations had made no difference to the nature of its clientele.[8]

Of course, the legislation affected the content of individual plays, as well as the operation of theatres. Sexual content was particularly investigated and viewed dimly by the examiners of plays. This was to some playgoers' satisfaction; in 1878, one reader of *The Era* wrote in to commend what he saw as a firmer hand being exercised by examiners of plays – 'There has occasionally been a terrible straining over a gnat, but this has been amply atoned for by a subsequent wholesale swallowing of camels.' This reader felt that sexually-suggestive plays could degrade the whole profession, and that some were calculated to 'give much offence' and could not, therefore, be regarded as satire. There was a belief by some, including this writer, that the degradation of the British theatrical tradition was being caused by alien influence – the English stage should be 'freed from the meretricious stuff which has hitherto disgraced it and kept clear from the dirt which some writers are so eager to borrow from our neighbours across the Channel'.

So it can be seen, therefore, that licensing caused both friction between the authorities or certain members of the public and those working within the theatrical industry and a restriction on what productions could be put on in British theatres. There was continual pressure on managers to ensure that their productions did not cause concern and that their audiences behaved themselves both within and outside the theatre, or face having their licence withdrawn. These were not their only concerns, though, and they faced legal pressures from other quarters.

CHAPTER 2

Theatrical Libel

In the latter half of the nineteenth century, libel was an occupational hazard in the theatrical profession, if press reports are anything to go by. Actors and others in the theatrical profession could be rather sensitive to perceived slurs and quick to take offence, bringing cases to the courts. This was, to some extent, understandable; a libel could have a drastic impact on their professional as well as personal reputation, resulting in fewer jobs, or in the case of managers, a perception of untrustworthiness that could affect their businesses. Problems could also arise from disputes within partnerships, or between contractors and sub-contractors – these were not all cases brought by or against actors, but involved a whole range of individuals employed in the theatres, from builders and decorators to architects and designers. Money and reputation were inevitably intertwined and were the cause of many libel cases brought before the courts and eagerly reported by the newspapers.

In 1873, a long account of one particular libel case was reported 'exclusively' for *The Era*. It was heard at the Court of Common Pleas at London's Guildhall and was brought by Charles Morton, manager of Islington's Philharmonic Theatre, against Charles Head, for both libel and slander. Libel, of course, was written, and slander spoken. Head denied both charges, stating that 'the words published and spoken were true in substance and in fact'. The charges and Head's defence, together with the men's status, led to a lot of publicity and interest in the case and on the day it was heard, 18 February, 'a number of members of the theatrical profession [were] present in court'.

Charles Morton was a very experienced theatrical manager, having worked in the industry for years and being known as 'The Father of the Halls' because of his association with the British music hall.[1] He had built South London's Canterbury Hall – 'which was a favourite place of resort for a considerable period' – and the Oxford Music Hall, near Tottenham Court Road, which he had also managed, before a company took it over. That company had subsequently been wound up and Morton had been left without an income. The libel, he stated, was therefore very damaging for him as he had 'nothing but his knowledge and experience to rely upon for his success'.

The man he accused of libelling and slandering him was a bookmaker. He had been introduced to Morton by others and they had at some point reached an agreement to turn the Philharmonic – originally a music hall – into a theatre and to operate it on that basis. Charles Head would put up the money and Morton would provide the knowledge of the industry. Morton believed that their agreement gave him absolute control and management of the theatre for three years and in return, he would receive a salary and a share of the net profits. The theatre had duly opened, concentrating on *opéra bouffe* – a form of comic opera that offered a more farcical than satirical experience – and achieving some success.[2] After a while, though, Head started to feel resentful that he had been financially responsible for the theatre, yet it was Morton who was getting all the credit for it. He started to interfere, until there was bad feeling between manager Charles and financial Charles.

As was common with the London theatres, which did not make as much money during the summer season, it was decided that the actors and actresses currently employed in Islington should go on a provincial tour during that time, with the theatre duly closing at the end of May. Head argued that Morton had not kept him informed, or sought his consent, about these arrangements; Morton insisted that Head had been kept fully aware and seen the advertisements that had been drawn up and published in *The Era* itself. But Head kept complaining. He had called Morton a 'bloody scoundrel', a 'damned scoundrel' and then shouted, 'He is indebted to me for everything he possesses, but I'll ruin him before I've done with him'. He accused Morton of defrauding him and on another occasion, said he'd 'robbed' him. On another occasion, the men had had dinner with one of Charles Dickens's sons (which one was not recorded), where Head again complained about Morton in similar terms. He then had some pamphlets produced, stating his complaints and accusing Morton of 'violations'. He ensured that others connected with the theatre received these publications; Edward Winder, former proprietor of the Metropolitan Music Hall in Paddington, stated that he had met Head a month earlier, 'and he inquired whether I had seen the pamphlet. I told him no and he said he would forward me one. I afterwards received one by post.' Morton was worried that if people believed those complaints, his character would be damaged and 'it was not likely he would be appointed to management by gentlemen of means who wished to possess a theatre. They must be satisfied as to his integrity.'

The case ran into a second day, with one of the theatre check-takers stating that Head had paid him to post around ninety pamphlets to various people. Others recorded hearing Head call Morton a scoundrel. But in the end, the judge ordered the jury not to concentrate on the slander, as spoken at the dinner, or the 'vulgar abuse' that Head was alleged to have shouted on various occasions, but on the written pamphlets – the libel being a more serious offence. The judge made clear that this was not 'a speech made on the spur of the moment, but a written statement deliberately made'. He cast doubt on Head's insistence that he had not seen adverts about the provincial tour in *The Era* – for that newspaper was, as well as being a theatrical one, also a 'sporting paper' and Head, as a bookie, was therefore 'likely to read' it. He considered that Head, in 'ill-humour or an undue desire for profit, had rashly uttered unjustifiable libellous matter' and the jury quickly agreed, awarding Charles Morton £200 in damages, thus giving restitution to his professional character.

The press could also become part of the story in libel cases – and in one particular case, brought its own case against a theatre proprietor. *The Era*, in 1862, made clear that it aimed to 'elevate, improve and encourage the theatrical profession' (despite its coverage sometimes contributing to the image of actors as raffish rakes and actresses as loose women) and was prepared to go to court to protect its image as a serious theatrical newspaper. In February 1862, its editor instigated an action for libel against Benjamin Webster, the proprietor of the Adelphi Theatre. The action was brought by Frederick Ledger, who was both proprietor and editor of *The Era*, and was heard at the Court of Queen's Bench at London's Guildhall.[3] Ledger sought compensation for 'a libel calculated to injure himself personally and diminish the circulation and profits' of his newspaper. He noted that *The Era* was 'partly a sporting and partly a theatrical journal, but it chiefly devoted its pages to subjects connected with the drama' and that as editor, he had tried to offer encouragement to the theatrical profession.

Webster's encouragement went beyond the newspaper's endorsements. In 1858, it had been proposed to form 'an institution called the Royal Dramatic College for building residences and giving pensions to actors and actresses who were unable to pursue their avocation on the stage' and Webster stated that he taken a leading role in its establishment. The proposal had been discussed at a meeting at the Princess's Theatre on 21 July 1858, attended by the likes of Charles Dickens and William Makepeace Thackeray – and, presumably, Ledger.[4] This was not the Royal Academy of Dramatic Art, which was only founded in 1904 by Herbert Beerbohm Tree, but a separate institution. A site had been found in Woking and the parties involved were now busy trying to raise funds to build and operate the home. Ledger stated that in 1860, a 'fancy fair' had been held at the proposed site, followed by a similar fair at the Crystal Palace the following year. He noted:

> Some true friends of the drama thought that these entertainments were not consistent with the object in view, namely, elevating in the estimation of the world the character of the ladies and gentlemen who appeared upon the stage. At these fairs there were Cheap Johns, Aunt Sallies, magic caves and wheels of fortune, in addition to the stalls kept by celebrated actresses.

Ledger said that although he approved of the institution and its aims, he, 'along with many others', didn't think the exhibitions would be popular with the public and so he censored references to them in the articles published in *The Era*. On 21 July 1861, he published an article commenting on the fair and a week later, published a letter from an individual that commented on the 'questionable taste of the committee appointed to carry out the arrangements for the fetes'. Ledger then received an angry letter from Benjamin Webster, acting as chairman of the committee of the Royal Dramatic College fete, demanding to know the identity of the letter-writer and wanting an 'apology from him, or you' – 'or (and my circulation is larger than yours) I will post you, both in London and every town in England, as sure as my name is Benjamin Webster'. Ledger, ever the newspaperman, duly published Webster's threat and added in an editorial note that Webster was trying to 'dictate to us the language, opinions and honest criticisms, our gentlemanly and independent writers are to pen'. After this, matters got worse. Webster, who had regularly advertised with *The Era*, withdrew all advertising and tried to prevent others from advertising too. Then, on 2 September, 'there appeared at the top of the playbill of the Adelphi a note' that accused Ledger of a 'gratuitous insult', the act of a 'very low-minded person' and one that Webster had 'forbidden'.

In court, Webster insisted that Ledger *was* a low-minded person, because 'for money, he inserted in his papers advertisements stating where improper books and prints could be purchased'. This was seen as an extraordinary defence, for in that case, most newspaper editors could be accused in a similar way and it was pointed out that some of Webster's productions were 'not quite consistent with the high moral tone which he assumed'! In return, Ledger was accused of having acted in order to annoy Webster – he denied this, but then added that 'he knew it would have that effect'. The two men admitted having been good friends up until this affair. The jury found in favour of Ledger, but made clear how absurd they thought the case was by awarding him damages of just one shilling. The Royal Dramatic College finally opened in 1865, with the Prince of Wales, later Edward VII, conducting the official opening. However, echoing the problems and disputes over funding it, it closed just twelve years later due to financial problems.[5]

It was not just *The Era* that had libel issues. In 1885, a weekly sports newspaper called *The Referee* – or, more specifically, its proprietor, Henry Sampson – was accused of libelling an actor named Owen Dove by publishing a bad review of his performance in a play entitled *Hush! Not A Word*. Mr Sampson had argued that the review 'was a fair comment and justified it as true'. The review, which was read out in court, referred to Mr Dove 'tottering' on the stage and it went on to state: 'A good many present thought this tottering was part of the business. It wasn't. Mr Dove is terribly afflicted. Therefore, he has my warmest sympathy, but this must not prevent me from saying that he should not upon the stage thrust his affliction before the public.' The review stated that Dove had nearly fallen over in a couple of scenes and that it was, in effect, painful to watch his difficulties. It then declared: 'God forbid that I should say one word needlessly to add anything to his suffering, but while he suffers good taste should induce him to abstain from acting, or else to devise for himself parts in which he can scarcely be accused of endeavouring to make buffoon-like capital out of serious illness.'

Dove himself gave evidence whilst seated, after asking permission to do so. He said that he suffered from a condition called *locomotor ataxia* and that although it impaired some movement, he could still take exercise – in fact, his doctors had told him that 'the excitement of the stage was good for him'.[6] He had been employed on this play at a salary of £20 a week and although it had been a failure, this was not due to him – and none of the other newspapers had found fault with his acting. He added that up until this time, the 'peculiarity' of his walk had never been noticed and that he had always tried to hide it by playing 'parts suited to his peculiarity' and by writing parts for himself. He had, for example, written for himself the part of a lame Spanish guerrilla in *Hush! Not A Word*.

He felt there was some animosity between him and Sampson; he did not like the man and he felt that Sampson disliked him as well. He admitted that Sampson had the right to criticise his acting in his newspaper, but this was a criticism based on a personal matter – it was malicious and false. He felt that the review made him 'on a par with the beggars outside foreign churches who got a living by displaying their sores and deformities'. But more importantly, since the review had appeared, he 'had no engagement and no manager had made any offer to him'.

Dove's solicitor argued that it was not 'obvious' to any member of the audience that Dove had a mobility problem, before admitting that Dove had had to lean on his arm and use a stick to even get into court. The defence then called various witnesses to state that they had noticed Dove's problems – part of its mission to show that the actor was 'ill-advised in attempting to improve his present position' by bringing a legal case. Yet the witnesses admitted that the 'tottering' was in keeping with the character Dove was playing and that his condition, in some ways, helped him with his characterisations. The jury had sympathy and found in favour of the struggling actor, awarding him £300 damages.

Publishing was certainly a dangerous profession. In another case from 1886, Monsieur Claude Marius Duplany, a French actor and manager known professionally as Marius, brought a case for the rather incredible sum of £1,000 (nearly £50,000 today) damages against James Davis. Davis, 31, was by trade a solicitor in Charing Cross, but he was sued for libel in his other career, as printer and publisher of a newspaper called *The Bat*.[7] The 36-year-old Duplany complained about a specific passage that appeared in *The Bat* on 23 March 1886:

> The Café Royal not only finds the money for the Empire Theatre, but has since found the way to the door for Charles de Chatelaine and others concerned in the production of *Round Leicester Square in Thirty Seconds; or, the Best Record from the Empire to the Alhambra*. Marius is now the sole manager of that badly built house. If Nicol [*sic*: Daniel Nicols, the proprietor of both the Café Royal and the Empire Theatre] would only persuade his patrons to dine comfortably at the Café Royal, would engage Marius in his old profession – that of a waiter – and would permanently close the Empire Theatre, he would confer the greatest benefit ever bestowed on the playgoing public.

Duplany argued that the innuendo of this piece was that as an actor or manager, he was incompetent and that his only skill lay in being a waiter. Davis argued that it was published without malice, but that he had already made an apology in *The Bat* and paid £10 into court to satisfy Duplany's claim – rather less than the £1,000 the latter was now arguing for. His written apology had been rather sly; although he had apologised for mistakenly thinking that Duplany had been a waiter, he had then argued that he did not agree that calling someone a waiter was bad – 'the profession of a waiter, if humble, is pre-eminently respectable and, indeed, so is that of an actor and I fail to understand how an actor of M. Marius's standing can be injured by a report that before he embarked in his present career he occupied a position equally trustworthy and certainly as useful. However, I have been sorry that his feelings have been hurt.'

Duplany's counsel argued that although 'at first sight it might not appear to be a serious thing to call a man a waiter', to call a man who had been a professional actor since the age of 15, when he had first appeared on stage in Paris, was indeed a 'very serious thing'. Duplany's personal qualities were stressed; he had only had a break from being an actor when the Franco-Prussian War broke out; at this point, he had returned to France and enrolled in the Chasseurs d'Afrique.[8] He served until the end of the war and then promptly returned to the London Lyceum to perform in *The Great Pink Pearl*. He had never been a waiter and Davis's apology was, in fact, 'no apology . . . but was simply an aggravation of the original libel'.

Davis had already made clear that if the case was brought to court, it would be:

> interesting, inasmuch as it will to some extent decide the social status of the actor. Is he inferior or superior to a waiter and if superior, how much? For my part, I do not consider that if I inadvertently called a tailor a hosier, or a butcher a baker, that I should injure him in his trade and M. Marius's grievance amounts to about the same thing.

The jury agreed. They found in favour of Duplany, but only awarded him £110, one-tenth of the amount he wanted, suggesting that although it was an insult to be called a waiter, it was not really that much of one.

A further Victorian newspaper proprietor who took on the role of defendant in a theatrical libel case was John Corlett, the first editor of *The Sporting Times*.[9] He appeared at the Mansion House Police Court on 24 January 1887, charged with publishing a false and defamatory libel concerning a chorus girl named Violet Davis, known professionally as Violet Dashwood. Violet had been in the chorus of the Avenue Theatre, but she and the other chorus girls had been reviewed by *The Sporting Times* and taken offence to a paragraph that referred to the girls as 'tarts'.

Unsurprisingly, the girls had taken the word to mean they were nothing more than persons 'of immoral character'. In court, there was absurd debate between the male counsels as to whether 'tart' really did always mean this and whether the character of the Princess in Captain Frederick Marryat's book *The Pacha of Many Tales* was being referred to as an immoral woman when she was described as 'the cream tart of delight' – a debate that caused laughter in court. One of the London aldermen then made others in court laugh again at his reference to having tart at dinner; the *Cardiff Times* simply headlined a piece on the case, 'What is a "tart"?'.

But in all fairness to the defendant, Corlett, he immediately stated that he was 'extremely sorry that the words should have been used, although he denied altogether that the word was used in the sense imputed to it. He wished to express his great regret to the prosecutrix that her name should have been mentioned in such a connection as to cause her pain.' He explained that he had been ill at home at the time the paragraph was published; it had been left to the sub-editor to deal with. Although that hapless sub was not to blame, had Corlett been in the office, 'he would not have passed the paragraph with the name of the young lady attached'.

Violet's character was then detailed by her lawyer. She was of irreproachable character, he said and had not just been in the chorus – she had had a part in the play and her name appeared on the bills. Violet lived at home with her parents and siblings and was maintaining herself by her own work, as an actress – 'she hoped, by her study and industry, [for] a good position in her profession'. Therefore, to be called a tart in a public review had caused her much pain. But Violet was both fair and careful. She knew that, at an early stage in her career, she could not afford to be labelled as a troublemaker. All she wanted was her reputation cleared; and so she accepted Corlett's seemingly sincere apology and stated that this and the payment of her legal costs, was all she wanted; she had no interest in being awarded financial damages. She agreed to both her summons and the case being withdrawn and that was the end of the matter.[10]

1887 was a bit of a bonanza year for lawyers dealing in theatrical libel suits, if the press reports are anything to go by. In May that year, David de Bensaude, the 29-year-old husband of actress Violet Cameron, sued H.S. Jennings, the owner of *The Umpire*, a three-year-old Manchester publication that specialised in sports and theatre news, and his editor.[11] De Bensaude wanted damages of £2,000 for libel in a report of an interview the paper had conducted with Hugh Cecil Lowther, the 5th Earl of Lonsdale the previous year, which had, in turn, resulted from proceedings brought against the earl for assault. In the interview, as published, there was an 'inference' that David de Bensaude was 'a thief, a liar, a drunkard, brutal to his wife, spending her earnings, cheating her out of her money and pawning her jewellery'. It was, his lawyer said, 'about as bad a libel as anyone could well conceive'.

De Bensaude and his wife certainly had a volatile relationship; the previous October, he had been in a New York police court charged with intent to kill, maim or shoot Violet Cameron 'because of her refusal to pay him £1,500 to go to Morocco or some equally remote place'. Violet gave evidence saying that she had been married for two years, had one child, but that David had never supported her and so she currently had a petition for a divorce pending in the London courts. David had also previously accused her of having adultery with the same Lord Lonsdale. Lord Lonsdale had also given evidence – with the papers noting that when he was called, 'he said that he was 29 years old and everybody looked surprised. He looks at least ten years older.' He admitted that he had previously assaulted de Bensaude and been fined 40s for the offence; they had been friends until David had 'tried to cut his wife's throat' one day. David was duly held for trial in the Court of General Sessions for his threats to Violet's life.

When the libel case then came to court the following year, the judge made it clear which side he stood on – and surprisingly, perhaps, it wasn't the earl's. The judge said 'he had more sympathy with a man who, being at odds with another and hating him, published a downright libel upon him, than he had with a man who published an atrocious libel on a man about whom he knew nothing, for the mere purpose of putting money into his pocket'. It was stated that *The Umpire*'s editor was young, didn't believe a peer of the realm would ever lie and therefore had felt safe to publish his interview. At that, there was laughter in court and the judge said, 'It really did require a considerable amount of credulity on the part of the court to accept that version of the case'. After an hour of deliberation, the jury agreed and found in favour of de Bensaude, awarding him damages of £390.

Two months later, David de Bensaude was back in court, after his actress wife sought a judicial separation from him – on the grounds of cruelty. He had then cross-petitioned, alleging that Violet had 'misconducted' herself with the Earl of Lonsdale. This may have come about as a result of the earl's original newspaper interview, for now, de Bensaude admitted that he had since made inquiries about the 'circumstances of the case upon which he had founded his petition', including 'interviewing' Violet and 'was happy to inform his lordship that there was no foundation whatever for any charge of impropriety of conduct' between the earl and wife – although 'undoubtedly the business relations between them were indiscreet and had led to exaggerated rumours'. He now wished to withdraw his divorce petition and to 'express his satisfaction that, in his opinion, his wife had completely cleared her character'. Violet then asked for her petition for a separation to similarly be withdrawn. De Bensaude wrote to Lord Lonsdale 'regretting that he should have caused him anxiety and trouble'.[12] Perhaps inevitably, it then emerged that Violet had indeed been having an affair with Lonsdale – and in fact, had given birth to his child in May 1887. It was suggested that de Bensaude had known about the child and was simply after Lonsdale's money.[13]

Even the editor of the seven-year-old newspaper *The Stage* was not immune from accusations of libel. In 1887, Charles Carson appeared at the court of Queen's Bench, charged with libelling Herman Merivale and his wife, the authors of a play called *The Whip-hand*. Merivale was a lawyer and keen amateur actor, who on the death of his father, the Permanent Under-Secretary at the India Office, had become a dramatist, writing several farces and burlesques.[14] As the next chapter will show, he was not averse to protecting his professional integrity in the courts. But in this case, he appeared both for himself and on behalf of his wife; the Victorian press did not regard her as important enough to have her own name mentioned – but she was Elizabeth, née Pittman, Merivale's wife of nine years.

The case centred around one particular part of *The Stage*'s review, which described the Merivales' play as 'a hash-up of ingredients which have been used ad nauseam, until one rises in protestation against the loving, confiding, fatuous husband, with the naughty wife and her double existence, the good male genius, the limp aristocrat and the villainous foreigner'. Merivale appeared in court to state that *The Stage* had 'imputed' that *The Whip-hand* was 'founded upon sexual impropriety', by conveying the impression that it was adultery on the part of the wife that formed the main plot of the play; Merivale denied this and argued for the 'purity' of *The Whip-hand*. *Reynolds's Newspaper* reported his argument further: 'The object of Mr Merivale had been to introduce to the public a class of play undefiled by any immoral suggestion and therefore he felt very keenly the language of the article.'

Charles Carson was not impressed. As his counsel stated, it was a matter of 'considerable importance' to the owners of public journals, who should not be subjected to unnecessary, 'vexatious and, he might add, foolish' actions for libel, as long as they restricted their criticism to the subject matter under discussion. He added that authors were notoriously sensitive creatures, over-analysing the motives of others, and Mr Merivale was not an exception to this rule. Mr Carson was a bit bewildered by the action, as he 'had not the slightest idea of suggesting that this was an immoral play and the words used in the article did not suggest such a thing'.

The judge, however, was not convinced. He found in favour of 'Merivale and Wife', but regarded the case as rather petty, awarding them damages of just one shilling. But the fact that Merivale had won the case was greeted with approval by another publication, *The Spectator*, which had regarded it as an important decision. It stated that the defence had been an 'attempt to deny the liability of journalists in actions for libel' and that it was glad, therefore, that the attempt had 'met with no success'. Late nineteenth-century editors regarded their publications as privileged and that therefore, their articles should not be allowed to be the subject of libel cases. *The Spectator*, rather loftily, thought that if they were allowed to be privileged in this sense, newspaper critics would, as a result, be 'practically irresponsible in their writing and so able to indulge in prejudicial and unfair criticisms without any fear of the consequences'. It was clear that Merivale and wife *versus* Carson was seen as something of a test case, with the freedom of the press on one side and those concerned about irresponsible reporting (and its effects on the business of writing and producing drama) on the other.

As can be seen, theatrical libels involved different people, for different reasons. Those who brought cases, or who defended them, could be from all levels of theatrical life. One libel, heard at the Westminster Police Court, did not at first sight appear to involve the theatre. The case was brought against Henry Ashford, a 44-year-old builder's clerk from Euston Square, by Edmund William Bradwell, a builder and decorator living at Great Portland Street. Ashford, it was heard, was formerly employed by Bradwell. He claimed to have been libelled in a letter written by Ashford to George Morley Dowdeswell, QC, one of the official referees of the High Court of Justice.

But to go back a bit. Bradwell had been employed by Francis, the 3rd Earl of Kilmorey to rebuild the St James's Theatre – Kilmorey owned the land the theatre was situated on.[15] Although he had finished the job, a dispute arose about the amount due for the work and eventually, Bradwell had to bring a case against Lord Kilmorey. He referred to Mr Dowdeswell, who found in Bradwell's favour. Months later, Ashford had written to Dowdeswell, alleging that Bradwell was guilty of falsifying his accounts and books and that he had tried to defraud Lord Kilmorey. Ashford detailed credits that hadn't been given for various items and deliberate errors made in calculations. A copy of the letter had also been sent to 'various theatrical persons with whom the prosecutor did business', including those involved in the rebuilding of the new Novelty Theatre – Ashford had been employed to work on this and as a result of the letter, building work had been stopped. Bradwell was understandably concerned that the letter might ruin his reputation and his business in the theatrical world, on which he depended.

Bradwell gave evidence that his books had been examined 'carefully' at the original case involving Lord Kilmorey and that the earl and his representatives had had access to them for more than a week before the case. He denied the allegations made against him and added that 'Lord Kilmorey's architect never expressed any doubts as to the accuracy of his accounts'. Ashford was committed for trial, but after discussion, a 'substantial' bail was agreed. When the case came to trial, 'a number of witnesses' were called and showed 'that there was not a tittle of truth in the charge'. Ashford withdrew his defence of justification and was bound over to come up for judgement if he was called on to.

These are just a few of the 'theatrical libels' – as they were termed by the press – that were reported on during the Victorian era. Reputation was everything in nineteenth-century society and it is therefore unsurprising that actors, writers and directors were keen to spot any potential libels and sue accordingly. Reputations, though, were important to all strata of theatre workers, from the well-known actors down to builders and other people without whom the theatres wouldn't have existed. There were also increasing concerns about the press having too much freedom and critics not being fair in their reviews of productions; and these concerns were played out both in court and in the pages of newspapers. There was a lot at stake in such cases. Editors were often the proprietors of their newspapers and a substantial loss in a libel case would have a major impact on their businesses. They had to balance the need to provide entertaining copy for their readers and to increase their audiences through their reputation for entertaining news, whilst at the same time not going so far that the subjects they wrote about could successfully sue them. Finding an equilibrium in this respect was a difficult task, as the court cases show, and it is not evident that this debate has been resolved even in the twenty-first century.

CHAPTER 3

Bankruptcy

Bankruptcy was an occupational hazard of theatrical management. Although it was attractive for actors to take on management responsibilities, as it gave them the chance to choose their own roles (the plum ones) and offered them and other individuals the chance to develop a career where they might make both their fortunes and reputations, in reality it was a 'risky business'.[1] You had to be a certain type of person to undertake the job; theatre lessees were 'entrepreneurs and speculators, known for their dabbling in multiple projects and their occasional monetary difficulties'.[2] Large sums could be involved, from hiring a company, to advertising productions and when times were bad, it could be the theatre managers who lost out.[3] Edward Tyrrel 'E.T.' Smith, for example, who had the lease of the Drury Lane theatre in 1852, 'continually embarked on new ventures' but never seemed to make money from them.[4] When manager and producer George Edwardes was reported to be in financial difficulties in 1897, his theatre company stepped in to help; one of his favourite 'Gaiety Girls', Marie Studholme, who was performing in America at the time, wrote to Edwardes to offer him her savings of £200 to help and added that she was confident she could raise £1,000 amongst the other actors, who were also willing to continue acting for him without pay. Edwardes, however, was able to refuse her kind offer.[5]

Initially, at least, there was a clear distinction between insolvent debtors and bankrupts – the former were individuals who were unable to pay their debts, whereas bankrupts were supposed to be traders, although many described themselves as such in order to qualify for bankruptcy. From 1861 onwards, however, insolvent individuals were also able to apply for bankruptcy. Cases could be heard both in London and at the district bankruptcy courts that had been established outside the capital in the 1840s. The newspapers could get information about bankruptcy proceedings from court records, petitions or advertisements placed in the *London Gazette*.[6] Until 1869 debtors could be sent to prison in England and so in such cases, court cases and prison records were invaluable sources of information for reporters.

One case from 1862 shows how debtors and bankrupts could now be one and the same thing – actor Gustavus Vaughan Brooke was reported to be a bankrupt who had appeared in court 'in custody of the gaoler of Warwick Debtors' Prison' to surrender to his bankruptcy petition and apply (successfully, as it turned out) for his discharge. Brooke was a heavy drinker with a history of unsuccessful partnerships and ventures, as well as a previous bankruptcy, and by the time he put on an unsuccessful run of *Measure for Measure* at Melbourne's Theatre Royal – where critics focused on the weak acting and saw it as a failure from the start – he was sinking financially. His biographer stated that 'things were all at sixes and sevens in the theatre and the public were soon to learn, in the most explicit manner, of the distress under which the management laboured'. At a benefit soon after, his business partner went on the stage to tell the audience that Brooke had 'disastrous losses' financially as a result of this latest partnership. Brooke had then made a speech, where he recognised the risk inherent in taking on the management of a theatre and noted: 'The receipts are diminished when the times are depressed . . . I have lost a fortune in it, but I trust that I have preserved my self-respect and my good name.'

Soon after, he returned to England, with an extra £1,500 debt to his name. He then succeeded in getting an engagement at Drury Lane, but in a 'wretched' theatrical company. This engagement was unsuccessful, poorly paid and was terminated prematurely. It was the man who had employed him, E.T. Smith – a man with a chequered career himself – who sought payment of debts and brought Brooke to bankruptcy. Brooke said he put in his petition for bankruptcy to stop the 'constant anxiety' he was under. His liabilities came to £2,267. His situation got no better; five years later, en route to Australia, his ship sank in a storm. He was seen standing on the ship as it went down, 'calmly surveying the scene, with his chin resting on his hands'.[7] The death of this actor saw long obituaries in the press that reported that 'the billowy curtain has fallen tumultuously on the last scene of the chequered life-drama of Gustavus Brooke, the tragedian' – but, as though the obituary writers were sucking lemons, went on to describe him as 'the lately too much despised remnant of wasted gifts and frittered faculties', who had failed in business through 'bad habits and financial mismanagement'.

Many actors doubled as theatre managers, or tried to move into management as a replacement for acting – and they could frequently have financial problems resulting from unsuccessful productions. William Charles Macready, the celebrated actor and manager, had a habit of trying to put others off following in his footsteps, describing the profession as 'unprofitable and demoralising'.[8] Macready's own stints as manager of the Covent Garden theatre in the 1830s and the Drury Lane theatre in the early 1840s had both been financially unsuccessful, so he was speaking from bitter experience.[9] Victor Stevens certainly found it unprofitable. He had been touring the provinces in a burlesque entitled *Go Bang*. In four weeks' time, in June, the tour would end – and then he had no further acting engagements booked until Christmas, when he would appear in panto on wages of around £35 a week. In the meantime, though, he had accumulated losses from a previous tour, in 1893, of *Bonnie Boy Blue*. Coal strikes had affected its success, he argued, and his main creditor was the Great Northern Railway Company. When he appeared in the bankruptcy court, he stated that he had no other productions in the pipeline; when asked why *The Stage* was currently advertising several burlesques he 'had up his sleeve', he answered: 'Oh, that goes for nothing. They have called me a good actor before now and I am not.' To laughter, he added that these burlesques were embryonic – 'I am prepared to write [them] to order if I can find a purchaser'. This highlights the speculative nature of theatrical workers, often living day-to-day, advertising plays that did not exist in the hope that someone would pay them to write them later.

As Macready's experience shows, bankruptcy could affect those who were deemed otherwise successful, or who gained later success despite their earlier problems. Back in 1854, the 'eminent actor' Charles Mathews of the Lyceum Theatre had become bankrupt. His financial problems had started some time earlier – in fact, back in 1838, when he and his wife were 'tempted' to go on tour to America, leaving behind their successful management of the Olympic Theatre. Their tour was 'disappointing' and while they were in the States, the Olympic, lacking Mathews' touch, also became unsuccessful. He lost

£3,000 as a result. He then took on the management of the Covent Garden theatre, but 'struggled through three seasons' before he had his properties seized and found himself charged with rent arrears amounting to several thousand pounds and sent to the Insolvent Debtors' Court. From this point on, he veered between extravagance and debt, coming to various arrangements with creditors that were all ultimately unsatisfactory. Newspapers recorded the fact that since 1838, his life had been a 'constant struggle with difficulties – he was always in the position of a man trying to swim with a stone round his neck – he was overweighted with debt'. The only thing that was free from debt, it was said, was his talent. However, his creditors gathered together to write a paper expressing their 'unabated confidence in him'. In court, the bankruptcy commissioner, Mr Fane, said that he would have been 'glad to have relieved Mr Mathews's anxiety at once' and it was only the fact that he felt he should examine the relevant case papers at home that had delayed granting him a certificate. His decision, somewhat surprisingly, led to applause from the creditors in court, especially when Mr Fane said, 'I hope his future career may be more fortunate in its pecuniary results than his former exertions have been'.

In another case, in 1891, the Manchester-born author, actor and comedian John Shine – known as J.L. Shine – came before the London Bankruptcy Court, with liabilities amounting to over £9,000, despite steady work at the Adelphi and Opera Comique theatres. He was said to have lost £10,000 on a production at the Globe Theatre and to also have speculated unsuccessfully on the stock market.[10] Shine was later to perform in a George Bernard Shaw play; he wrote to Shaw in 1904 to praise his 'god-like patience and courteous consideration'.[11] As can be seen from these cases, actors often branched out into theatrical management in the hope of getting a successful production or three and making more money than they would just acting. Yet it tended to be this move that caused their monetary problems. In 1893, Frank Owen Chambers, who used the stage name Frank Gilchrist, had his story covered in the *Gloucester Citizen* under the headline 'A Bankrupt Actor's Tale of Woe'. Chambers had been both an actor and theatrical manager – and, ironically, a former bank clerk. It was his bank earnings, together with some money from his father, that he had intended to use to put on a tour of a play, *Victory*. He had formerly put on a provincial tour of two plays – *Fatal Beauty* and *Never Despair*. These made some money and so he was confident that *Victory* would do well. But unfortunately, the day before the play opened in Kidderminster, the Duke of Clarence was buried and this affected his audiences. He only took £20 over three days. In another town, the local mayor was lying in state and the newspapers criticised him for having the 'indecency' of putting on a play whilst their mayor lay waiting to be buried. This second untimely death and the bad reports again affected his takings. In the county court at Kidderminster, to gales of laughter, it was suggested that if Chambers put on a play about his misfortunes, the unfortunate man might well make some money.

In court in Exeter in 1886, actor Charles Collette's case also showed a precarious financial situation arising both from his leasing of the Torquay Theatre Royal and a succession of short-term acting engagements. His average income for the previous four years had been between £300 and £400 a year; he earned £25 per week in pantomime in Manchester and a similar amount both as part of the Vaughan-Conway Company and at the Empire Theatre. He was due to be receiving a similar salary for a forthcoming engagement at the Alhambra Theatre. He had got into arrears with the rent on the

Torquay theatre, but had expected that 'the business in the winter' – pantomime time – would 'make up for the losses in the summer'. Collette gave the impression of a naïve man who had failed to take responsibility for his finances – he claimed that he didn't know what capital he had and 'knew nothing about the books or receipts' because he left all the finances to his manager, Henry Ebling Marston.[12] His bank account was even in Marston's name, although Collette was keen to stress that Marston 'was his servant and not his master'. He was clear, though, that he could not agree to pay a fixed annual sum to his creditors to pay them off, 'his earnings as an actor being so precarious'. They may have been precarious, but this did not prevent Collette from having a forty-year career on the stage.[13]

Although Collette blamed both his acting and his theatre management for his financial predicament, George Rutland Fleet, an actor who was known professionally as Rutland Barrington, put the blame purely on the latter for his own situation. He was examined at the London Court of Bankruptcy in 1891, where he stated that he was insolvent because of his unsuccessful leasing and management of the St James's Theatre, which had lost him over £3,000. He had only been the lessee for four months, from September 1888 to January 1889, but this had led him to borrow money from a friend and created liabilities of over £4,000. After giving up his lease, he was engaged by Richard D'Oyly Carte at the Savoy Theatre for £25 per week, to perform in *The Gondoliers* – but this successful job, playing Giuseppe in a long run of the comic opera, did not stop him being brought before the bankruptcy court. This run of *The Gondoliers* continued until 1891. Although he became a star of musical comedies in the Edwardian era, particularly those put on at Daly's Theatre on Cranbourn Street, near Leicester Square, he died in poverty in 1922 – a paralytic stroke having prevented him from working and earning for the previous three years.[14]

As Barrington's case shows, illness could affect an actor's ability to earn money – but in some cases, debt could also be caused by an actor's own inability to control his spending. In the case of the French-born Anglo-Irish actor Charles Francis Coghlan, both were factors in his debts. He was examined by the courts in February 1891, when he was 49 years old. At this time, he had, ironically, a good job, playing the male lead in *Antony and Cleopatra* at London's Princess Theatre, at a salary of £50 a week. Yet he had liabilities of over £3,000, which he blamed on 'his improvidence and also through illness'. He admitted that he always spent whatever he earned, but obviously did more than this, as he had a substantial debt – nearly £700 – caused from hiring carriages for himself and also had 'kept up a large establishment' in Hertfordshire. This was long-term financial mismanagement and excessive expenditure for, as he admitted to laughter in the court, 'he was enabled to make out his list of creditors from memory and from reference to writs and summonses with which he had been served'. Life was not completely smooth for the actor after this; his play *Citizen Pierre*, which he put on in New York, with himself in the title role, failed in early 1899 and he died in October that year.[15]

Some bankruptcy cases involved large sums of money, but others were far smaller and reflected the precarious finances of even well-known Victorian performers. So for every Frederick Morton Vokes – an actor whose debts were nearly £9,000, after the 'failure of theatrical speculation' when he tried to build a theatre in America – there was a Charles Sugden. In 1888, Sugden, who had been known professionally as Charles Neville until the previous year and was described as 'the well-known actor' in the newspapers, had a receiving order made against him at the London Bankruptcy Court.[16] It was stated that the debts were 'small' and that his only assets were items of furniture, presumably from his rooms on Gloucester Road and being 'covered by a bill of sale'.

But whether the amount was large or small, by the 1890s, the press enjoyed detailing the minutiae of an actor's finances, making public the rickety arrangements and precarious nature of theatrical life. So when Alfred Stevens, known professionally as Victor Stevens, went through the bankruptcy process in 1896, a long piece on him, headlined 'An Actor's Failure' was published in the *Sheffield Evening Telegraph*, describing him as 'the bankrupt, an actor, author and composer, [who] was also engaged taking companies on tour'. Stevens had unsecured debts of nearly £2,000 and no assets. He had managed a burlesque of *Little Boy Blue* in April 1892 which had resulted in a loss of £75; in June and July of that year, he had toured the same show and made a profit of £420, but when he repeated the tour in 1893, he made a loss. He then toured with two other burlesques, 'which just cleared expenses', before getting an engagement at the Lyceum Theatre. He then went on tour again, but then 'failed' in March 1895, which he blamed on the failure of the 1893 burlesque tour, as well as on 'the expense of his large family and certain relatives'. He had previously been made bankrupt in 1881. His income was laid bare in the court and the press; since March 1895, he had earned £96 in fourteen weeks, getting £40 for appearing in two pantomimes, paid in advance. He had, however, been unemployed since the previous Christmas. When asked if he had any prospective acting engagements coming up, Stevens responded: 'I have been managing for some time and do not consider myself on the London market. I am not the only first-class actor out of an engagement in London; better actors than myself are out of employment.'

It is clear that Stevens saw bankruptcy as something to be expected in his career and that the actor's ego enabled him to not see this as a sign of failure, or of a lack of talent – he was still a 'first-class actor' and unemployment was something that all actors should expect, regardless of their talent. In fact, that is how many of these cases come across, to modern eyes, although it should be remembered that we see these bankruptcies through the sometimes distorting mirror of the press. However, despite this, it appears that debt, insolvency and bankruptcy were not necessarily seen as matters to be ashamed of in the theatrical world – they occurred too often. The risk that actors took in choosing a life on the stage, where they took on often poorly-paid engagements and inevitably had quieter periods or periods of unemployment, was magnified when they attempted to take on a theatrical management role. A lack of awareness of the financial risks, or of finances generally, meant trouble often lay ahead – and some actor-managers saw this trouble as an inevitable part of their job. It was also, though, a worthwhile gamble, for there was always a hope of future success just around the corner.

CHAPTER 4

In Breach of Contract

Actors in Victorian Britain appear to have been a litigious lot, frequently bringing cases for breaches of contract against their management. This was understandable, however, given the reliance actors had on precious engagements that would enable them to earn a regular income – even if only for a while. A breach of contract was a civil, rather than criminal, matter that involved the plaintiff suing for damages. Cases in Victorian England and Wales after 1875 were heard at the Queen's Bench Division of the High Court, which had – and continues to have – responsibility for both breach of contract cases and libel, slander and negligence cases, all involving claims for damages. Prior to 1875, the Court of Queen's Bench served the same purpose as a court of common law, but this was abolished by the 1873 Supreme Court of Judicature Act and replaced with the Queen's Bench Division of the new High Court of Justice.[1]

Actors might sue simply because they had been dismissed from a production – such as when in 1892, George Sinclair ('an actor both in London and the provinces') was awarded £120 in damages after a touring company manager, Charles Wybrow, dismissed him from his production of *Paul Jones*. But they might also use the civil courts to establish their own legal rights as actors. In a case just three months after Queen Victoria's death, one comedian, G.A. Warden, claimed damages from the proprietor of the Theatre Royal in Bolton. He had been engaged by the proprietor, James F. Elliston, who ran more than one touring company, to play Atkins in a pantomime of *Robinson Crusoe* at the Broadway Theatre in Deptford. On 19 January 1901, Elliston put up a notice giving two weeks' notice to the company. The Queen died three days later and then another notice was put up saying that the theatre would be closed the following day out of respect and would close again for the Queen's funeral. A further notice stated that due to the Queen's death, the pantomime would be terminated immediately. However, another pantomime that Elliston was running in Stoke Newington continued and so Warden believed his panto was really being cancelled as it wasn't paying, and the Queen's death was a handy cover. The court found that 'there was no occasion to close the theatre for the death of the Queen excepting what is usual in such cases' and for those 'usual' days, Warden's salary would have been deducted as 'the rule of the profession was "no play, no pay"'. It was obvious, though, that Elliston had not needed to close the theatre for as long as he did and the clause in his performers' contracts relating to what would happen in the event of 'a public calamity' did not apply, even to the death of Queen Victoria. Warden received £18 damages; other suits were then brought by an actress in the pantomime and its stage manager and both won their cases too.

Other cases were watched eagerly by others, aware that they might need to have recourse to the law at some point in the future. One case in 1900 had 'excited a good deal of interest in the theatrical world' when it was heard at the Queen's Bench. Dramatist Herman Merivale had sued Martin Harvey – the professional name of Sir John Martin

Harvey (1863–1944), who was an actor, producer, playwright and theatre manager – for damages, claiming he had not produced Merivale's version of *Don Juan* at the Prince of Wales Theatre in London. Harvey then counter-claimed for libel, as Merivale had written a statement claiming to have been 'shabbily treated'. Merivale won both cases and was awarded substantial damages of £500. This was not, perhaps, unsurprising, as Merivale had an advantage in being a former lawyer.

These cases, as Harvey's suggests, did not always result in success for the actor. In 1900, actor Robert Loraine sued another actress, Florence West – referred to by her married name, Mrs Lewis Waller – for breach of contract, after the actress engaged Robert at a salary of £30 per week. Mrs Waller in turn claimed that she had the right to dismiss Robert, as he had 'broken the terms of the agreement relating to attendances at rehearsals'. She had engaged him to play D'Artagnan in a production of *The Three Musketeers* in Dublin; at the Queen's Bench, the judges found in favour of Mrs Waller – the *Northamptonshire Evening Telegraph* gave its piece on the verdict the sub-head 'Plaintiff at the Theatre of War'. This case highlighted the issue of rehearsals, which during much of the Victorian era could be rather haphazard affairs and usually unpaid, although by the end of the nineteenth century some theatre companies had started paying actors half-pay for attending them.[2] If an actor was not being paid to attend, it is clear that he might not always see his attendance as his priority, but try and do something else to get money in instead.

Many cases were brought against theatre managers and the managers of touring companies by actors, claiming breach of contract, but on occasion, managers had to sue the actor. One such case was in 1893, when William Hunter Kendal sued another actor named Philip Cunningham for breach of contract. Cunningham had entered into an agreement with Kendal to undertake a tour of the 'provinces' and America. All was well until they were in the States, when Cunningham abruptly left, saying that Kendal had 'failed to carry out certain verbal promises' to him. On arriving back in Britain himself, Kendal was granted an injunction by magistrates that restrained Cunningham from appearing 'in his professional capacity in any theatre for 20 weeks, or until the trial of the action for alleged breach of contract'.[3] Twenty years earlier, a Shakespearean actor, William Henry Pennington – best known for being a survivor of the Charge of the Light Brigade in 1854 and who regularly performed Tennyson's poem of the same name on stage – failed to perform a six-night engagement at the Nottingham Theatre Royal.[4] The lessee of the theatre, Frank Musgrave, stated that the annual rent of the theatre was £1,000 and the taxes £250. He had agreed to share the takings with Pennington, but instead had lost £54 1s and his share of the proceeds, which was estimated to have been about £125. At the Queen's Bench, the two negotiated damages and Pennington agreed to pay Musgrave £60.[5] In 1898, Walter Somerset, who was managing a touring company that was currently performing a play called *The Sorrows of Satan*, sued actress Alice de Winton for breach of contract. Alice was starring as Margaret Foster in the play; she had reached Brighton with the company when she 'threw up her part without notice'. Alice claimed that Walter had broken her own contract, which stipulated she would be his principal star and have a dressing room 'for her exclusive use'. The judge hearing the case was unsympathetic towards Alice's diva-esque demands, stating that 'it would be impossible to carry on the theatrical profession if the leading actors or actresses could throw up their parts at a moment's notice'. Alice was ordered to pay Walter damages of £50.

Other cases involved actors who tried to go into partnership with each other in order to put on productions. Scott Buist was one such actor. In 1889, he and William Drew discussed taking on Toole's Theatre – the Folly Theatre on King William IV Street in London, which had been renamed under the management of John Lawrence Toole – in order to put on a production called *Our Regiment*. They would each put in £500 to this end. However, it soon emerged that Drew did not actually have his share of the money. Buist duly took on the theatre for four months – December 1889 to Easter 1890, put on the production and it failed, losing him £1,600. He took Drew to court for breach of contract and won. A year after his failed venture, he had had the last laugh, gaining a glowing review in the *Illustrated London News* for his production of Ibsen's *Hedda Gabler*, in which he also played George Tesman and where he was described as a 'dramatic radical'.[6]

In the Queen's Bench in 1895, actor-manager George Manners and the well-known actor Fred Storey brought separate breach of contract actions against financial journalist Charles Wilbraham Perryman of Charing Cross and Major W.H. Hand of Richmond in relation to a theatre syndicate they had organised to put on the comic opera *Wink The Other Eye-vanhoe* – later renamed *All My Eye-vanhoe*. Fred Storey was seeking to recover just over £90; he also worked as a scene painter and the previous August, Perryman and Hand had engaged him to paint the scenes for the production, to be staged at the Trafalgar Theatre, through their agent – J.L. Shine. Storey was promised £100 for the work and was subsequently engaged, again through Shine, to play a principal role in the play. He would start his performances in September and work for eight weeks, on a weekly salary of £17, with half-pay for matinees. He had been paid the full amount for the scene painting and £45 6s 8d salary, but now wanted the balance of the eight weeks' salary. Perryman and Hand denied that they owed Storey money, saying they were not partners for the production and that Shine had not been their agent, but the agent of a syndicate called the Burlesque and Comedy Syndicate (Limited). Regardless of whether or not this was the case, Storey won his case and Perryman and Hand were ordered to pay him the outstanding salary arrears. George Manners had brought a very similar case against the two men, having agreed to be the acting manager of the production. After the production only ran for five nights, Manners was offered £20, but wanted half his agreed salary (he had been engaged at £10 a week). The case was settled in his favour and Perryman and Hand were ordered to pay Manners £40 4s and costs. Their lack of success with their comic opera syndicate cost them dearly.

A further type of dispute could be caused between theatre proprietors and copyright holders. In 1899, Albert Fredericks, the proprietor of the three-year-old Borough Theatre in Stratford, east London, brought an action for breach of contract against Lewis Waller, a 39-year-old actor and writer – and husband of Florence West. Waller owned the acting rights of a particular adaptation of Alexandre Dumas's *The Three Musketeers*. He had promised to appear in the production at Fredericks' theatre with his 'No 1 Company' the previous October, but, when October arrived, he was performing at the Globe Theatre. In his defence, he claimed that he had never signed an agreement to perform in Stratford and also that Fredericks had not suffered any financial damage. Fredericks had based his claim for damages on a return of his receipts for the relevant week, 'arguing that with an actor of note in a piece, the total week's income was always higher'.[7] In court, there was debate as to whether Waller's play was the same as the one currently being performed at Her Majesty's Theatre; the judge, Sir Alfred Wills, responded, 'Certainly not. Anyone who has seen them would not say so; and, as a matter of fact, I think Mr Lewis Waller's much the better of the two'. Others in court laughed and Waller said, smilingly, 'Thank you, my lord'. This did not, however, stop the court from finding in Fredericks' favour and he was awarded damages of £275.

In 1889, Brompton County Court was the location for another breach of contract case brought by Henry Plunkett Gratton, the 'dramatic author', against comedic actor Herbert Sparling. The two men had met two years earlier and had discussed Gratton rewriting a drama called *Dawn*. This conversation took place at Sparling's home on the Strand, with one of the play's authors, comedian Frank Oswald, present.[8] At the end of the discussion, Gratton was engaged to rewrite the play, with payment in stages – £10 after rewriting Act 1, £10 on production of the play, £15 at the end of thirty nights' performance and a royalty of £2 per week at every theatre it was performed in. After Gratton had worked on the play for some time, he was notified that the second author objected to the play being altered by 'any other party'. Gratton asked for the first instalment of £10, but was told that Sparling was 'short of money and had only enough to carry him over the Bank Holiday'. Gratton then called on him when he heard no more and found, to his astonishment, that Sparling had suddenly left his rooms without giving information of his future whereabouts. It was only when he bumped into Frank Oswald some time later that he found out Sparling's new address. Sparling's solicitor responded, 'I presume you know of the existence of a paper called *The Era*?' Gratton said he did. The solicitor said, 'You don't know that the columns of that paper are always used by actors and actresses for the purpose of giving their address to those whom it might concern? You didn't take the trouble to look into the columns of *The Era* to find out where Mr Sparling was?' 'Certainly not,' responded Grattan. It then emerged that the second author had consented to the adaptation of the work and that therefore, 'the agreement still exists if the plaintiff is willing to continue the work'. Grattan was therefore only awarded £10 – the amount owing for the work he had done so far.

At the other end of the financial scale, actress Louie Freear, then aged 28, received £800 damages when she won a breach of contract case at the London Sheriff's Court in 1900. She had brought the case against two New York men, the Sire Brothers, who were the lessees of the New York Theatre and owners of the Greater New York Amusement Company; George Lederer was their agent in Britain. It was Lederer who, in May 1899, had asked Louie if she would like to go to New York to take on the principal role in the play *The Man in the Moon* for twelve weeks. She would be paid £150 a week, with expenses. The play was produced and was a great success in the theatre. However, the Sire Brothers then asked her to perform in the open air, at the Magnolia Grove Roof Garden – she refused and they wrote to her stating that if she didn't, they would cancel the rest of her engagement. Her business manager, Bernard Soane Robey, stated in court that 'if she had appeared on the open-air stage it would have injured her as an actress'; presumably, they were both concerned about the acoustics of an open-air event, where Louie's voice might have been lost or appear too quiet for the audience. Louie sued for five weeks' salary and £50 expenses, stating that she 'came before the jury in the interests of the poorer members of the profession. She thought it right to bring the action and got what she was clearly entitled to.' The court agreed.[9]

Not all cases involved adults. Many actors on the Victorian stage had started as child performers; 15 or 16 was a common age anyway to be in the theatre, but frequently the offspring of theatrical families and those whose talents were seen by their parents as a way to supplement the family income, were put on the stage at far younger an age. In 1899, a county court action in Westminster involved a ten-year-old boy, known as Little Garnet Vayne. He was the son of a Mrs Clara Butler, who had brought the case against Messrs Eliot and Sedger. Her son had, apparently, 'held a prominent position of "some years' standing" in the profession' and in 1898 had been engaged in a production of *Macbeth* at the Lyceum for £4 a week. During the run, he was also engaged, at a higher salary of £4 10s a week, by Arthur Eliot and Horace Sedger, to perform in *Alice in Wonderland* at the Opera Comique. Many parents would have been as keen as Clara Butler to have a child on the stage, as 'rates for theatrical boys were . . . attractive compared to alternative employment'.[10] Indeed, in one newspaper's coverage of the case, the boy's salary was news enough to make the headline: £4 a week at ten years of age'. However, in this case, it appears that the boy was from a theatrical family – Garnet's mother, Clara, was 'professionally known as Miss Gwennie Vayne' and she was herself an actress. A look at the 1901 census for Putney shows a widowed Clara Butler, 39, living there with her daughters Marguerite, Ruby and Coralie and son Garnet, all of them listed as actors.[11] Clara clearly recognised her son's earning potential, though; in August 1898, she had placed an advert in *The Era* that put his name in larger letters than her own:

Miss Gwennie Vayne and
LITTLE GARNET VAYNE
(the Original Katie, 'How London Lives')
supporting Mr Charles Warner,
Lyric Opera House, W.[12]

Although it was not unusual for adult actors to have to learn and perform more than one role at a time, it must have been incredibly demanding for a ten-year-old. In 1903, this age was set as the minimum age at which a child could act on the stage.[13] Perhaps Garnet Butler's performances suffered as a result of the hard work; certainly, he was dismissed by Eliot and Sedger about a month before the *Alice* run was due to end. Rather than recognizing the problems inherent in getting a child to work so hard, Clara Butler thought about the lost income and brought a case against the two men. She won, but did her son? He had to give evidence in the case and was described in the following terms: 'The boy was attired in a Little Lord Fauntleroy costume and gave his evidence very brightly.' Perhaps he saw the court case and his appearance in it, simply as another performance, coached in the details by his actress parent.[14]

Clearly, some of these cases wouldn't have needed to be brought if the plaintiffs had had been part of a unionised profession. In the 1870s, there had briefly been a 'protection association' for Manchester musical artistes and the 1880s had seen a revival of trade unionism, thanks to the efforts of low-paid workers. Musicians had been represented by the Amalgamated Musicians' Union (AMU) since 1893, the union seeking to improve their pay and working conditions. Unfortunately, though, Equity – the trade union for professional performers – was only established in 1931. Performers therefore had to fight their own causes and sue for damages for breaches of contract. These breaches could have been caused by management who were somewhat slapdash in their approach to business, or, at worst, who wanted to get rid of certain performers and cancelled engagements, taking a gamble that actors wouldn't want to sully their reputations or risk their money in bringing a case against them. Although actors clearly brought cases that were in their own interest, they were also helped by those such as Louie Freear, who recognised that in taking a firm line, she was both encouraging others to do the same and warning employers that they should stick to the contracts, or face court themselves.

CHAPTER 5

Celebrity Culture

The Victorian era was one of celebrity culture, where the famous were written about and commercialised, seen as public figures and appropriated by their admirers. This was not a new phenomenon: as mentioned earlier, there is clear evidence of a celebrity culture back in the eighteenth century. However, the growth of the newspaper and periodicals industry and the development of technology greatly aided the dissemination and publication of gossip in the nineteenth century. Celebrities could be writers or poets and when they died (or even before), their admirers adopted their homes, turning them into tourist sites in their desire to know their favourite authors on a personal as well as intellectual level.[1] Although in the 1840s, the press expressed anxiety over why and how this admiration was shown, it soon became part of this culture, with its own gossip columns detailing the private lives of individuals. *The World*, for example, offered a 'Celebrities at Home' series and, of course, *The Era* had its 'Theatrical Gossip' column.[2] By the 1880s, there was one periodical entitled *Our Celebrities: A Portrait Gallery* and another called *Celebrities of the Day: British and Foreign*, featuring biographical sketches – such publications were an 'indication of the shift from biography to personality and celebrity which was taking place in the last decades of the nineteenth century'.[3]

Actors and actresses were very much part of this celebrity culture. The Victorian press included advertisements from companies selling 'Photographs – actresses, celebrities' for a penny each; collectable postcards enabled fans to have pictures of their favourites in their own homes, and bedrooms. The power of actors and actresses over their fans was recognised and exploited by companies, who paid them to endorse their products; for example, in 1899, 'the celebrated actress' Cora Urquhart Brown-Potter advertised 'Tatcho' hair restorer, one newspaper advert stating 'Mrs Brown-Potter, renowned for her wealth of glorious hair' 'only' uses Tatcho.[4] Conversely, being forgotten about was seen by the press as something no actress would want – when Mrs Leigh Murray died aged 75 in 1892, the *Manchester Courier* commented that she 'had so long retired from the exercise of her profession as an actress that many playgoers must almost have forgotten her'. Fame was transient, but by the end of the nineteenth century, it was regarded as being something to be desired and aspired to.[5]

Actresses were seen as having 'pulling power' in terms of advertising, but also in terms of encouraging charitable donations. They were frequently called on to take part in charity events, having a vital role in fundraising by encouraging others to participate – those who were keen to get 'unique encounters with celebrities'.[6] As Catherine Hindson has noted, though, these events broke through the confines of the theatre, where the actress was separated from her audience, enabling fans to gain public access to these women and a degree of intimacy that might not be afforded by a trip to a theatrical performance.[7] There was an increasing expectation that the lives of performers – both professional and private – would be reported on and in some cases, actors and actresses used the press to promote either their own charitable work, or to publicise their own complaints or grievances. Perhaps the most notorious example of this was when American performer Ilda Orme publicised a fourteen-year dispute with the father of her alleged former lover through the pages of the press. Ilda, who may have been suffering from paranoid delusions, claimed to have been persecuted and shot whilst in London in 1898; however, it was believed that she may have shot herself to create an image of herself as the victim and she was duly sent to Colney Hatch asylum in Middlesex and kept in a padded cell until the American ambassador intervened. She then returned to America, where she next turned up on a ship to publicly horsewhip theatrical manager Marcus Mayer, believing that he had lost her professional engagements. Throughout and after these very public incidents, Ilda gave long interviews to the press, further criticizing those who 'persecuted' her, and placed advertisements stressing her availability for theatrical jobs. What is particularly significant about Ilda's tirades to the press is that the naming of the man she held mainly responsible for her troubles – Boston lawyer Micah Dyer – was not deemed libellous, despite a clear lack of evidence that he was in any way involved.

As Ilda's case makes clear, performers of both genders were watched by audiences and newspaper readers who felt, through this process of watching and reading, that they were part of both the theatrical experience and of the performer's life. An individual theatregoer might become fixated on a performer, reading obsessively about his or her idol and hanging around theatre stage-doors in the hope of a 'hello' or an autograph. They wrote love letters to their favourites, to the extent that, in 1885, the *St James's Gazette* remarked that 'love-letters are not to actresses what they are to other women. They come in such quantities and they are so foolish, or so impertinent and so very much alike in their own kind, that they have little more charm at last than the wine circular that is sent onto you with fourpence more to pay.' This correspondent was asked to burn many letters sent to an actress friend and noted that 'this lady has proved specially fatal to youths of a tender age . . . Had she preserved them there would by this time have been quite a sheaf of letters dated from schools; as it is, a few characteristic specimens fell to my share. Some are respectful and some are not.'

These letters – what we would call fan letters – varied from the innocent to the obsessive. One boy had written to the actress after seeing her in a pantomime, 'I was at the pantomime on Thursday and I love you very much and I know you do not care for me and you do not know me. When I was at the pantomime, I looked at you all the time and I would like to come again to look at you . . . I love you because you are beautiful, but more because the inner man is displayed; for beauty is skin deep, but virtue will endure.' These boys were seen as essentially harmless – although they clearly placed their own views of morality and virtue onto these actresses who they only knew through their professional roles – but adult writers were more problematic and seen as 'sentimental or desperate'. They held candles for individual actresses for years; they wrote poems or detailed how they had wandered the streets all night after watching the actress perform, 'thinking of what might have been'. Others demanded to be met at specific places and at specific times, or offered to call at the actresses' houses. Unrequited love – as these male fans saw it – could lead them to become suicidal, especially if they felt the actress had slighted them. This was what happened in 1894. Jane Hading was a member of the Comedie-Française when they had visited London; she then went on a tour in the

US, where a riding master named Pierre Brady tried paying her a visit; understandably, he was 'rather coldly received'. He tried writing a passionate letter to Jane and got no answer. He wrote again: 'Madam – my last thought is of you. At the moment of quitting the world, I send you a passionate adieu.' His body was found in his lodgings; he had committed suicide by poisoning. In another case, closer to home, a 'lovesick boy', not out of his teens and an amateur singer, had fallen for the charms of an actress at a Bristol theatre – 'she looked with cold disdain' on him. Ignoring this slight problem, he decided to write her a love letter; but he didn't know how to write and so had to ask a literate friend to do so for him. Unfortunately, he couldn't read what the friend had written; and it was so appalling that the actress wrote back: 'Your presumption hardly deserves a reply. Permit me to request you never to address me on such a subject again. I have something else to do besides making singers' hearts "musical".'

As can be seen from these examples, the press tended to mock the actions of these lovelorn fans, seeing the concept of adoring theatre-lovers as a rather strange, absurd fact. In 1881, *The Era* wrote that 'there is a certain class of idiots that infests stage doors to worry actresses with silly attentions'. It drew attention to one particular case – a man (who sounded rather young) who was spending a lot of time 'haunting' the Crystal Palace in the hope of seeing one of its pantomime actresses. He had left a letter for her at the stage door, which the paper had been passed. It quoted the letter in detail, including sections where the actress was described as 'so awfully lovely and I have fallen in love with you' and a conclusion that pleaded:

> If you are not cross at my writing this, will you please throw two carrots at your mother (you know who I mean) in the scene where you find yourself at home? Do please. Ever yours, SILLY. PS – You have seen me before with my sister, near the stage door.

The Era described the letter sarcastically as 'the precious document', but it is clear that infatuations could result from visits to the theatre. This letter-writer desperately wanted to form a 'link' with the actress – a bond that only the two of them would share. Hence the use of 'you know who I mean' and a request to convey a secret message to him during a performance. The press genuinely did not understand this element of the theatrical public, regarding the public as being too easily pleased, willing to 'patronise [anything] that is superlatively exquisite' in terms of special effects and extravagance. In 1899, *The Era* went so far as to describe Sarah Bernhardt's fans as 'ridiculous':

> The worship which Madame Sarah Bernhardt has lavished upon her by American and English people in Paris is almost extravagantly enthusiastic. When she is in the French capital two middle-aged ladies wait before her house in the Boulevard Pereire every morning to see her go out. When their divinity appears she gives these ridiculous 'Saralatresses' her hand to kiss, with a gesture of condescension worthy of an empress.

The theatre enabled ordinary people to get a glimpse of glamour way beyond their normal lives and it is not surprising that as the industry boomed and diversified into music halls and later into film, that fans 'worshipped' individuals who were a part of that glamorous life. The press made out that they were only interested in the 'seriousness' of the theatre

– its artistic merit and the performances of those on stage – yet its mocking attitude towards 'ordinary' fans failed to recognise the press's own prurient interest in actors and actresses, as reflected through their coverage of their private lives.

On occasion, individuals would become more dangerous and present behaviour that today, we could describe as stalking. A Mancunian lad named Newton had 'attached himself to a travelling company as an admirer of one of the actresses' in 1893, but paid for the bouquets he presented her with by robbing apartments, so keen was he to present himself as an affluent suitor. In 1884, a New York case reported in the British press had involved 20-year-old actress Grace Leslie. After she had finished performing in *Seven Ravens* one night, she had got the streetcar from Third Avenue to Fulton Ferry, in order to get home to Brooklyn. A young, blond, rather stout man in the car tried to get her attention; she ignored him and got off the tram at Fulton Street. He got off as well and followed her to the ferry house, before sitting directly opposite her in her cabin, trying to 'mash' her. She went onto the deck to avoid him and he followed her again, trying to put his arm round her waist and to cuddle her. She balled her fist and hit him hard between the eyes, sending him sprawling. 'Oh darling, don't hit me like that again!' he cried, to which the actress responded, 'Don't you call me darling. I will teach you to be insulting to young ladies.' She then hit him repeatedly with her parasol, until he 'begged for mercy'. The *Aberdeen Evening Express* reported the case as an example of what happened to young men after 'stalking actresses in America'.

Back at home in Britain, some actresses could not respond with Grace Leslie's presence of mind. This is understandable in some cases. In some, the persecution was a slow seep of increasing menace – such as was the case with Mary Fitzpatrick's 'admirer', Ernest Bryham Parsons, who showered her with unwanted attention for five years between 1897 and 1902. This attention included sending her 'abominable' letters and pornographic drawings, frequently asking her to marry her and culminating with seizing her by the arms while she was out walking one day. His defence in court was that he had an 'excess of affection' for the actress that 'had led him to do these things'.[8] With George Boynton, a 20-year-old unemployed Londoner who appeared before the Bow Street magistrates in 1871, charged with assaulting and threatening Cornelie D'Anka, the stalking might have eventually resulted in murder. The singer and actress was performing at the Globe Theatre at the time. Boynton had been writing letters to her and had pretended that he was an heir to a fortune in order to get an introduction to her. He said that he had wanted to marry her, but she had rejected his advances. He continued to 'pursue her in a most offensive way' – calling for her at the theatre's stage door, hiring a hansom cab to follow her around as she travelled in her carriage, calling at her home; all without any encouragement from her that she was remotely interested in him. He then posted her a parcel, containing a single bullet and the next time the actress was in her carriage and saw George in a cab behind her, he lifted his pistol and pointed it towards her head. At this point, Cornelie called the police. Sadly, although the police took the case seriously, the defence did not, laughing at elements of the actress's evidence, arguing that as the prosecution couldn't prove the pistol was loaded, that an assault charge couldn't be proved either, and suggesting that George's actions were simply the 'foolish' ones of a very young man. George was simply bound over to keep the peace for six months and then released.[9]

George's violence was ostensibly caused by unrequited love for an actress. But on other occasions, individuals might have a financial motive in making life difficult for the jobbing actor. In such cases, these were individuals who believed they were the people with power, rather than the actors being powerful. They sought control; and they believed that actors had something they could benefit from – namely, money. The next chapter looks at the cases where actors were seen not as objects of desire who were admired or obsessed about in that context, but instead as people to threaten, to extort, to blackmail, or simply to humiliate while they worked.

PART 2:
CRIMINAL LIVES

CHAPTER 6

Blackmail

In 1891, one actor appeared as a witness in a lawsuit, stating that he had been threatened by an individual who said 'less than half a dozen men acting in concert could make such a disturbance [during his performance] to render it wholly impossible for an actor to go on with his part'. He had been asked to pay this blackmailer in order to prevent such a disturbance, but had the strength of mind to refuse. It was, apparently, not uncommon for 'stage-door loiterers' to demand money from actors either to refrain from making noise during a performance, or, conversely, to applaud loudly and make the actor look more popular than he might be in reality.[1] In 1895, it was noted in the press that 'a system of blackmailing is being applied to pantomime artistes employed at two or more of the London theatres'. The best-known actors at one theatre were 'molested' when leaving after a performance one night and threatened with 'the bird' – the colloquial term for hissing and shouting complaints – unless the actors paid them to keep quiet. On New Year's Day, 1895, one young actress was threatened with violence unless she gave the blackmailers money – 'and being alone and seriously alarmed she handed over the whole contents of her purse'. A year earlier, it was noted that Birmingham theatres were particularly notorious for incidences of blackmail during the panto season – 'for some years it has been a common practice at this season for a number of ruffians to accost the pantomimists after they leave the theatre and endeavour to extort money by promising them in return plenty of gallery applause and in the event of refusal, to resort to threats'. The number of incidents had gradually increased until the actors found that 'the nuisance has become unbearable'. One of the Birmingham Theatre Royal's leading actors had reported his daughter, also an actor, being 'shamefully ill-abused' by blackmailers and it had got to the stage whereby some of the actresses were refusing to enter or leave the theatre by the stage door. Eventually, the situation was reported to the police.

This practice was widespread. In 1885, Bessie Bonehill, the vaudeville singer and male impersonator, was performing in *Aladdin* at the Alexandra Opera House in Sheffield, was followed after leaving the theatre by several 'costers', the Victorian street traders whom Henry Mayhew had been so brutally honest about twenty years earlier. These men demanded money from 30-year-old Bessie 'for the applause they had given her during the evening', arguing that others had paid them for doing this on other occasions. Bessie refused to pay them and so the following Saturday evening, the men took their seats in the opera house and as soon as the actress started to sing, hissed her 'in a most brutal and disgraceful manner'. They had tried to blackmail the wrong woman, though. Instead of getting upset, Bessie walked up to the footlights and told the audience exactly what the men were doing and why. To a hearty round of applause, the men were removed from the theatre. Despite this act of courage, Bessie subsequently walked home from the theatre each night accompanied by a police constable, 'in order to guard her against personal violence'. And in Birmingham in 1889, it was again reported that 'once more during a pantomime season in Birmingham, disgraceful blackmailing has occurred'. In the four years since the blackmailing was reported to police, the blackmailers had become steadily more determined, becoming 'a band of guerrillas against whom the managements of the various theatres long since declared a traceless war of extermination'. They had tried to steal Jenny Hill's diamonds as she walked from the stage-door to her carriage after a performance. Millie Hylton was less fortunate, being attacked in the street after an evening performance and left bleeding and unconscious. It was noted that the blackmailers tended to leave male actors largely alone, focusing on women in order to 'avoid a hiding' by their victims.

Bessie's bravery was still commended by the press in 1889, as was the action of Marie Loftus, who had been so 'terribly annoyed by the importunities and threats of many sturdy ruffians' that she had called a police officer to her house and had him hidden behind her drawing-room curtains. Four 'hulking ruffians' duly turned up at her door, one of them saying, 'Now then, Maria *sic*, you'll have to tip up. The others tip us and you'll have to do the same'. Marie invited him in, where he found three other actresses – Florrie West (presumably Florence West, Mrs Lewis Waller), Annie Dunbar and Alice Leamar – sitting there. He was not intimidated by these ladies and again demanded money from Marie. After he had incriminated himself, out stepped the policeman from behind the curtains. This did intimidate the youth, who fell on his knees, 'bellowing for mercy'. It was said that all the while he was led to Moor Street Police Station, he was begging for mercy and making promises that he would 'never annoy another pantomime artist so long as he lived'. His horror at being caught by the police was so intense that Marie Loftus ended up withdrawing her prosecution against him.

Marie told the press that gangs of youths would knock on her door every day demanding money and would then make 'such a row in the gallery that my songs were spoiled and I could not make a word heard. I was very nearly stopping and making a speech, but I did not like to lose my temper.' She added the commonly-held view of Birmingham: 'Birmingham is the worst place in England for blackmail. I know no other town where the gallery boys look for pay.' Her views were backed up by her colleague Florrie West, who described Birmingham as '"the hub" of the blackmailing system – it produced an ample income for the gallery boys, who work in perfectly organised gangs'. Annie Dunbar only escaped the blackmailers because they knocked on her door when her husband was home and he 'threatened to thrash the intruders'.

A simpler form of blackmail was carried out by those engaged to carry out minor work in the theatres. One actor, Frederic Dobell, was not prepared to accept such blackmail attempts. A versatile actor, Dobell played theatres across Britain, acting in everything from Shakespeare to melodrama.[2] In 1881, the 37-year-old was playing Harry Huntingford in a production of *The World* at the Grand Theatre, Leeds – a performance described in the press as being acted by him 'with power and intelligence'. It was also a part that required him 'falling down a trap, nightly, onto a bed'. Four men were employed to stand around the bed, to ensure that the actor landed on it – if he missed, he would end up falling 30 feet down into the theatre's cellar. One night, as he did his usual fall, one of the men commented, in a 'half bullying, half cajoling' tone, that 'I should expect something for myself . . . that cellar is 30 feet deep'. Two nights later, Dobell did his fall again and this time, the man made his demand more explicit, saying, 'Now, then, where's that half-dollar you are going to give us?' The actor stepped out of the trap and said, 'I've got a shilling for you, lads, who shall I give it to?' The blackmailer demanded it at once, saying if it was not paid, he would ensure Dobell was dropped into the cellar the following week. The actor pocketed his money and 'expressed my opinion of the man and his abominable threat in the most forcible terms at my command and laid a formal complaint before the management'.

No criminal action seems to have resulted; the theatre management tried to make out that the threats were simply 'chaffs', made in jest rather than being serious attempts to extort money by threats. However, they weren't 100 per cent sure, evidently, as they immediately dismissed the blackmailer from his job. Dobell reported the case to the newspapers as a warning to other actors. However, he also drew attention to the type of blackmail that the Birmingham theatres had been particularly prone to. He noted the 'well-known fact' that during the pantomime season, particularly, many actors and actresses had to buy their own safety by paying weekly instalments to men, a payment known euphemistically as 'beer money'. It was basically a protection racket that targeted the theatrical profession. Dobell raised the question of how it was allowed to exist and thrive, arguing rather reasonably that theatre managers should co-operate with their actors and work together to end the practice of blackmail, perhaps by putting up notices backstage to the effect that 'any workman demanding money from artists engaged would thereby subject himself to instant dismissal'.

One such plan had already been put into place at the Surrey Theatre by its managers, Messrs Conquest and Meritt and the manager of the Cork Theatre and Opera House, James J. Scanlan, had written to *The Era* back in August 1885 to make it clear that he also found 'these harpies' a 'bane' that 'make the travelling acting-manager lose his temper and make use of "plain" language', to the extent that he had a notice in his green room stating that the stagehands were adequately paid and that if he heard of any attempts made by them to blackmail actors, they would be liable to instant dismissal. He noted that 'this notice has had a most salutary effect'. So it is clear that some actors made attempts to stand up to blackmailers and that some theatre managers were willing to state publicly that they would not tolerate attempts to extort money from performers. However, the consistent reporting of such cases, particularly during the pantomime season and over a course of at least a decade, suggests this was a long-standing problem that was difficult to eradicate.[3] In 1898, Henry Irving gave a speech at a meeting of the Actors' Benevolent Fund, where he pointed out that 'certain individuals, who seemed to possess all the murderous points of vanity and ill-will' attempted to 'levy a sort of blackmail under threats'. Irving, in a position of security compared to many actors, told the other actors present that if they, or any colleagues, were blackmailed, they should immediately 'hand the offender over to the police for prosecution'.[4]

As these cases show, for every star-struck theatre aficionado who waited outside a stage door in the hope of seeing their favourite actor or singer, there was an individual or group wondering how to make money from them, or causing other problems. In some cases, they simply sought to embarrass them; in others, again, they were attempting to blackmail those they saw as better-off than them. In Birmingham in 1880, a gang of youths, known in the press as 'roughs', caused trouble by attempting to blackmail actors in the city. One of them, a young man named Mitchell, ended up in the Birmingham

Police Court on Monday 8 March. On the Saturday, 6 March, he appears to have watched the pantomime, *Aladdin*, with his mates at the Prince of Wales Theatre. He was armed with an unusual weapon – a large cabbage. After the performance, he left the theatre's gallery and threw the cabbage at a male actor, presumably one he had been attempting to blackmail. Unfortunately, his aim was poor and he hit the female star of the panto – Miss Jenny Hill. It struck her in the eye and knocked her down. Mitchell was found guilty of assaulting Miss Hill and given two months' hard labour.

In another case, at the Belfast police court, two soldiers and a merchant accused Mun Noble Paumier, a veteran Cumbrian actor, of assaulting them at the Belfast theatre one evening the previous week. The performance that night was *The Hunchback*, with Paumier taking on the role of Master Walter. It was perhaps not a well-performed piece and the actors became aware of laughter from the audience. Paumier took offence and, noticing the three men in their private box laughing, went and spat in each of their faces, before striking one of them – the Honourable Arthur Annesley. The performance, surprisingly, continued, but afterwards, the three men went backstage to ask Paumier the reason for his actions. They insisted they had done nothing wrong, but Paumier retorted, 'You lie!' and left the theatre. The men had subsequently asked Paumier to make a public apology, but he refused. He then failed to turn up to court; his defence muttered that the 42-year-old actor was 'likely by this time in the Crimea', the war being underway at this point. Paumier, who was back in England by 1861 and continued performing, appears to have had something of a reputation for what was euphemistically called 'eccentricity', having once evicted a drunken audience-member from his box during a performance, kicking him literally into the gutter outside the theatre before coolly returning to his role.[5]

A more serious case was heard at the Court of Exchequer in London in 1871. Solicitor Leopold Lewis brought a case against the manager of the Queen's Theatre in Long Acre, Covent Garden, Ernest Clifton, for assault, wrongful imprisonment and malicious prosecution, demanding damages. Lewis stated that on 17 April 1871, he had paid to see a performance of *Joan of Arc* at the theatre, standing in the pit section. Halfway through the performance, he asserted that there was 'some noise and confusion on the stage and lots of people could not hear'. Victorian audiences could be quite vocal and Lewis duly called out for the cast to speak up. A policeman, Constable Bampton, who was employed by the theatre (the Queen's Theatre paying the police authorities directly for their use of the Met's finest), tapped him on the shoulder and asked him to be quiet. Lewis refused, said he had a right to call out and duly 'again called upon the performers to speak up'. He was then 'brutally dragged out of the pit by the officer and some person connected with the Theatre down stairs into the street'.

A charge of causing a disturbance was brought against him but dismissed the next day, at which point Lewis brought his own case against the theatre. At court, one witness stated that he too had called for the actors to speak louder. Another man, E. Trevor Twiss, stated that 'the performance was dragging and the actors were inaudible. In his opinion Mr Lewis acted quite right in saying, "Speak up!"' Ernest Clifton stated that he had been in his manager's room on the night in question and had been unaware of any disturbance:

> He was coming down stairs, having been in his room a couple of hours, when he was met by Bampton, the constable. He then learned that the plaintiff had been removed from the theatre and Bampton requested him to go to Bow Street Police

Station. There he saw Mr Lewis. Witness was informed that Mr Lewis had been creating a disturbance. Mr Lewis asked whether he [Clifton] intended to sign such a paltry charge and he replied, 'We cannot have any disturbances in the theatre and I am compelled to do so.'

As seems to have been common with these cases, those involved with the theatre were rebuked for behaviour that was deemed unbecoming – class was clearly an issue, with theatrical types being looked down on by the legal profession. One witness, John Wicks, who was the money taker at the pit entrance of the Queen's Theatre, was told off for 'assuming sundry airs and graces while giving his evidence'. The assistant manager, Morris Jacobs, argued that Lewis had shouted out during a particularly quiet scene on stage, but the prosecution refuted this, casting doubt on his evidence by stressing 'the occasional temporary noises which must occur on the stage when there was such elaborate scenery to be prepared at the Queen's'. It was also argued that 'with respect to the witnesses for the defence, there was not a single independent one. They were either persons connected with the theatre, or their friends.' In addition, Lewis 'had as much right' to tell the actors to speak up,

> as the judge or jury had a right to tell a witness to speak louder if he spoke inaudibly. Even if plaintiff chose to hiss, supposing the piece was bad, or the actors acted badly, he had a right to do so. Managers were not employed to regulate whether the audience was to hiss or applaud.

The jury recommended damages of 40 shillings for Lewis's initial prosecution. However, on the other charges, of assault and wrongful imprisonment, the jurors found in favour of Ernest Clifton, with one juror 'remarking that they thought what had occurred in the theatre the plaintiff had brought upon himself'.

All of this might lead readers to suspect that actors and others involved in the theatrical life, such as managers and directors, were rather violent creatures – but, of course, they could be victims themselves. Even in the case of Mr Paumier, above, he had some justification for his violence. Signor Caldi, who was in the corps of the Hull Theatre Royal, appeared to be a victim. He complained that he had been assaulted by one George Simpson, who had struck the Italian actor several times in the face. But again, things were not straightforward. Although the assault was proved, Caldi admitted that Simpson had been angry because Caldi was in debt to him and had failed to pay him. Simpson had approached Caldi and asked him to pay five shillings; Caldi had offered him just half, which Simpson took offence at. The assault was seen as rather trivial by the magistrates, who made Simpson enter into his own recognizances of £5 to keep the peace for three months.

Theatre audiences could, as Paumier's case shows, be difficult themselves. At the Olympic Theatre in London, on the evening of Friday, 22 June 1856, a riot started in the theatre pit. There was due to be a benefit for Mr Wigan, who held the theatre's lease and was also an actor-manager, as was usual. It was a production of *School for Scandal* and it was looked forward to. Therefore, at an early hour: 'the pit entrance was besieged by a highly-respectable body of individuals, including a great many ladies, who waited with exemplary patience and good humour until the doors were opened'. It became quite full, but then it emerged that there weren't enough stall seats for everybody – certainly not enough for all the people who had been queuing by the pit. A man demanded, 'Where's the pit?' and Wigan was asked to come forward to explain why not enough cheap seats had been provided. There was soon an 'uproar', someone called for people to 'jump over' – and over fifty men and women jumped over into the stall seats that had previously been set out. At this point, Wigan finally came out and said, 'those who had wrongfully taken possession of the stalls must give them up – and if they did not they would be turned out'. People continued to complain, until Wigan stated that he would have to get the audience to settle the matter. 'The seats, however, that had been taken by assault were retained by the possessors.'

A different sort of riot occurred in 1890, in what became known as 'The Gold Craze Case', after the name of the play at the centre of the case. This focused on an objection by one grand individual to a character being based on him. The play, *The Gold Craze*, was a new, four-act production with a complicated plot, written by Brandon Thomas. It was first performed at the Princess's Theatre in London on 30 November 1889.

One of the main characters in the play was the Baron de Fleurville, a swindler, adventurer and villain, described in the press as a 'pseudo-baron' whose real name was the more prosaic Raoul Cadona. This character bore some similarities to an infamous figure in Victorian society – the self-proclaimed Marquis de Leuville, who was himself said to be a charlatan whose real name was William Redivivus Oliver. He was understandably worried that the character of the baron was based on himself and 'protested against the production of any portion of the play which might be considered a caricature of himself'.

Given the rumours about de Leuville's own background, it is unsurprising that he did not want any lampooning of himself to be carried out in public. He therefore tried to cause a riot by sending in a group of men to attend the play and to hiss and hoot 'for the purpose of ruining' the production. Just after the rising of the curtain for the second act, the audience had become aware of a 'great disturbance at the right-hand side of the pit. There was a good deal of hallooing and shouting and cries of "Take the thing off!"' The policeman on duty at the theatre, Constable Gill, said he saw around six men on seats behind the stalls and two others at the door, all shouting. People sitting near the offenders were asking them to be quiet, but they continued shouting, 'hissing and hooting, using very bad language and making a great noise with their feet'.

The Marquis was, as a result, accused by theatre manager Henry Cummings of instigating a riot at the Princess's Theatre. George Haddens, William Cronin (listed as J. Cronin in some newspaper reports of the riot) and Edward Hill, together with unnamed 'others', were said to have been asked by the Marquis to cause the rumpus and had agreed to take part. They had been offered £1 2s to do so. Cronin said that he had hissed the 'villain' baron, 'against his opinion, because he very much liked the piece', causing laughter in court.

An actor in the play, George Dalziel, together with A.H. Chamberlain, said that he had been in an argument beforehand about a 'proposed caricature' – that of the Baron de Fleurville, who was played by 40-year-old actor John Barnes, known professionally as J.H. Barnes – that he had heard was in the play. The Marquis' defence appeared to admit the offence, saying it was justified because of the caricature:

> Mr Cook, for the defence, commented strongly on the scandalous manner in which
> the Marquis was believed to have been caricatured and maintained that any one so

insulted had a perfect right to have the character, though not the actor, hissed and hooted. The Marquis, therefore, was perfectly right in what he did by sending men to the theatre.

A witness for the defence, theatre critic and journalist A.W. Allen (possibly a newspaper typo for John W. Allen, who was a London-based reporter), said that although there was some hooting, it was 'little more to be heard than was generally the case on first nights'. He added that the make-up used for Barnes, playing the Baron, made him look 'strikingly like' the Marquis. The author of *The Gold Craze*, Brandon Thomas, was then called to give evidence, where he denied having based the character of Baron de Fleurville on the Marquis; instead, he argued, he was based on a 'relation of his own by marriage. He had but a slight acquaintance with the Marquis and had not him in his mind at the time he selected the name. The Baron de Fleurville was not intended to ridicule the Marquess [*sic*] in any way. It was a more natural accident that the names were so much alike.'

The case was not resolved until the following year, when it was heard at the Queen's Bench. The jury decided that the portrayal of the baron was not a libel on the self-proclaimed Marquis, because his reputation, such as it was, could not have been injured by an 'exceedingly innocent and harmless paragraph' – and they found in favour of the defendants.[6]

Another fairly common form of making a disturbance at the theatre was to hiss. Robert Dixon was accused of causing a disturbance at Southwark's Victoria Theatre in 1847. One night, he had been watching a play from the gallery. He stood up on one of the benches and started hissing the performance, trying to prevent the play from going on. Those around him repeatedly asked him to be quiet, but he refused. The constable on duty, Murray, then tried to eject Dixon from the theatre and was assaulted in the process. When Dixon came up before the local magistrate, he said that 'having reason to be displeased with the acting of a particular performer, he expressed his dissatisfaction in the usual way and thought he was justified in it'. Constable Murray, though, said that young men were recently in the habit of getting tickets for the gallery and then trying to interrupt the performance – any performance – 'out of mere wantonness'. The magistrate wanted a recognizance – a financial security to bind Dixon over to good behaviour – or gaol for the offender and although Dixon argued that he had been locked up since 10 pm the night before and 'that was punishment enough for hissing an actor', the magistrate was 'inexorable'. Young Dixon's father, therefore, had to pay the recognizance to get his son home.

Two years earlier, it had been an actor who had brought individuals to court for hissing at him during a performance – to the extent that he had been forced off stage. Barnard Gregory, better known as the proprietor and editor of *The Satirist*, a scandalous weekly newspaper that had been embarrassing London residents since 1831, was due to appear at the Covent Garden theatre on 13 February 1843, playing Hamlet.[7] However, as soon as the 46-year-old made his entrance on stage, there was 'such a tumult of uproar' that he could not be heard. The hissing was due to three individuals – the Duke of Brunswick, his equerry Baron Audlan and a Mr Vallance, the Duke of Brunswick's lawyer, who were in a box close to the stage. Barnard complained that he was unable to perform as a result and whereas he had been expecting to make £50 a night, the theatre actually made a loss that night. He brought a case for damages, arguing that the hissing had been part of a conspiracy against him.

Several witnesses were called in the Court of Common Pleas to give their opinion of Barnard Gregory's acting skills. This was to ascertain whether his reputation as an actor was so poor that the hissing was deserved. Their opinions varied; one said he was 'fine', another 'good'. But then one said, 'He was a fair actor and, if fairly heard, would not have been hissed off.' Lord Beaumont, though, said that although Gregory had been good as Shylock and Othello, 'he did not perform either of the parts in the manner in which I think they ought to be performed'. The men involved denied being part of a conspiracy against Barnard, but admitted they had hissed more because they disliked *The Satirist* and the 'libels' it contained. Barnard had faced many libel charges before and the Duke of Brunswick had previously brought a case against Gregory for libel.[8] The defendants contended that the hissing 'arose from one great spontaneous burst of feeling from persons of all classes, in every part of the house, at seeing the man who assailed, weekly, all parties and classes, come forward to seek their support and suffrages as a public actor.' The hissing was significant as a choice of protest as the first page of *The Satirist* contained the line: 'Satire's my weapon. I was born a critic and a satirist; and my nurse remarked that I hissed as soon as I saw light.' The jury, unusually, found in favour of the hissing men; it was apparently valid to seek revenge on a journalist and actor's views by hissing him off stage. When the verdict was announced, the public present in court burst into applause and were sternly told by the Lord Chief Justice: 'You must be silent, for you are not in a theatre now.' Gregory's life, though, was something like a theatre play – full of events and drama. Less than a year after the 'hissing case', he was sentenced to six months in Newgate after the Duke of Brunswick and Mr Vallance won another libel case against him. He managed to drag the case through appeal, though, and the judgement was only confirmed seven years later. Even after his death, the feud between Gregory and the Duke continued; Gregory referred to him as his 'enemy' in his will.[9]

It is clear that both male and female actresses faced a number of problems when it came to audiences. The public felt it 'owned' them, or owned the theatrical arena and asserted that perceived power when it could. Although some problems were gender-related and others clearly financial, others were created out of a desire to cause trouble, to disrupt, or to make explicit public feeling about individuals, even if it had little to do with their acting. But the public were also keen to act as critics and if they were less than impressed with a performance, they made their views very vocal indeed.

CHAPTER 7

Assault

The threat of assault, of violence, was ever-present in Victorian theatres and particularly so in London's many places of entertainment. As Ros Crone has pointed out, 'cheap tickets attracted large crowds and with large crowds came the need for control'.[1] Many theatres employed security – usually police constables – to help prevent offences, or, when they occurred, to deal promptly with the offenders, as the previous chapter showed.

But for some, violence was part of the attraction of visiting the theatre. It could involve persons known to each other – a form of turf war, or a previous dispute aired again on the parties meeting at the theatre; or it could involve strangers wanting a bit of excitement. It might be inflicted on members of the cast by those in the audience, or by theatre proprietors and managers against audience members. Unfortunately, the constables employed to prevent violence could also be the subject of it themselves, attacked by those in the audience who resented their presence and attempts to control them. As Crone has argued, attempts by the theatre management to control their audiences were perhaps doomed to failure because of the nature of the Victorian theatre itself, with its lack of regular seats, dim lighting and other features that failed to separate the audience from those on stage – the effect being that the audience felt it was on the same level as the actors and actresses and was not awed or made silent by the drama of the stage itself.[2]

When the music halls and penny gaffs increased in popularity, leading theatres to focus their efforts on attracting the middle classes to the theatre (leaving the working classes to the music halls), they recognised that they needed to focus on altering perceptions of the theatre being a place of violence. In 1868, comedian Joseph Arnold Cave, the lessee of the Royal Victoria Theatre (now the Old Vic), noted on his playbills that 'any person whistling or making any other disturbance will be expelled by the police', but ultimately, it may have been the introduction of electric lighting and other technological innovations that may have helped more in stopping violence being as possible and unseen as it had previously been.[3]

However, the blame for theatre-related violence cannot be placed entirely on the part of the audience. Victorian actors could be a rather fiery bunch, their sense of the dramatic reflected in their private and professional lives. The newspapers were full of tales of assaults committed by those engaged in theatrical careers, with gossipy reports of their appearances before local magistrates, or even of their trials, in the more serious cases. Some assaults were on actors by theatre managers and stemmed from work disputes, others were the result of arguments between actors and their landlords, or between actors themselves. Domestic situations also resulted in actors appearing before magistrates either charged with assault or claiming to be the victims in such cases. Yet other cases had a more malicious intent, stemming from the precariousness of some actors' lives and the desire to maintain contracts and get paid. These assaults could be, to modern eyes, incredibly trivial – such as the case involving provincial actress Nellie Lionel, appearing at the Star Theatre in Wolverhampton in 1888. She accused tailor Henry Lowder of assault after he threw a carrot at her during a particularly sad scene in her play. Yet such cases were not trivial to the complainants, who wanted to protect their personal and professional reputations and ensure that those who criticised their performances, left them open to mockery, or who prevented them performing, were punished.

Newspaper readers eagerly read about these 'theatrical' cases, lapping up tales that seemed to prove that the theatre was a centre of vice and crime. Yet others resented this link. One night in 1877, Frederick Medex, a 'lecturer attached to Messrs Strange and Wilson's Diorama' in Ipswich, gave a lecture responding to recent attacks by George Williams, a former actor at the city's Theatre Royal but who now went around preaching the Gospel. Williams had 'cast certain stigma upon the theatrical profession' and Medex felt that this profession had 'been grossly insulted by the insinuations'. He argued in his lecture that actors were denounced by religious men as being 'blasphemers, vile sinners and contributors towards every form of vice', when he, Medex, had actually found that the 'morality, integrity, honesty, sobriety and chastity of the profession always compared favourably with that of outside society. How many charges of a disagreeable nature were found against that profession? A very small number . . . very insignificant.'

Medex then gave statistics for the period January 1870 to October 1877, stating that only six actors had been convicted of theft and one of assault, compared to nine clergymen being convicted of theft and two of assault. Unfortunately, it was not recorded where Medex got his figures from (were they for Ipswich, Suffolk, or nationally?) and only recorded cases that had reached trial and resulted in convictions. But it is clear that Medex, just like Williams, was rather subjective in his views – and his figures show, actually, that actors weren't at a significantly lower risk of convictions for theft and assault by their more religious counterparts. Ironically, immediately under *The Era*'s coverage of Medex's lecture – which concluded with his statement that actors 'were the most charitable and benevolent of any class in the world' – was a story about an actor, Thomas Webber ('a member of the *Pink Dominos* company, who concluded at the Gaiety Theatre on Saturday') being accused in the Dublin police court of assaulting a Trinity College porter. The newspaper reports of 'theatrical assaults', as they were invariably called in headlines, clearly show that these were not isolated cases. They also show that actors were not all the paragons of virtue that Medex believed them to be. The nature of acting or of putting on a show, the risks involved and the peripatetic home lives of those in the theatrical profession, meant that tempers could, and did, fray.

Actors lost their tempers with their colleagues, but spouses, siblings and friends could all be the victims of an actor's loss of equilibrium. Relationships between actors and theatre managers, stagehands and newspaper reporters all came under the media spotlight when assaults, or threats of assault, were brought to the police courts and magistrates. These were cases brought in London and across the provinces, with newspapers writing just as eagerly about cases in Liverpool as they did about cases in the metropolis, ensuring a wide audience for tales of blows being traded, black eyes given and blood flowing. Newspaper reports therefore shed light not only on the character of the individual actor away from his theatrical roles, but also on the type of family actors came from and their relationships with those who were not part of their theatrical family.

One woman, Marie Zievan, was assaulted because she was young and alone rather than because of her profession. Described as 'an actress, the wife of a London theatrical artist', she was attacked by a commercial traveller, Frederick Ashton, in a South-Eastern Railway train carriage halfway between Ashford and Tonbridge. Although Marie had made sure she had got on a carriage with two other women in it, when she got on at Folkestone, they had both got off at early stops, leaving her there alone with Ashton, who then indecently assaulted her. In a manner reminiscent of some of today's newspapers, the *Leicester Chronicle*, in reporting the assault, emphasised the fact that the actress was in the third-class compartment – hinting that her career was not quite a stellar one (although the *Sheffield Evening Telegraph* described her as 'a stylishly-dressed young lady'). Regardless of this, though, Frederick Ashton, of Lavender Hill in south London, was committed for trial at the next assizes.

Another perhaps sexually-motivated assault case ended in a trial for attempted murder. Again, it involved an actress on her own, but in this case involved one who was trying to make her way home on foot after an evening performance. In this case, though, it was used by the press to instigate a moral panic over the 'perils of London life'. This phrase was coined by the *Penny Illustrated Paper* in 1895, to highlight a series of incidents that, it said, exemplified the dangers of daily life in the metropolis. This case involved a 34-year-old butcher named Arthur Kilsby, who, it was said sniffily, 'dressed as a mechanic'. He was charged with attempted murder. His victim had been the fantastically-named Lydia Alexandra Hostage. Around 32 years old, Lydia was married but lived not with her husband Andrew – who may have been working in Africa – but with her widowed father, a French polisher and siblings at 28 Tenison Street, off the York Road, where Waterloo station is now.

She was an actress and had been performing in a show at the Palace Theatre on Shaftesbury Avenue one Monday night. It was around midnight when she had left the premises and headed home on foot. She would have made her way through Covent Garden and across the Strand down to the Embankment, and she stated that she had made her way through the Embankment underground station before climbing the steps up to the top of the Hungerford Bridge in order to get across to the South Bank. There were few people around and she became aware that someone was following her up the two flights of steps. Before she reached the top of the bridge, the man following her grabbed her round the neck before trying to snatch the purse from her hand, but she managed to keep hold of it. He then let go, but stabbed her several times in the shoulder. Lydia screamed and the man ran down the steps, throwing the knife away as he did so.

A policeman, who Lydia came across as she rushed back to the District Line, managed to stop the attacker as he ran up Embankment and arrested him. Once at the police station, the prisoner, Arthur Kilsby, denied having anything to do with the attack on Lydia, stating, 'I never attempted to steal the purse at all'. But he then changed his mind, saying, 'I give myself up: I did it'. His pockets were searched and in one was found a paper that stated that Kilsby had, until recently, served in the Canadian Militia and that he had only just returned to England. Kilsby said that he had been drinking heavily over the previous three or four days, although the police constable said that he was 'perfectly sober' when taken into custody.

He was committed for trial at the Central Criminal Court and once there, pleaded guilty to assaulting Lydia with intent to rob her. In November 1895, he was brought before the court for sentencing. Dr Walker, the Newgate gaol's medical officer, stated that Arthur was 'in a low state mentally and physically and had suffered from sunstroke', but it was more the fact that Lydia's wounds were deemed to be superficial that led to a relatively minor punishment – Arthur was sentenced to 12 months in prison. Lydia was asked in court to testify that Arthur was the man who had wounded her. She sounded understandably confused as to why she had been targeted: 'I had never seen the man before in my life. I cannot understand it. It is a most remarkable thing.'

Disputes could occur between those performing at the same theatre and artistic sensibilities sometimes caused eruptions between writers and actors. For example, Henry Beaumont, a comedian performing at the theatre in Derby, complained that Professor Abel, a star of Victorian provincial theatre, who usually appeared on stage with his performing dogs and who had written and directed part of Beaumont's play, had assaulted him and used threatening language towards him.[4] The alleged abuse had taken place after Beaumont's play had finished the previous Wednesday evening. Beaumont had returned to his dressing room and Abel burst in and charged him with 'not having used a sword knot which was introduced in the piece performed'. He waved his fist in his face and threatened to horsewhip Beaumont.

At Nottingham police court, Abel accused Beaumont of purposely 'spoiling' the performance, but Beaumont responded by saying, 'Mr Abel ought to have been there to direct his piece himself, but he was not; I am unconscious of having spoiled Mr Abel's performance.' Another comedian, John Simeon, gave evidence, having witnessed the threats. He had played the character of a general in the controversial play and stated, 'Mr Beaumont did his best for the success of the piece; Mr Beaumont only missed one rehearsal . . . [but] the sword knot is one of the chief points in the play.' It appeared that Abel had a reputation for fierce directing; Simeon had once been threatened whilst rehearsing and Abel had also been rumoured to have challenged the manager of the Theatre Royal in Preston to a fight. Another witness, an actor, failed to turn up to give evidence, but this was not regarded as important as 'he was drunk at the Shakespeare public-house, when he ought to have been prompting'. Stage manager Henry Dudley stated that Beaumont had failed to give as much attention to the play as he ought to have done and added, 'the sword knot is the plot of the piece and if left behind it destroys the whole plot of the piece . . . [Mr Abel is] justified in his complaint'. Despite his backing of Abel, Dudley ran scared when he was asked if he would act as his surety, arguing that 'he was here today and gone tomorrow'. But despite that, he was bound over to £10 and Abel to £20, to keep the peace for six months. The judge added that Abel's conduct was 'a disgrace to him in his profession'.

As this case shows, professional pride amongst those working in the theatrical arena could cause loss of tempers – and court cases – as could differing theatrical temperaments. One assault case from 1879 involved blackmail, opera and the Garrick Theatre. The case was originally covered in the 27 July 1879 edition of *The Era*, which reported that a case of assault involving vocalist Garret James Roche had been heard at the Thames Police Court the previous Wednesday. Garret had been accused of assaulting Richard Walter South, stage manager of the Garrick Theatre. South stated that at about 11.30 pm on Tuesday 22 July, he had been standing outside the theatre, having 'some high words' with the Garrick's general manager. Roche, who was a member of the Garrick's company, walked up to him and started 'abusing' him. Roche told South that he deserved a 'good thrashing' before punching him in the face, sending the latter to the floor. When he got up, he saw some other people trying to get Roche to leave, but he refused and instead, ran up to South and punched him again, before a constable came rushing up and promptly took him into custody.

The general manager who Roche had been having words with was one Charles Wentworth Dillon Sturgeon, known by the first of his middle names, who had disliked it when Roche had asked him for a fortnight's salary that was due to him. Roche stated that he did not use insulting language towards him, but simply called him a liar. He argued that South had approached him while he was accusing Sturgeon and had tried to intervene on Sturgeon's behalf, accusing Roche of having £5 from South that he had obtained by false pretences.

In his defence, South argued that Roche had been dismissed by Sturgeon after having been found to have received bribes – namely the £5 referred to before, which he had demanded from South as an 'entrance fee'. Sturgeon had made clear that this practice – although sometimes carried out elsewhere – was not acceptable at the Garrick. South said that Roche had been drinking and was very abusive, using 'some very ungentlemanly language'. Wentworth Sturgeon, who had an advantage in being a trained and practising barrister, then gave evidence to say that he had been putting the theatre's lessee, May Bulmer, into a cab when Roche had come up to him accusing him of being a liar.

> Complainant then called Mr Roche a liar and put his fist in his face and touched his nose. Defendant, on this, struck him and knocked him down. He got up and they then both put themselves into a fighting attitude, but were separated. I had had occasion to discharge the complainant from his post as Stage Manager and had prevented him from going into the Theatre that night.

The magistrate found that although Roche had made use of bad language and had been drinking, it was also clear that there had been 'some financial business between them which was doubtless the cause of the quarrel'. He simply ordered Roche to keep the peace for three months and he left the court surrounded by friends.

This was not, however, the end of the matter. All parties appear to have disliked how they were portrayed in *The Era*'s coverage of the case. South wrote to the paper on 14 August 1879, complaining of 'inaccuracies' in its coverage that were 'calculated to do me professional harm'. He argued that Odoardo Barri, a composer as well as treasurer at the Garrick, who claimed to be from Italy but who was in reality an Irishman named Edward Slater, had refused to give him two weeks' salary that was due to him. After being insulted by Sturgeon and told the money was not available, he left the theatre without pay – 'I naturally felt indignant and determined at once to resign'. Sturgeon then dismissed him and South responded with bad language. His letter stressed that he had worked 'night and day for six weeks before the opening without payment'.

When this letter was published three days later, Wentworth Sturgeon was angered so much that he wrote his own response, detailing the bribery that South had allegedly indulged in. Sturgeon said that following allegations that Odoardo Barri had received a 'bonus' of £25 for 'obtaining a lady an appearance upon the Garrick stage,' with another £25 promised if she gained a principal role, he looked into the matter and found that it was South who had actually taken payment from Roche in order to get him into 'Miss Bulmer's opera company'. He implied that bribery and blackmail were endemic problems at the Garrick at this time and that Sturgeon's work was cut out trying to stamp out the practice. Barri then wrote his own letter complaining that South had described him in his first letter as behaving 'insultingly' when, he argued, it was actually South who was both insulting and offensive. The letters were published together.

What this case and the subsequent letter show is that the theatrical court cases covered by *The Era* were read avidly by members of the theatrical profession, including those who featured in the cases themselves. Their public profile and reputation were, understandably, of great importance to them and so they read the reports and sought to clarify negative mentions of themselves where necessary. But the case also shows that positions and roles could be gained not just through merit, but on ability to pay the unscrupulous.

Arguments originating with discussions about contracts and pay were common. One case was brought against an actor named James Albert Arnold in 1878 by a Mrs Strickland; her husband was a prompter, currently working in Margate, but three weeks earlier he had been with Walter Seattle's Company at Brighton. James Arnold was the leading actor with the company. Mrs Strickland had called on Arnold, asking for money owing to her husband, but was told she could not see him until that evening's performance had finished. Arnold then said he would walk her part of the way home – but on the road, assaulted her. It is possible, although the newspapers did not record it, that the assault was a sexual one. Arnold was found guilty of assault at Margate Borough Court and sentenced to six weeks in prison with hard labour.

That case stemmed from the wife of a prompter needing her husband's wages, but in 1873, a more dramatic case was heard that stemmed from an actor's contract. The acting manager of the Prince's Theatre in Manchester, 46-year-old Frederick Haywell, brought an assault action against the German-born tragedian Daniel Edward Bandmann at the Manchester Assizes. Bandmann said a disagreement had started between the two men over the terms of their contract, with Haywell having told Bandmann that if the latter stopped a performance, he would be held responsible. Bandmann had torn up Haywell's contract and in response, Haywell called him a cad. Bandmann then hit him and a fight erupted – the men had to be separated by the stage carpenters.

Haywell was possibly the wrong person to mess with; after an initial spell as a scenic artist at the Prince's, under his real name of Frederick Hawley, he had then trained as a solicitor before returning to the stage as Frederick Haywell, where he was described as 'an actor of considerable reputation'. During the case, the defence argued that Haywell had previously received 'diverse complaints' about Bandmann, but it was then argued by the prosecution that this was relevant – 'You may as well call witnesses as to his character generally and if you did so I should be happy to call half the theatrical managers of England'. Laughter was heard in court when Haywell stated that recent performances of Shakespeare at the Prince's had not been very successful:

> The truth of the matter was that Shakespeare was somewhat at a discount right now. The immortal bard had been put upon the shelf, temporarily of course, by Mr [W.S.] Gilbert and people were now being enchanted with *The Wicked World* and had forgot the Bard of Avon.[5]

It was heard that Bandmann had a 'very violent temper [and] behaved with great rudeness to a great many of the company and caused great offence in the theatre'. However, the jury found in his favour, awarding him £5 damages – the equivalent of around £200 today. Ironically, given his dismissal of Shakespeare, in the 1880s Haywell became librarian of the Shakespeare Memorial Theatre in Stratford, dedicating the rest of his life to making the theatre library a centre of Shakespearian research.[6]

This was not Bandmann's only appearance in a newspaper court report, suggesting that the allegations of his temper had some foundation, despite his vindication in the earlier case. Five years after the Haywell case, Bandmann was accused at the Queen's Bench of assaulting actress Clara Rousby. Mrs Rousby was then the proprietor of London's Queen's Theatre and she had bought the rights to the play *Madeline Morel* from Bandmann, who had adapted it from a German play. She intended to take the starring role herself.

Actors started rehearsing for the play, under Mrs Rousby's supervision, but it was not until 15 April that Bandmann attended a rehearsal. He watched the first four acts, but then jumped up, having taken offence at some alterations that had been made to his text. 'I will be damned if I will see it done that way!' he allegedly shouted and tried to grab the manuscript, which was being held by Charles Morelli, the prompter. Mrs Rousby 'resisted' the attempt and Bandmann then grabbed her violently by the arm and hit her with 'such force that she had been scarcely able to use her arm since the occurrence'. Mrs Rousby then made things arguably worse by alluding to Bandmann's prior reputation – 'Mr Bandmann, this is not the first time you have struck a woman'.

Bandmann argued that he had been trying to protect the manuscripts, which he said were in his arms and were 'undoubtedly' his own property and that George Everett, a theatrical agent, and Charles Morelli had assaulted him to get them. The case was first brought to the Bow Street police office on the morning of 16 April 1878, the day after the alleged assault, but by June, the case had still not been heard. The indictment for assault had been sent to the Queen's Bench via certiorari from the Middlesex Sessions, as it was considered felonious rather than a misdemeanour – Bandmann was accused of inflicting grievous bodily harm, actual bodily harm and common assault. However, because it was seventieth on the court's list of cases to be tried, several months were likely to elapse before it could be heard. Bandmann's lawyer, Mr Serjeant Parry, applied for the case to be accelerated and therefore heard prior to the Michaelmas sittings that September. Bandmann stated in an affidavit that:

> he had already been obliged, owing to the charge, to relinquish his engagement in London as an actor at the Adelphi Theatre, owing to the excitement that existed in reference to this case, from its having been taken up and commented on by the theatrical and other newspapers; and that whilst the case was pending he would be precluded from obtaining engagements either in London or on the Continent. He also stated that he had followed the profession of an actor for 20 years and that it was his sole means of livelihood for himself, wife and family.

The application was refused; the Lord Chief Justice said Bandmann's engagement could not be broken and therefore, he should still be able to carry on his roles at the Adelphi. However, the case was not tried until 19 November. Mrs Rousby gave a suitably dramatic testimony, setting herself up as the innocent party, but doubt was cast on her account when she admitted that after the assault, she had visited a lawyer before going to the doctor's. Witnesses then blackened her character, accusing her of being a regular drinker – intoxication having caused an earlier accident she had been involved in. After the months of adjournments and delays, the jury finally only debated matters for forty-five minutes, before the foreman announced that Mrs Rousby's injuries were 'caused unintentionally by Mr Bandmann' and that he was therefore not guilty of all charges. The verdict was met with loud applause and when Mr Bandmann and his wife left the court, they were 'loudly cheered'. Mrs Rousby left the court with her reputation rather tarnished. She never recovered from the scandal, soon leaving England for the spa waters of Wiesbaden, where she died a year later, of tuberculosis, aged 30. Bandmann, meanwhile, retired in the 1880s and became a rancher in Montana, where he died of the effects of indigestion in 1905.[7]

At the New Theatre Royal in Rugby, Warwickshire, in 1890, a dispute over the breaking of contracts and a theatrical licence application turned into an assault case – but it could easily, according to the complainants, have been a more serious charge of arson or murder. The case brought to light the jingoistic nature of parts of Victorian society, with one complainant being viewed with suspicion because he was French and suggested also that actors and managers were constantly involved in a negotiation over their work and contracts that could lead to tit-for-tat court cases. John Henry Howard had applied for a licence to produce stage plays at the theatre, on behalf of his brother Walter, a former actor of several decades' standing. However, three actors – sisters Alice and Irene Aldercron and Paul Berton – opposed the granting of the licence and appeared at the Rugby Petty Sessions to formally oppose it and, at the same time, to apply for a summons against J.H. Howard for assault.

They argued that the previous week, after a performance of *The Lady of Lyons*, Howard had rushed onto the stage, called the actors 'hounds' and 'vipers' and tried to make his way into Alice Aldercron's dressing room. He was stopped from doing so, but then started sprinkling some kind of oil over the stage and threatened to burn the place down. He then turned on his brother and violently assaulting him, leaving him with injuries to his face. Monsieur Berton was next in line and he was seized by the throat, Howard telling him, 'I have a revolver in my pocket and mean to use it'. He also referred to the actor as a 'French worm' and suggested that they duel. The actors recorded that they had nothing bad to say against Howard's brother, Walter, who was 'a gentleman and who had from beginning to end protected and assisted the ladies in every way'. However, they said that he should not be given a licence if he then allowed his brother 'whose conduct was that of a madman, who carried loaded revolvers about with him and who attempted to burn the theatre down', to be the manager.

Because the opposition to the licence had been made at a late date, the case was adjourned for a week to enable the magistrates to find out what arrangements would be made for the management of the theatre. However, they granted summons for assault and for keeping the peace, because the actors were in fear of their lives. When the assault case was heard, though, Walter Howard stated that the altercation was Alice Aldercron's fault, because that morning, at rehearsals, she had 'refused to perform and left the theatre, together with M. Berton' and that as a result, his brother had wanted to serve them with notices to leave. He added that the substance spilt on stage was distemper and not flammable. The defence lawyer stated that the evidence for attempted arson was 'not sufficient to hang a cat on and was ludicrous from beginning to end' – it had been an exaggeration by the women. He added that Berton's challenge to fight with pistols 'in French fashion, was the product of the imaginative mind of a foreigner'. The magistrates agreed that no assault had been committed and dismissed John Henry Howard – after granting his brother an unconditional licence.[8]

Personal animosity clearly played a part in some assaults that took place between individuals working at the same theatre. Actor Walter Groves appeared at the Newcastle upon Tyne police court on 17 February 1881, accused of assaulting theatre 'super' (a minor actor) Samuel Carr. The case was said to have 'created a great amount of interest in the town, the court being filled by several of the chief artists in the Theatre Royal Pantomime and others'. Walter had been playing the part of Tornado in the Theatre Royal's production of *Sinbad the Sailor*, a popular pantomime. Tornado was the Storm King and so Walter was required to play the part of a 'blustering railer'.

Carr and another actor, who had been playing the part of Tiny Tim, had been going home together after one performance when Groves had apparently come up to them in Pilgrim Street and threatened to 'kick that part of Tiny Tim's person for which chairs were made'. It was about 11.15 pm and dark. Samuel Carr tried to defuse the situation, but Groves took off his coat and hat and rushed at him. It was noted that 'Tiny Tim was a man of small stature and the complainant readily attempted to protect his small friend'. Yet when Groves ran at Carr, Carr immediately ran round a lamp-post opposite the London Hotel. Groves caught up with him, pushed him down and hit him on the face. Carr shouted, 'Let me get up!' and then Groves kicked him twice. Only when Carr shouted, 'Murder!' did a policeman run up and stop Groves.

Groves was repeatedly referred to as a 'man of education' and Carr stated that he should have known better than to act the way he did. In his defence, the actor stated that Carr had used insulting language to him when he was in the company of two ladies. Carr denied it. Then, from the centre of the court, comedian Richard Hicks shouted out: 'This man is an impudent fellow. I have been insulted by him every night in going home.' The prosecuting counsel wearily sighed, 'We are going to have the whole pantomime here'. Soon, though, Groves was found guilty and fined 10s or the alternative punishment of fourteen days in prison – he paid the fine immediately. As his friends left the court, one was heard to remark, '10s? That's nothing'.

Unusually, in another assault case in 1874, the defendant, theatrical manager Frederick McFadyen, pleaded guilty from the outset – although he argued that there were extenuating circumstances. McFadyen was accused of assaulting Edward Higginson Jolly, the not-so-jolly theatrical reporter for *The Era*. Jolly had been sitting in a box at the Leicester Theatre one Saturday night, close to the stage, watching McFadyen's production of a burlesque entitled *Chilperic*. He alleged that McFadyen came up and hit him three times across the nose, covering the reporter with blood. The audience in the pit immediately started hissing and booing – to them, this was part of the drama. *The Era* duly stated that the attack on its reporter was 'most brutal and most unprovoked'.

In court, McFadyen said Jolly had been 'grossly insulting' towards McFadyen's wife, the burlesque actress Carrie Nelson, by 'getting up and leaving the house when singing was commencing' on stage. McFadyen said there was no animosity between the two men, but whenever Carrie appeared, Jolly had got up and turned his back on her. He had gone up to Jolly to ask if he had meant to write that Carrie couldn't act or sing and Jolly apparently answered in the affirmative. However, the judges were not impressed with McFadyen's mistaken act of spousal loyalty, stating that they were surprised that a theatrical manager, whose duty was to maintain order, would himself cause a breach of the peace in a public place – 'such things would not be allowed'. McFadyen was duly fined 40 shillings and warned that if he didn't pay, he would be imprisoned for two weeks.

In the same edition of *The Era*, the newspaper reported yet another theatrical assault case, this time involving an actor and one of the stagehands – a theatre carpenter at the Royal Amphitheatre in Liverpool. This case had attracted a lot of public attention, resulting in a 'densely crowded' police court when the two parties appeared and many more people having to wait outside due to lack of room. John Boardman, the carpenter, had worked at the Amphitheatre and the Theatre Royal for over twenty years. He had been waiting at the back of the stage one evening to change the scenery for the final scene of the fifth act of *Richard III* – his job being to pull half of the scene across to the left-hand side of the stage. Actor Barry Sullivan's son was waiting on the other side, with second carpenter William Barton, the latter being required to shift the other half of the scenery to the right-hand side. While they were waiting for a bell to be rung to signal that the scene was ready to be changed, Sullivan, who was appearing in the play, came over behind Boardman and hit him with his prop, a sword, saying, 'Why don't you make the change, you . . . fool?' Boardman immediately did so.

It was argued that the dispute arose because Boardman should have taken his cue not from the prompter's bell, but from Sullivan himself. Boardman disputed this and stated that he was waiting for the bell. The bell had been a long time coming and he blamed Sullivan's son for the delay. But then Boardman made a mistake, by mentioning that his wife had told him not to return to work at the theatre previously, 'when I had another case'. When questioned, it emerged that he had brought a similar case before, which had been settled out of court. In that case, against Mr J.C. Cowper, the latter had made an 'ample apology in presence of the company and paid his (complainant's) solicitor's costs'. A clear comparison was made between Boardman – the lowly stage carpenter with a habit of complaining of his treatment by actors – and the great Sullivan who, his defence lawyer stressed, was so successful that wherever he appeared, whether in England or Australia, 'he was sure to draw large audiences'. The lawyer, Bremner, scoffed at the allegations of assault, calling them 'frivolous'. The two magistrates hearing the case disagreed and, on establishing that an assault had been committed, did set a fine. However, it was only for five shillings, because Mr Sullivan was found to have committed the act 'thoughtlessly and without intending to do the man any harm'. On conclusion of the case, the crowds left the court and gathered outside to cheer Sullivan as he walked out, in the company of several of his friends.

The relationship between the different strata of theatrical workers and between them and their public, is clearly visible in these assault cases. Theatrical managers were distrusted, seen by some actors and reporters as abusing their considerable authority, being biased when it came to actors they were personally involved with and caring, ultimately, about money and profits. Actors saw themselves as better than the stagehands, prompters and other theatre staff, despite the fact that without them their productions would fail to be performed; they were blamed for anything that went wrong, but ignored when things went right. Off stage, actresses were vulnerable to assaults from husbands, landlords, co-workers and strangers – yet their willingness to press charges and complain about these assaults shows a steeliness and determination to bring others to account and to protect their own reputations that is rather admirable and counters the image of a subservient Victorian woman. These, instead, were women used to being independent and earning their own money, having careers that by necessity involved a strong will and perseverance. This attitude is also evident in their giving of evidence to police and magistrates and expressed clearly in the pages of the nineteenth-century newspapers. It is all the more notable in that great credence was paid to women's morality and reputation – and if they had skeletons in their cupboards, both press and the courts would take pleasure in finding these out and publicizing them. It took some nerve to report cases to the police.

And the public? They lapped up incidents in theatres and eagerly read about them in the papers. In some case, they even queued to attend court cases involving actors and cheered them on during and afterwards. In this light, court cases involving theatrical people were a form of theatre in themselves.

CHAPTER 8

Theft

In 1856, a 22-year-old prisoner at the House of Correction in Coldbath Fields, London, wrote a 'glossary' on thieves, recording the practices of London gangs. The practice of 'flimping' that they carried out involved simply snatching small goods from an individual – such as a watch or a necklace. The prisoner, recorded only as 'W', stated that flimping was 'most frequently practiced at theatres; on entering or retiring'.[1] Crowded places were good targets, as the mass of people exiting hid the activities of thieves.[2] Therefore, it is not surprising to find various accounts in the newspapers of theatregoers being targets by thieves during their nights out – such as when a lady named Miss Williams, who was heading to the Drury Lane theatre for an evening with her married sister and her children, was jostled by two men at the pit entrance and had her opera glasses stolen. She failed to notice the loss until she had reached her box, because the jostling had disguised it. In 1892, a bookmaker's clerk was charged with attempting to pick pockets after a police detective spotted him in a doorway near the Strand Theatre with another man. As soon as the audience came out, the men mingled with them and the clerk was spotted trying to put his hands into a man's pocket. He was afterwards identified as a man who had picked the pocket of a local doctor when he had visited the Strand Theatre two weeks earlier, stealing a gold watch. Two years earlier, in Edinburgh, two men had been picking pockets at the Theatre Royal and again took a watch – this time from a Dunfermline iron-moulder who had been in the audience. These men were sentenced to a year in prison apiece.

On occasion, thieving was carried out by those who were desperate to attend the theatre themselves, but who could not afford it by any legitimate means – The *London City Mission Magazine* in 1840 had reported the case of 'C.H.', aged 16, who was sent to prison for picking pockets. He had lived with his father, but 'was constantly robbing him for the purpose of frequenting theatres and concerts at public houses'. Theatres could also be seen as dens of iniquity and where crime was fostered; another 16-year-old, J.F., ended up in prison after being encouraged six months earlier to spend his wages on going to a play – 'since which time he has been a constant frequenter of theatres and the associate of thieves'. Likewise, 15-year-old T.C. stated that he had been a 'constant frequenter of theatres' for the past three months and 'he states that the theatre has been a great inducement to him to thieve'.[3] These lads tended to gather at the penny theatres, or gaffs, rather than the more salubrious places; the penny gaffs served up an entertaining range of plays, often based on real-life murder cases, for the affordable entry fee of a penny. Right at the start of the Victorian era, it was noted that so many working-class boys – aged primarily between eight and 16 – attended the penny theatres that they were able both to form associations with each other and to formulate plans for 'thieving and robbing houses and shops and other places' – so these theatres became seen as being 'most destructive of all moral principle'.[4] In the 1850s, Henry Mayhew believed that the stage of the penny gaff, 'instead of being the means for illustrating a moral precept, is turned into a platform to teach the cruellest debauchery. The audience is usually composed of children so young, that these dens become the school-rooms where the guiding morals of a life are picked up.'[5]

The boys who learned their 'trade' in the penny gaff often became career criminals, repeat offenders with certain *modus operandi* and many teens and young men progressed to robbing the wealthier clientele of more 'traditional' theatres, who had small, valuable items on them, such as jewellery or watches on chains. This was the only life they knew. Although they were often fairly young, pickpockets could be of any age – when James Milcoy was charged with picking the pockets of a Mrs Ellson at the Princess's Theatre in London in 1887, he was described repeatedly as an elderly or old man, who was working with two younger men, in a set-up that has echoes of Fagin training his young thieves in *Oliver Twist*.[6] Other thieves worked on a larger, more organised scale, targeting theatres specifically, not just audience members. In 1886, one group of thieves targeted the Theatre Royal on Bedford Street, Sunderland, overnight. It was the first night of a play called *The Vicar* and the thieves were believed to have hidden themselves in the theatre after the play finished. After everyone had gone, they lit the gas-lamps in the theatre and then went from dressing room to dressing room, 'breaking the locks of the boxes belonging to the company and scattering the contents over the rooms. Not a box or basket escaped search.' Three actresses – Grace Otway, Mabel Harrison and Rose Stapleton – lost their jewellery.[7] Grace Otway had been keeping some valuable diamonds in her dressing room and she offered a reward of £10 for their return. Luigi Lablache, whose company were due to open in *Blind Justice* at the theatre the following week and who had already left his box there, also lost items and offered a reward of £5.

But when an actor hit hard times, he might resort to theft himself (or herself). There were many opportunities for a provincial actor to steal, taking items from local stores or houses, or even from the theatre in which he was working and selling goods onto pawnbrokers, strangers or to other actors, unaware of where these goods had come from. This was not an unlikely scenario – as many actors on the lower rungs of the provincial ladder had second jobs, it was feasible that goods might be shown that the actor claimed came from another job. In 1880, one actor, 25-year-old Herbert Clarence Evans, appeared at the Birmingham Quarter Sessions, charged with stealing a parcel containing eleven gold chains. The parcel had belonged to a Manchester jeweller and Evans, seeing it in a carriage at Birmingham's New Street Station, had filched it. Evans had been in Birmingham for professional work – he had a short-term engagement at the Theatre Royal. He took advantage of his position to sell several of the chains to the other actors and actresses he was performing with. Herbert pleaded guilty to theft and was sentenced to nine months in prison.

In another case, in 1893, a travelling actor named Frank Danvers – described in the press as 'a young man with a profession [*sic*] of hair' – was charged at Castle Eden Police Court in County Durham with stealing some more mundane items of dress – three pairs of linen cuffs and a pair of socks. Danvers was the actor's professional name, although the press reports of his case failed to report his real name. It was alleged that Danvers had been lodging at the house of Ralph Welsh, in the middle of December 1892 and had stayed until 16 January. Ralph had then noticed some items missing, but it took until

11 February before he saw Danvers again, at Hetton, where he accused him of stealing items from his house. Danvers first denied everything, but then admitted they were in his box at his new lodgings in Haswell, around five miles from Castle Eden. A police officer was called to the lodgings, where the cuffs and socks were found. Danvers was fined 20 shillings, with the warning that if he failed to pay, he would be sent to prison for fourteen days.

A more ambitious crime was committed by another actor the same year, 1893. Reginald Reid, described in the press as a 'gentlemanly-looking fellow', appeared with another man named Charles Johnson at the Quarter Sessions in Southampton, indicted with obtaining money by false pretences. It was alleged that the two men had obtained £9 10s from a local hotel proprietor and money changer, Henry Charles Herring, who was based on Southampton's Oxford Street. Reid was a well-known actor, who called himself, according to the press, Rix Russell. Actually, this appears to have been a misprint – Rex Russell was a 'celebrated' character actor of the 1890s, who was certainly travelling around the country performing, and it is likely that this was the actor who was charged – the fact that he was 'well known in the theatrical profession' made his story immediately more newsworthy.[8]

It appeared that Johnson was Reid's 'innocent agent' – he had been told by Reid to get money from Mr Herring from a postal order, only it turned out that it was not a postal order, but simply 'a receipt for money paid to the Post Office for transmission abroad'. Johnson was acquitted, but Reid was found guilty. He had already been in prison awaiting trial for two months and so received a more lenient sentence of ten weeks' hard labour. However, a message soon arrived from Brighton asking for Reid to be re-arrested – he was said to have committed a similar offence there.

Many 'theatrical' thefts reported in the press were committed by men, but on occasion, there was a female perpetrator. In 1886, 19-year-old Jessie Vyner, described as being of 'prepossessing appearance', was charged in Edinburgh with stealing £6 10s from a box in the house of her landlady in the city's Grindley Street.[9] Jessie was an actress who was performing in the annual pantomime at the Lyceum Theatre; this theft was perceived in theatrical circles as being particularly bad, as the money had belonged to another actress who was lodging with her. When she was arrested, Jessie admitted what she had done; in court, she was fined £2, with the alternative of five days in prison. Two years later, an even younger actress, 16-year-old Amy Coates, was in Preston Police Court, charged with stealing a diamond ring from Robert Scanlan, who owned a jeweller's shop on Orchard Street. He had shown the ring to a customer – Amy – who later left the shop without buying anything. He then noticed the ring missing, and on running after the girl, found it on her. Although he later said he was willing to drop the case, the court would not let him; but Scanlan worried about the effect on a 16-year-old girl being sent to prison. A theatrical manager, John Evans, was called to give a statement. He said that Amy was an orphan and he had adopted her when she was five years old, she was of a previously good character and if the magistrates let her off, 'he would take her back'. The arguments of both Evans and Scanlan won round the magistrates, who said they were 'inclined to take a lenient view of the case and give the prisoner a chance to redeem her character'. She paid a 20-shilling fine and was allowed to leave.

In another case from 1895, an actress who had several aliases was charged with stealing nearly £600 worth of jewellery from a Mrs Gibbings in Ridgemount Gardens, Bloomsbury, London. Mabel Stanley, also known as McLean, Willett and Vaughan, appeared at Bow Street Police Court to answer the charge, despite an (unsuccessful) attempt by the victim to withdraw the charge. Four years earlier, actress Florrie Dytch was arrested at her Birmingham lodgings, accused of committing fraud and thefts on lodging house keepers in Wolverhampton and Walsall. Florrie had previously been engaged with the New Babylon Theatrical Company, but since that engagement had ended some time before, she had been unemployed and facing homelessness. She therefore moved around local lodgings, pretending that her father was about to give her a sum of money and relying on the sympathy and trust of lodging-house keepers.

Women were more commonly featured as the victims of thefts – such as in 1894, when the actress Eva Westlake, who was appearing at the Prince of Wales Theatre in Birmingham, was the victim of a theft committed by clerk George Campbell.[10] He duly appeared at the Quarter Sessions charged with stealing two of Eva's brooches. He had apparently called at Eva's lodgings in Birmingham, claiming that he sought apartments himself and on being shown round the house, took the brooches from Eva's dressing table. He had also taken a gold watch from William Frost, either another tenant or the landlord. He was found guilty of theft and got six months in prison. In 1886, Nellie Farren was appearing in *Jack Sheppard* at Nottingham's Theatre Royal. This was the 1885 burlesque *Little Jack Sheppard*, written by Henry Pottinger Stephens and W. Yardley, which was originally performed at London's Gaiety Theatre.[11] Farren, then aged 38 but still playing principal boys, had been with the original London production before touring with it.[12] The play depicted the life of the notorious eighteenth-century criminal – a thief and housebreaker. Other plays and burlesques about Sheppard had been banned by the Lord Chamberlain in the 1840s, due to fears that audience members would try and copy Sheppard's behaviour.[13] This may indeed have been the case in Nottingham, when one person carried out a theft after a performance. It was evening and after finishing at the theatre, Nellie Farren took a cab from there to her apartments at the George Hotel, carrying with her a jewellery case containing 'gems and jewellery of a considerable value', most of which were apparently gifts from her admirers. It was very foggy that night and it was reported that Farren had been 'nervous' during the short journey. She put her case down on a sideboard in her sitting room, but forgot to take them into her bedroom with her when she went to bed, as she usually did – and in the morning, they were missing. The Nottingham detectives were called and made inquiries, but, as the *Sheffield Independent* commented, they 'have not any clue to the thieves yet'. It was stated that Farren was particularly distressed, not because of the financial value of the goods, which included an oyster-shaped locket of gold, diamonds and sapphires, but because 'they were presents commemorative of some of her artistic triumphs'!

Another actress, Dorothy Hayward, was dining in a London restaurant on 26 November 1890 and left her purse, which contained a cheque for £10, on the table. She then went to the Prince of Wales Theatre and there realised what she had done. She returned to the restaurant and questioned waiter Anthony Romani. He denied knowing anything about it. Dorothy notified the police and had the cheque stopped. The next morning, another man, Gorringe, tried to get the cheque cashed. The police were sent for and Gorringe, on being arrested, put the blame for the theft squarely on the waiter. At trial, Gorringe was dismissed with a caution, but Romani was sentenced to six weeks in prison with hard labour. Actresses were commonly targeted for their jewellery, however, as Nellie Farren's and Eva Westlake's cases show. The well-known actress Amy Sedgwick, who lived in Brighton, had several items of jewellery stolen from her house by her lady's maid, referred to as 'Fogg, alias Carter'; Florence St John, who had just arrived at Princes Street Station in Edinburgh, ready to start performing *Faust Up To Date* at the Lyceum Theatre, had her jewel case stolen after a porter placed it in a cab for her and then got distracted. While he was looking elsewhere, a thief managed to take it without the cab driver noticing. It is clear that actresses were the targets of both opportunistic thefts and those that were planned and although many were carried out by people previously unknown to the victim, on occasion, even their servants could be tempted by the goods they saw actresses with.

One of the notable features of some of these theatrical thefts is the age of the perpetrators. Amy Coates was 16; Jessie Vyner was 19. Percy Moore, another 19-year-old, who worked as a clerk for the Actors' Association, received eighteen months' hard labour after being convicted of theft in 1894. He had previously been convicted of false pretences and only got out of a prison sentence after promising to enlist in the navy. Once he had reached his first port, though, he had deserted. He had then gained his clerical job, but during it, opened a letter addressed to actress Miss Sidley, found a blank cheque in it, entered the figure of £10 on it and cashed it. His conviction was a blow for the three-year-old Actors' Association, whose establishment as a professional organization (a precursor to trade unionism and the formation of Equity in 1931) was aimed at making the acting industry appear both socially and professionally respectable.[14] Having a clerk who opened actress's letters and stole money was not a good reflection on it.

In cases such as Amy Coates, there was considerable sympathy for her as a very young, orphaned, vulnerable first offender. In the case of Percy Moore, though, there was far less. He was male, a repeat offender and a deserter. He was not seen as deserving of another chance, or as being as capable of redemption – even though he was still, by our standards, young. The motives of those convicted of theft differ; in Florrie Dytch's case, unemployment and the resulting financial hardship moved her to commit fraud; in Anthony Romani's case, it was a spur-of-the-moment decision motivated by a customer leaving her purse behind – an example of an opportunistic theft where the victim's profession was not a factor in the crime. But other individuals appear to have targeted actresses, knowing that there was a reasonable chance, particularly with more successful women, that they would have jewels and belongings in their homes or with them after performances – jewels that may have been worn on stage, or in their personal lives to highlight their status as successful theatrical performers.

CHAPTER 9

Prostitution

Elements of the Victorian press and politicians had frequently tried to shut down particular theatres because of the perceived link between theatres and prostitution, most notably, as discussed earlier, in the case of the Empire Theatre. In the nineteenth century, prostitution was referred to as the 'Great Social Evil', such acts being seen as a threat not just to the individual but to the 'nation's moral well-being'.[1] Commonly, it was the theatre building itself that was associated with prostitutes; its environs being a place where prostitutes could both ply their trade and meet with clients. Some theatres were also attractive places for prostitutes to socialise – and if they paid their entrance fee like any other audience member, there was little theatres could do. Newspapers sometimes blamed the theatres themselves for encouraging prostitutes by the choice of production they put on; for example, in 1855, when the Drury Lane theatre put on a masquerade, *Bell's Weekly Messenger* commented:

> We utterly object to this class of entertainments, as being in every respect demoralising and degrading. The scenes after midnight beggared all description; the house was filled with unfortunate women . . . It is really high time that the magistracy of the metropolis should interfere to put down these abominable repetitions of vice and profligacy. If masquerades are prohibited at Vauxhall, because of their immorality, why should they be tolerated at Covent Garden and Drury Lane? That Drury Lane should be prostituted to such purposes under its present management, we are not surprised at.

There was clearly a dichotomy between what the press thought the theatres should show – productions of 'high operatic character' and morality – and what was actually popular and would get audiences through the door. The press acted as guardians of morality, even though they relied on the salacious, sexual stories for their own revenue.

Although stories such as the one above saw prostitutes as theatregoers, engaging in prostitution or paying for prostitutes was also something that actors might engage in. Sometimes stories took an almost xenophobic approach, with European actresses being seen as particularly sexual and immoral – for example, in 1864, the *Glasgow Morning Post*'s reporters licked their lips over a story from Paris, where there had been a 'revelation of immorality such as ought to shock even the conscience-hardened Parisian'. This story involved a young man who had fallen for 'a woman who, professionally an actress, was privately a prostitute'. The youth left all his property to the woman in his will and then died – 'Thus prostitution is triumphant'. In other cases, the link was a throwback to more decadent eighteenth-century or early nineteenth-century times; in 1879, one paper was still referring to Dorothea Jordan as 'a prostitute actress'.[2] There were certainly a few cases in the newspapers where women admitted to being both actresses and prostitutes. In 1844, Jane Thomas was accused in court of owing £8 8s to a Finsbury linen draper,

Timothy Thomas, for goods. She was described in court as an actress who performed under the name of Jane Mordaunt and who had played in *Jack Sheppard* in one of the 'minor theatres'. Her defence was somewhat unorthodox – or, in the words of the *Evening Standard*, 'extraordinary'. She pleaded that she was a prostitute and that the draper had known this. The drapery goods were delivered to her in order to continue this prostitution and Mr Thomas 'expected to be repaid out of the wages and gain of prostitution'. Jane won her case. In 1861, a letter writer told the *Morning Post* about a shelter for outcast boys, where the mother of one had been traced. She had been said to have been a 'drunken prostitute', but it emerged that she had also been 'an actress at one of the minor theatres, has been of the most drunken, dissolute habits, [and] has lived with several different men . . . surely she is not fit to have the charge of a child'.

In another case that came after the passing of the Contagious Diseases Acts, a libel case was brought by a William Simpson against Captain Harris of the Metropolitan Police, on behalf of the daughter of a Mrs Percy, who had committed suicide in 1874. Mrs Percy was an actress, living with her daughter, who had complained that the Contagious Diseases Acts were 'attempted to be put in force in reference to her'. She and her 16-year-old daughter had been seen in Aldershot in the company of soldiers, who had then gone to their house and stayed until midnight; they had then been asked to go to the local hospital to be examined. Mrs Percy was found drowned in the local canal a few days later.[3] The highly-controversial Contagious Diseases Acts were passed between 1864 and 1869. They enabled police to arrest women suspected of being prostitutes – initially, only if they lived in certain areas – and force them to be examined for venereal diseases. The Acts stigmatised women, but not the men who used prostitutes.[4] Captain Harris had given evidence to the House of Commons that both Mrs Percy and her daughter had been acting as prostitutes. The press regarded the libel action as unlikely to succeed, due to a clause in the Act that 'protects from all sorts of consequences those who perform any public duty under its provisions' – in effect, that any woman could be accused of being a prostitute under the Act, as it was seen as a public duty to do so.

The link between individuals and prostitution was most commonly seen in divorce petitions as a tit-for-tat action, or on occasion, as a malicious action on the part of a partner seeking to blacken the name of the person they were trying to divorce. Of course, some cases may genuinely have had prostitution as a basis for a split, but there was certainly much name-calling amongst the suits, which the press reported with varying degrees of modesty.

This book has already mentioned the actress Grace Otway, who was the victim of theft whilst performing at the Theatre Royal in Sunderland in 1886, but four years later, she was in the press again as part of a far juicier story – her divorce – during which allegations both of adultery and prostitution were aired. The airing of such rumours and gossip, and their subsequent reporting in the press, showed the vulnerability of actresses to both be tarred as prostitutes and the use of such terms by those with grudges against them, to deliberately influence how they were seen by press and public. Grace's husband was the impressively named Charles Fitz Roy Alex Hallifax (*sic*) Bagot, who was unsurprisingly known professionally simply as Fitzroy Bagot. Born in Simla, India, in 1850 to Alexander Bagot, an army colonel, he had, by 1881, become the stage manager at the Prince of Wales Theatre on Tottenham Road in London, under Edgar Bruce.[5] On

17 August 1881, he married young Grace, then aged 22 – her marriage registered under her birth name of Emily Maynard Palmer Oldfield. She was also the child of an army colonel, Charles Oldfield, but both her father and Charles' had died prior to the wedding at the parish church of St George, Hanover Square.[6] Four years after their wedding, in April 1885, a daughter, named Viva Brabazon Bagot, was born at St John's Wood in London.[7]

On 29 January 1890, Charles filed for divorce on the grounds of Grace's adultery, stating that there was no way he could be Viva's natural father.[8] He named a Morton R. Selton as having had an affair with Grace at the Langham Hotel in Adelaide, Australia, around 18 June 1884, leading to Grace giving birth to a baby girl at 40 Grove Road, St John's Wood, on 13 April 1885.[9] Charles then decided this was incorrect and amended his petition to state that the adultery had been committed in Melbourne, rather than Adelaide and on 19 July 1884, rather than in June, or possibly on 19 August.

Grace's reply was firstly to deny any adultery and to claim that Charles had deserted her over two years previously – but then, curiously, added that Charles had both conduced to and connived at, her adultery – 'if any'. She argued that Charles had forced her to obtain large sums of money from different men and to give the money to him – and that he knew the money was obtained 'by immoral intercourse with the said men'. During the period of her marriage, she said, Charles failed to provide her with a home and instead 'lived upon her earnings and the money she obtained from men by immoral practices'. Therefore, rather than commit adultery, she had actually been prostituting herself, at his orders.

Charles, describing himself in the divorce documents as a journalist now, stated that Grace had written him a letter in December 1888, admitting to adultery with Morton Selton and stating that the child she had registered as hers and Charles's was not his. Charles stressed that the baby could not be his, as he had not seen his wife since 20 December 1882 and had been living with his mother since then. At the time of the baby's conception, he had been living on his own in lodgings in Charles Street, Westminster, then had gone to Dublin, Brighton, Dieppe and Paris. He had continued travelling around the world – from France and Belgium to Tunisia, Libya and Malta – until August 1885.[10] Meanwhile, as of 1890, Morton Selton was in the USA and not contactable – or, as Charles put, it 'his exact address there is unknown to me and in all probability considerable difficulty would be experienced in finding him'.

The divorce court agreed with Charles that Grace had committed adultery; they failed to believe her allegations of forced prostitution. Charles was granted his divorce. Although the press coverage eagerly covered the divorce, the newspapers refused to mention the prostitution, simply referring to the allegations of 'connivance' and stating that Grace had said, in cross-examination, that 'she had told her husband that she had committed adultery with several men and made no secret of it'. Grace was also reported to have been 'very extravagant and insisted upon having her own way', to the extent that her husband had ended up filing for bankruptcy. It was also reported that Grace admitted that her child wasn't her husband's and that although, when Charles met her (he was stage manager at the Prince of Wales, which was about to show *The Colonel*, a play that Grace was appearing in) he thought she was 'a respectable woman', 'after the wedding he heard certain matters about the respondent. He told her what he had heard, but she said it was untrue, but she admitted she had been the mistress of someone. [Charles] was greatly distressed.' Therefore, the press ended up presenting a very one-sided view of the relationship and omitting, out of its own strange perceptions of morality, to put her side of the story across. Although her admittance of prostitution would have backed Charles's comments about her background, her allegations of connivance and being threatened to commit such acts by her husband, were dismissed by the courts and therefore the newspapers – which only appear to have covered the story once the decree nisi had been issued – failed to mention it at all, apart from one line in the *York Herald*, where Charles Bagot was simply quoted as saying 'It was utterly untrue that he had ever benefited by his wife's immorality' and an unnamed lawyer was quoted as saying that when Grace had sent money to her husband, he 'must have known the means by which she obtained it'. As the paper had failed to mention prostitution at any point previously, these two lines must have raised a few quizzical eyebrows among Victorian readers.

Only months after the divorce, on 16 February 1891, Grace remarried. *The Era* reported that the wedding of Francis Nicholas Evans, AB, BL, son of the late Captain Nicholas Evans, RN, JP and grandson of the late Admiral Evans, MP of Newtown, County Cork, to Emily (Aimee) Maynard Palmer Bagot, 'daughter of the late Colonel Charles Oldfield, professionally known as Miss Grace Otway' had taken place at Richmond in Surrey. The marriage announcement was placed in the following week's newspaper, too, to make sure everyone had seen that Grace Otway had made a good second marriage. She also continued to perform and in 1899, appeared at Her Majesty's Theatre in a performance of *Carnac Sahib* that also starred Herbert Beerbohm Tree. In 1932, the 'Birthdays of the Week' round-up in *The Era* noted that it was Grace Otway's birthday on 3 June; she died three years later.[11]

The detailing of female sexual behaviour was presumably enjoyed by the newspaper's readership and hence the amount of words spent describing it. Yet a Victorian woman's reputation was based on her morality and innocence – and so it is unsurprising that when allegations were made, those who felt they could be impacted by it retaliated. The young actress Edith Bruce, well known as the subject of the London Stereoscopic Company's publicity material, was caught up in a case of mistaken identity in 1880, when a divorce case, Aveling *versus* Aveling, was heard at the Divorce Court. The case was brought by Florence Mary Aveling, née Winn, against her husband of less than three years, Ernest Henry, in October 1880. with the decree nisi issued on 9 February 1881.[12] Ernest Aveling was an auctioneer and son of a Congregationalist minister; Florence the daughter of a gentleman. They had married at 22, had a daughter, Olive, at 23 and were divorced at 25. Theirs was just another middle class divorce – with Florence alleging that her husband had neglected her from an early stage of their marriage, 'coming home at all hours after midnight in a state of intoxication and absenting himself from time to time from home for days without communicating'. Her more serious allegations against her husband involved his alleged tendency to sleep with other women, primarily prostitutes. It was rather appropriate that Henry's home in Stamford Hill was on Cazenove Road. Florence alleged that from the date of their marriage to the date of her divorce petition, he had 'been in the habit of visiting one Edith Bruce, a prostitute at 10 Sutherland Place, Pimlico'. Rumours rapidly spread that this was the actress Edith Bruce, who was a member of the Criterion company and who had recently drawn good reviews as part of the Crystal Palace Pantomime. *The Era* noted that her name had been 'dragged' into the press reports of the divorce and mentioned that they were able to categorically state that the named woman was not the 'clever young actress'. They reported that such a statement was necessary because 'enemies of the stage' had 'as usual' taken great pleasure in gossiping about the case in order to suggest that it was an illustration of the immorality of the theatre and those who worked in it.

The implication was clear – actresses were still considered little more than prostitutes in some circles and therefore, the prostitute Edith Bruce might be mistaken to be the actress Edith Bruce. Yet the divorce petition made no link to the acting profession; indeed, Henry was more likely to find prostitutes at the Royal Aquarium at Westminster, according to his wife. One several occasions, he had left his wife alone there and she had had to 'wait for him in the Ladies' Room among 20 to 30 prostitutes, thereby outraging her feelings'. But although the divorce petition did not make the link between acting and prostitution, the newspapers did. It was clear that personal cases in the courts could be used by the press for their own political or moral diatribes against the theatrical profession, or against women generally (according to this divorce, London's public places were thronged with prostitutes waiting to take advantage of married men, or to outrage respectable married women). *The Era*, as the leading theatrical newspaper, was keen to refute such insinuations and maintain the loyalty of the actresses who read it.

Individual actors and actresses, too, tried to ensure that the local press got a more positive picture of the theatrical profession. In 1877, comedian Frederick Medey wrote from Darlington to Middlesbrough's *Daily Gazette* as part of an ongoing correspondence in the paper about the morality of the acting profession (the question being posed was 'Is theatregoing consistent with a Christian profession?'). He was responding to an article from David Eades, who claimed, Medey wrote, to be a Christian, yet 'he knows the names of filthy books that certainly I never heard of' and who had insinuated that the acting profession was immoral. The two men had had quite a discourse – both in the pages of the paper and in private letters – and Medey had challenged Eades to a public debate on the issue, which Eades refused to take part in, 'on the ground that the "heat and excitement which invariably attach to a public discussion would render it almost impossible to discuss the same with any good result"'. Medey stated his pride at his profession, writing: 'I would like to remind him that, as an actor, I am a gentleman by Act of Parliament – I am proud to know that I am a member of the same profession as William Shakespeare.'

Although Medey acknowledged that some actors, on leaving the profession, had fallen into disrepute, he believed that the wider profession was being stigmatised by 'ignorant and bigoted people'. He noted that, conversely, the theatre was seeing remarkable growth – both in the number of theatres worldwide and in the number of reputable actors commanding higher salaries within the profession. He added that he had been in the theatre for twenty years, 'and during that time I have never known an actor or actress sentenced to penal servitude: have never heard of an actress becoming a prostitute; have never heard of an actor being convicted of indecent assault or bestiality; and I have known of hundreds of such charges proved against "professing Christians"'.

There was undoubtedly hyperbole and professional pride in Medey's comments; for actors had been sentenced to penal servitude and had been convicted of various offences (although possibly not bestiality) within this period. But perhaps he was simply speaking from personal experience, using the examples of his own friends; either way, it was clear that for every person who equated acting with crime and prostitution, there was an actor to stand up for his or her maligned profession – a profession that, as Medey made clear, was responsible for a form of entertainment that was hugely popular with the wider Victorian public.

CHAPTER 10

Murder, Murder!

The Victorian press loved a good murder. Crime reporting increased over the course of the nineteenth century; prior to 1868, public executions were a good source of stories for reporters, but after they became private affairs, carried out in the courtyards of prisons, murder trials continued to be eagerly covered for the titillation of readers. Acting was regarded, at least to a certain extent, as an occupation for immoral individuals – a perception that renowned actors tried to combat. When the actor Charles Kemble said that 'no actor was ever, ever suspended on the gallows, or sentenced to death', the *Gloucestershire Chronicle* was keen to refute his assertion, stating that a decade earlier, an actor named Bartlett was executed at Gloucester after being convicted of murder, although the paper added that he had been 'an actor to the life, though only a stroller'. This was 23-year-old Charles Samuel Bartlett, who was hanged for murdering his mother-in-law, a Mrs Lewis. At that time, he was described in the press as 'a person of good education and address, [and who] had with his wife for some time obtained a livelihood in the character of strolling players'. He was regarded as behaving very confidently on his way to his death and gave an impressive speech immediately before he dropped. Despite attitudes towards actors gradually ameliorating from 1860 onwards, the coverage of crimes, particularly murders, involving the theatrical profession continued to be covered by the press as though they were something to be expected; perhaps the fact that actors had to express a range of emotions in their professional lives meant it was assumed that they were emotional in their private lives too.[1]

But in part, these crimes were seen as something 'foreign'; and the cases covered in the press in the mid-nineteenth century tended to be about actors outside of the UK; as Kemble's assertion may have suggested, the British actor was more respectable, less emotional, than his European or American counterpart. In 1862, the press covered the criminal trial of a 19-year-old actor named Dumont, described as a 'jeune premier – player of "lovers" characters – at the little theatre of Montparnasse'. He was at the Parisian Assize Court charged with attempted murder; his trial was attended by 'a well-dressed audience, among whom were several actors and actresses' and was seen as something of a dramatic character himself:

> He appears to have been a sort of Cherubino, sighing after every lady within his ken. The actresses to whom he made love, laughed at him and treated him as a child and their husbands or protectors never considered him as a rival worth notice.

His most recent passion was the actress Madame Demongeot, who had been playing at the Island Theatre in the Bois de Boulogne; after she had got home from a performance, she and her husband had gone to bed – 'in separate beds', stressed the pursed-lipped British press. Dumont, who had been hiding in their apartment, then leapt up and stabbed

Monsieur Demongeot fifteen times. He claimed to have wanted to kill the husband and then rape the wife; luckily for them both, his plan failed.

Three years later, the British newspapers covered the murder in Balachef, Russia, of the actor Koulebiakine by a local landed proprietor named Mr Dokoukine, who told the actor he had performed his most recent role badly, and when Koulebiakine suggested that Dokoukine replace him to see if he could do it better, Dokoukine took offence and later turned up a Koulebiakine's hotel room and shot him at point-blank range. Before he died, Koulebiakine asked why Dokoukine had shot him; his killer replied, 'Because you deserved to die like a dog!'[2]

Throughout the nineteenth century, the British papers were able to get stories from the other side of the Atlantic and their readers enjoyed stories about the American stage.[3] They also enjoyed stories from *off* the American stage. Back in 1842, the UK press had covered the murder of an American actor, Mr Ewing, shortly after he had finished performing in the first act of a play in Mobile, Alabama. The curtain dropped and Ewing immediately engaged in an argument with an actress on his production, Miss Hamblin, which ended when she stuck a dagger in his heart, causing death almost instantaneously. Panicking, Miss Hamblin immediately jumped out of the nearest window, still in her costume – that of a page. Hours later, she had still not been found. The events happened on 25 March, but due to the time it took for the American newspapers to reach Britain, it was not reported over here until nearly two months later.

By the 1890s, the British newspapers were able to obtain their American stories far quicker, via telegraph. In 1890, the *Hull Daily Mail* covered the tale of Charles Crumley, a black actor who performed under the name of Charles Webster. He had been playing 'Clen the Nigger' in Barclay Campbell's White Slave Company since around 1880. He had married a Canadian woman, a Miss Ernest, in 1875, when his bride was 21 years old. She was described in the newspaper as being 'of a very lively disposition', a nice euphemism for a woman who was not a demure, stay-at-home wife. Crumley had been touring with his company and on returning to his home in New York heard rumours that had been going round in his absence, involving his wife and an engineer named Robert McNeill. He lay in wait for McNeill outside his house and on seeing him approach, 'immediately drew a revolver, from which he fired two shots, causing instant death'. There were no more details, but this basic story, involving love, cuckolding, the theatre and a dramatic murder, was enough to get it covered in newspapers across England and Wales.

Reports of theatrical murders and attempted murders frequently specified a personal motive, such as in 1879, when Mark Gray shot actor Edwin Booth – the brother of John Wilkes Booth, murderer of Abraham Lincoln – while Booth was performing at Chicago's McVicker's Theater.[4] *The Cornishman* newspaper reported that Gray had 'declared personal revenge against Mr Booth', but failed to report why he sought that revenge.[5] The *Chicago Tribune*, conversely, reported the case in far greater detail, noting that Booth stepped out into the footlights when the shot was fired and when the theatre manager, Louis Sharpe asked, 'What is it, Edwin, who is it?', he pointed to Gray on the balcony and said, 'There he is; that's the man'. Gray was taken into custody, where he told the police, 'My reason for attempting to shoot Booth is that he mocked me. I saw him a few nights since in Richelieu and Booth said in one of the scenes, "Mark where she stands!"' Gray felt that Booth emphasised the 'Mark' and was therefore referring to him – he was immediately sent to the nearest insane asylum. Obviously, this was a local story for the Chicago paper; for the British press, the fact that an actor had been targeted like this was news, but because it happened so far away from home and to an American, made it unnecessary to report in detail.

A further American case reported by the British press, from 1895, was equally short in detail, as the murder was more obviously the result of a personal relationship – the actor Joseph K. Emmett, known as 'Fritz', had had an argument with his wife which culminated in his fatally shooting her. The *Sheffield Evening Telegraph* thought this incident, which it learned of from a 'San Francisco despatch', was newsworthy enough to report, but not newsworthy enough to name the wife, or provide more details about where and why the murder took place.

A case with a more tangible link to Britain came in the autumn of 1895, when *The Times* was telegraphed by its Sydney correspondent to report that a well-known English actor named Arthur Dacre (the professional name of Arthur Culver James) had shot his wife, the actress Amy Roselle, while she slept and had then cut his own throat. The couple had been on tour in Australia and it had proved to be disastrous, leaving them 'despondent'. The deaths appeared to have been the result of a suicide pact, as both Arthur and Amy had left 'most pathetic letters'.[6] The couple's English origins were stressed – for example, Amy was 'but little over 40 years of age and was born in Glastonbury, where her father was a schoolmaster'. She had been on the stage since she was 16 and had been married to Arthur Dacre for nine years; he had originally been a surgeon and *The Times* stated that 'in him the stage loses a singularly handsome, intelligent and cultivated actor'.[7]

It was two years later that the UK got its own home-grown drama involving the dramatic profession – and it was, perhaps, the most infamous theatrical murder of the nineteenth century. This was the murder of actor William Terriss by Richard Archer Prince. It was on the evening of Thursday, 16 December 1897 – a few minutes before 7 pm – that the actor arrived at the stage door of the Adelphi Theatre in London; he was due to play in the drama *Secret Service* there that evening. He arrived in a cab with fellow actor John Henry Graves and was stepping across the pavement to the stage door when 'a man of foreign appearance' in a long black cloak ran up to him and plunged a stiletto into the left-hand side of Terriss's chest, just below his heart. Terriss shouted, 'My God, he's stabbed me, he's stabbed me. Don't let him escape!' as he fell down. Members of the crowd who had gathered round the stage door to see the likes of Terriss arrive grabbed his assailant, whilst others carried the dying actor into the theatre, placing him on the stair landing. Doctors were summoned from the nearby Charing Cross Hospital, but within a few minutes of the attack, Terriss was dead. With him was his leading lady, Jessie Millward, who broke down in tears as he died. Meanwhile, his attacker was secured by police who took him to Bow Street Police Station.

This man was soon identified as Richard Archer Prince, who had been a 'super' – a minor actor – during an Adelphi production some years earlier called *In The Ranks*, which Terriss had taken the lead role in. Initially, there was uncertainty about what his motive for the stabbing could be, for 'the deceased actor's genial nature made it inconceivable that anything like personal vengeance can have prompted such a tragedy'. However, one press reporter, on making inquiries, found that Prince had regularly 'haunted' the Adelphi and the day before the attack, had asked the stage door keeper where Terriss was. His behaviour had been seen as so disturbing that another actor had to come and order Prince to leave the theatre. It was noted that this affair was treated simply 'as one of the many unpleasant little scenes to which actors high in the profession are subjected by those occupying humbler and less successful positions in connection with the stage'. Another member of the Adelphi cast said that Prince had been known for some time by the other actors as 'Mad Prince'.[8]

The murder was so out of the blue, so shocking, that even the press seemed genuinely upset and almost lost for words. Of course, they covered the story in depth, but the initial obituaries were less formal than usual. The *Liverpool Mercury* had, on its front page, an obituary by Joseph Hatton, which started: 'Terriss was a fatalist', detailing his lack of fear of death which was the result of facing it 'often enough without flinching during a singularly adventurous career'. Hatton commented that Terriss had actually received medals from the Royal Humane Society for saving lives at sea.[9] The obituary ended, 'Poor fellow, he had rare and good qualities and on and off the stage the world is the darker for his death'. Hatton had known and worked with Terriss and his somewhat stunned obituary reflected the horror the theatrical world felt towards the violent death of an actor who had been benevolent and charitable towards those less fortunate than himself. This shock extended to the wider community. In one North London boarding house, which was particularly popular with actors, the female general servant, for whom a trip to the Adelphi was 'her one and only source of enjoyment', had fallen in love with the actor. On her night off, one night in 1897, she had gone to the Adelphi in the hope of spotting Terriss – 'a mad desire to have a look at him, off the stage, suddenly seized her'. She arrived at the stage door just as Terriss was stabbed and fled in horror at what she saw. The next time she was spotted cleaning the front door steps of the boarding house, she was wearing a 'tiny piece of draggled black crêpe', pinned to her old, torn, print bodice – a symbol of respect from a poor girl for whom Terriss had represented an escape from her mundane, hard life.

On his arrival at Bond Street – although another report says Bow Street Police Station – Prince had claimed that he had killed Terriss because he had refused him aid from the benevolent fund that morning. At the Old Bailey on Monday 10 January 1898, the Recorder of London, Sir Charles Hall, directed the Grand Jury to return a true bill against Prince, saying that it was unnecessary to enter into details of the murder again, except that 'it was sufficient to say the accused was seen to stab Mr Terriss and was really caught in the act'. The murder was of such great interest that the press reported the nitty-gritty of the court procedure, which it often omitted. It speculated as to who the judge at the trial would be and although it noted that three doctors had agreed that Prince was insane when he committed the murder, 'the question as to whether Prince is now sane enough to plead is one with regard to which it is understood the medical men are not so unanimous'. After the murder, other actors realised they had had a lucky escape from Prince. Wilson Barrett, who was performing in *Claudian* in Melbourne, Australia, when the news of the murder reached him, was said to be 'greatly shocked at the sad tidings' and, reported the newspapers,

> said he was almost certain that the assassin was identical with a man named Prince, who followed him (Mr Barrett) about with a revolver when he was lessee of the Princess's Theatre, London. One day, Mr Barrett called Archer into the office of the

theatre and accused him of intent to murder. Archer admitted the charge and said Mr Barrett was his brother and had robbed him. Then he knew the man was mad.

The *South Wales Echo* commented that if this was the same man – and it seemed likely – then Wilson Barrett should shoulder some of the blame, as he had 'neglected' to 'have the madman locked up'.

On 10 January 1898, Prince was tried at the Old Bailey and found not guilty, by way of insanity, the jury stating that 'they found the prisoner knew what he was doing and to whom he was doing it; but that upon the medical evidence, he was insane so as not to be responsible for his actions according to law at the time he committed the act'.[10] As was usual with such cases, he was ordered to be detained until Her Majesty's pleasure was known, which meant that he was sent to Broadmoor Criminal Lunatic Asylum. Although many thought this was a lenient sentence, with Sir Henry Irving saying that Prince was not executed simply because his victim was an actor, this is not true; lunatic murderers were usually sent to Broadmoor, where they could end up incarcerated for years.[11] This was certainly the case with Prince, who was still in the asylum when he died in 1936.[12]

The press had to wait thirteen years for a domestic theatrical murder that would gain as much coverage as the killing of William Terriss.[13] There were other cases of attempted murder during the late nineteenth century – such as in 1878, when actor Thomas Harry Jones, 'a man of haggard appearance' who had been performing in Hanley, Staffordshire, met a woman named Ellen Major as he was walking to Crewe. Without saying a word to her, he tried to cut her throat with a pocket knife before stabbing her in the chest. She was later found unconscious, lying on the road. In court, Jones said 'he had been drinking heavily' and committed the offence in the belief that he was playing a part in *Maria Marten, or the Murder in the Red Barn*. He was tried at Chester Assizes. Another attempted murder was carried out by 'well-known London actor' John Webb, who 'takes the part of the villain in the *Passion of Life* play'. He had also tried to cut a woman's throat – this time, though, it was his actress wife, Nellie Webb. When he was charged at Cradley Heath in the West Midlands in 1900, he was said to have become 'very strange through over-study'. But these cases did not receive much press attention, despite them being committed by actors and one having a link to one of the most notorious crimes of the early nineteenth century – the Red Barn Murder of 1827, which spawned a series of plays and ballads.[14]

What made some cases more newsworthy than others? Obviously, attempted murders were not seen as important as cases where the victim had died, but this was not the only consideration. Domestic crimes and sexual crimes, were generally seen as less interesting as crimes where there was no such relationship between the individuals. The exception would be cases such as Amy Roselle's, which involved British actors in a foreign country, or which highlighted the insecurity and therefore dangerousness, of a life on the stage. The coverage of such stories had a moral purpose. However, William Terriss's murder was awful because it came out of the blue and it took place both almost within the confines of the theatre and in England's theatrical capital. Provincial cases might have been of interest to local newspapers, but London cases were important both to the London-based press and to those in the provinces.

PART 3:
PERSONAL LIVES

CHAPTER 11

Sex and Seduction

It was really the personal lives of performers that the press was interested in, and increasingly so as the Victoria era progressed. Yes, there were still plenty of theatrical reviews being published and articles about the profession, or about professional engagements, but *The Era*'s 'Theatrical Gossip' column was so named for a reason. The interest in the personal encompassed things that we might today find rather innocuous, or not newsworthy. For example, one item in 1896 drew attention to actress Kate Rorke's religion:

> It is mentioned as a strange coincidence that the well-known actress Miss Kate Rorke, who undertakes the part of the beautiful Protestant who had been given the name of St Hilda by Martin Luther in the new play at the Shaftesbury Theatre, London, is a member of the Roman Catholic Church.

Was the newspaper simply drawing attention to the 'strange coincidence', or was it using the role as a hook to bring in Rorke's Catholicism? After all, actors might be reasonably expected to take on roles that did not reflect their real lives, so the story was not news unless it was being used to stress Rorke's 'otherness' in terms of not adhering to the established church. As was with the case with many stories about the stage, the press was distinguishing between 'ordinary' people and those who lived a different, more unconventional life by being theatrical performers. Likewise, the wider coverage about their personal lives also served to stress this unconventionality. Weddings were notable because of their theatrical participants; but of far greater interest were the stories about sex, seduction, bigamy and divorce, breathlessly told for an eager audience keen to maintain this perception of actors as having exciting, unconventional lives – even when the reality was a more mundane one of stress, financial insecurity and the impact of one's profession on one's ability to maintain a stable home life.

Some offences committed by or on performers did not fit a simple box. This chapter looks at some of the varied incidences that affected performers in Victorian England – some the result of actors' complex private lives or peripatetic lives and others the result of audiences' desires to communicate with actors. Again, some of these incidences show how the lives of nineteenth-century 'celebrities' in the acting world were similar to those today – and the problems that could arise from them were eagerly covered by the press for the delectation of their readers just as celebrity magazines and the *Daily Mail*'s 'sidebar of shame' covers celebrity scandals today. Then as now, too, there could be problems with obsessed fans of particular actors or singers, wanting to get a bit too close to their idols. Ex-girlfriends and mistresses might cause problems after they had been discarded; if their finances took a turn for the worse after a relationship with an actor ended, they might resort to blackmail or worse. Here are some of the diverse problems in the theatrical world that the nineteenth-century press covered.

It was Spring 1856 and a tall, genteel-looking 30-year-old woman named Harriet Collins was brought to the Marlborough Street police office one Tuesday, charged with threatening the life of comedian John Munroe Graham. Harriet stated that her name was Harriet Graham, implying that she was married to the comic – but she was not. A second charge was also made against her by another comedian and friend of Graham's, named Thomas Brazier, who accused her of 'being drunk and annoying him at his residence, No 2 Nelson Street, Camden Town'. Harriet had been the mistress of John Munroe Graham, having lived under his protection for over twelve years. However, several months prior to her appearance before the magistrates, the couple had separated, 'by mutual consent', with Graham agreeing to give her a regular amount of money each week as maintenance.

However, in May 1856, Harriet accosted Graham as he was leaving the Princess's Theatre, where he was performing. She drew a pistol and tried to shoot him in the chest. 'The pistol, fortunately for Mr Graham, missed fire.' She was grabbed by several other people who were passing by and taken into custody. On 12 May 1856, at the Old Bailey, Harriet was tried for an 'attempt to shoot to murder and do bodily harm' but that judgement was respited. A month later, the records stated that she had been 'convicted at the last session of felony – feloniously attempting to shoot to do bodily harm – judgement respited – four calendar months from conviction'.[1] She was in prison from May until September that year and then released – but 'ever since then she has subjected Mr Graham to such a vexatious system of annoyance as to become almost unbearable'. Harriet had taken to following Graham around and when he would stop and tell her to leave him alone, she would use 'language of such a threatening nature that he went in fear of his life'.

Graham eventually went to one of the magistrates at Marlborough Street, Peregrine Bingham, to get a warrant against Harriet, but before it could be executed, Harriet turned up in Camden, at Thomas Brazier's house.[2] She caused such a scene that Brazier had to take her to the police. When asked by William Beadon, another senior magistrate at the Marlborough Street Police Court, why she had gone to Brazier's, Harriet said she thought Graham was there and she had wanted to see him.[3] Mr Beadon said it was 'very clear' that Graham did not want to see Harriet: 'Why did she not keep away from him, especially as she had promised him she would do so? Why did she persist in annoying Mr Graham?'

Harriet denied annoying or threatening Graham, stating that she had lived with him as his wife for more than twelve years and 'had earned and saved money for him, which he had squandered away in low, profligate company'. She had come out of prison with no money, not even a change of clothing, and had sought him out in order to get enough money to travel to an engagement in Yorkshire with a spare set of clothes. Graham, however, stated that he had given Harriet maintenance of £1 a week, on condition that she kept away from him.

Women who had cohabited with men and who had been left in financially-precarious situations when the relationship ended, often received a sympathetic hearing from Victorian judges, who felt that men had a 'moral obligation' to support women they had treated as wives in all but name.[4] Harriet, though, had overstepped the mark in her reaction to Graham. When she complained that 'Mr Graham always tried to avoid me', the magistrate displayed a distinct lack of sympathy:

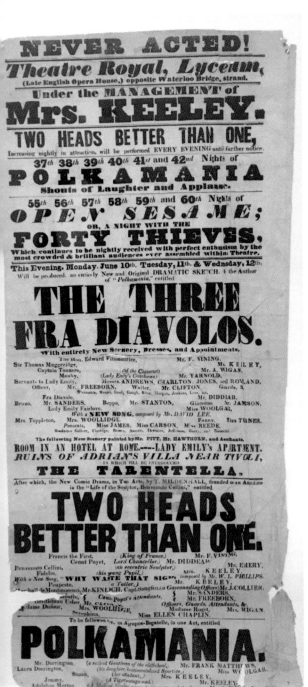

Kate Rorke, whose religion was the focus of newspaper gossip in the 1890s. (Author's collection)

A playbill from the 1840s, with the successful, long-serving actress-manager Mrs Keeley at the top. (Author's collection)

Rutland Barrington as Captain Corcoran in *HMS Pinafore*. (From Rutland Barrington, 'A record of 35 years' experience on the English stage' (Grant Richards, London, 1908))

William Horace Lingard in drag – he was the subject of a bigamy case. (Public domain)

Josephine 'Cassy' Casaboni and Lytton Grey in a publicity shot; Grey divorced his second wife after she had an affair with fellow actor Dick Neville. (Author's collection)

William's most famous spouse – actress Alice Dunning Lingard. (Public domain)

Violet Cameron, whose husband successfully brought an action for libel against a newspaper editor in 1887 – part of a scandal involving Violet and the Earl of Lonsdale. (Author's collection)

Actress Clara Rousby brought an assault case against Daniel Bandmann in 1878, but found herself accused of alcoholism. (Author's collection)

Cornelie D'Anka, who found herself the victim of an unpleasant stalking case in 1871, where she had a pistol pointed at her and a bullet delivered to her at a theatre. (Author's collection)

Gaiety Girl Marie Studholme, who offered her manager George Edwardes her savings when he ran into financial difficulties. (Author's collection)

Eva Sothern (1862-1945). She gave up her successful acting career when she married at the age of 21. (Author's collection)

J. L. Toole (1830-1906), the comedian, actor, actor-manager and producer, who ran Toole's Theatre – formerly the Folly Theatre – in London. (Author's collection)

Statue of Edwin Booth at Gramercy Park, New York. Edwin Booth, brother of the notorious Charles Wilkes Booth, was nearly the victim of murder himself – a fact that the British press lapped up. (Author's collection)

The plaque to pantomime artist Sarah Smith – whose dress was set alight in 1863 – at Postman's Park in London. (Author's collection)

'Tragic death of an actress' – a typically understated scene from the *Illustrated Police News* of 12 August 1899, p.6. (Newspaper Image © The British Library Board. All rights reserved. With thanks to The British Newspaper Archive (www.BritishNewspaperArchive.co.uk))

Grace Otway Oldfield, the actress who was involved both in a theft case, and a more complex marital situation. (Author's collection)

'Exciting scene on board ship: an actress horsewhips a well-known theatrical manager' – a mid-Atlantic tale involving manager Marcus Mayer and performer Ilda Orme, from the *Illustrated Police News*, 17 June 1899, p.1. (Newspaper Image © The British Library Board. All rights reserved. With thanks to The British Newspaper Archive (www.BritishNewspaperArchive.co.uk))

The Royal Dublin Hospital, where 18-year-old actress Alice Harper died – whilst her 'husband' Fred Solomon went on stage at the Gaiety Theatre. (Author's collection)

A plaque outside the stage door of the Adelphi Theatre in London marks the spot where William Terriss was murdered. (Author's collection)

514 Broadway, Soho, New York. It was on a building at this site - Wood's, later the Theatre Comique - that William Horace Lingard and his wife Alice first appeared; he took over the management of the theatre after leaving England. (Author's collection)

Ellen Terry, whose relationships kept the British newspapers agog. (Author's collection)

William Terriss, victim of the most famous British theatrical murder of the 19th century. (Author's collection)

Performers sometimes took action against unruly audience members, as this 1899 image shows. 'A Variety Actress and the Dudes' from *Illustrated Police News*, 10 June 1899, p.12. (Newspaper Image © The British Library Board. All rights reserved. With thanks to The British Newspaper Archive (www.BritishNewspaperArchive.co.uk))

A production of W.S. Gilbert's *The Wicked World* being performed at the Haymarket Theatre in 1873 – as featured in the *Illustrated London News*. (Public domain)

Amy Roselle, the English actress shot dead by her husband Arthur Dacre in 1895 as part of a suicide pact. (Public domain)

The actor Charles Francis Coghlan (1842-1899), who was successful on both sides of the Atlantic. (Public domain)

The actor Squire Bancroft, whose 'secret' son's marriage made the news because of him. (Author's collection)

Madge Kendal, the actress and theatre manager – later Dame Madge. Being married to actor William Hunter Griston, it was inevitable that the press would be fascinated by her family. (Public domain)

It was not a very astonishing fact that a man should endeavour to avoid her, or refuse to give her money, especially after she had held a loaded pistol to his breast. Her conduct could not be for one moment tolerated.

He made Harriet promise not to follow or annoy Graham again and not to visit Brazier. He then ordered her into a recognizance to keep the peace for the next three months. Harriet paid the surety immediately – despite her protestations of poverty – and was duly discharged. The case showed how a performer's past could catch up with him – but it also showed the precarious situation of women who lived with performers as their mistresses, without the security of marriage. Once discarded, they lost their financial security and could soon be reduced to acts such as Harriet's rash threats to her former lover and his friend.

When married women engaged in extra-marital relationships, husbands might bring actions against their lovers, arguing that their wives had been seduced. In 1874, in Dublin, an actor named Norrall brought a criminal conversation case against Captain William Roger Snow, demanding compensation of £1,500. 'Crim con' was a common law tort that was the result of adultery, where the husband would seek compensation for his wife's infidelity. Although it had been abolished in England back in 1857, it still existed in Ireland at this time.[5]

Norrall stated that he had met his wife, also an actress and known professionally as Miss Thompson, when she was taking part in an amateur performance at Dublin's Theatre Royal. She had subsequently been engaged professionally at the Gaiety Theatre. There, Captain Snow – an officer in the Army Service Corps – had frequently seen her. Norrall travelled to Belfast to try and get an engagement and while he was away, he argued, Snow seduced his wife. On his return to Dublin, he found Snow in his wife's rooms at night-time – the two men fought and the case came to court. Before the Queen's Bench, Captain Snow admitted that he had seduced Miss Thompson – Mrs Norrall – but 'denied positively that he knew she was married'. Mrs Norrall corroborated this, stating 'she had concealed from him the fact that she was a married woman'. Since the fight, she had left Norrall and was now living with Snow. She argued that Norrall was an unkind man who had neglected her; the jury, although finding in favour of Norrall, awarded him just £100 damages rather than the larger amount he had been asking for.

The case had wider repercussions for the hapless William Roger Snow. Outside of his army career, he had a successful sideline as a writer and artist, under the pseudonym Richard André.[6] After the crim con case, he abandoned his wife and started using a second pseudonym, Clifford Merton, in order to prevent her knowing his whereabouts. Eventually, she discovered him and petitioned for a divorce. Their case was heard in London in February 1882 and duly reported by the press, who noted that all four of the couple's children had died, and that they had been 'happy' until 1872, when the affair between Snow and Mrs Norrall had taken place. He had then been dismissed from the army and disappeared until 1881, when his wife discovered him living in Camberwell with another woman, under the Merton name. Mrs Snow went to his house and 'claimed her right to remain with him as his lawful wife. He flew into a violent passion and turned her out of the house with violence.' She was allowed a judicial separation due to his adultery.

In the 1850s, another case had highlighted the xenophobia and racism inherent in

Victorian society. It raised issues of how mixed-race relationships were perceived and their lack of acceptability amongst many. It revolved around a black actor named Ira Aldridge, who was 'known in the theatrical world as The African Roscius'. It was noted that 'he was well calculated to play certain parts, being "coloured" by nature and he had amassed a considerable sum of money' – and even that 'he was a black star, but rather a desirable one'. Today, he is remembered as the first black actor to become famous in his time. Ira was, like many other black actors in Victorian England, originally a performer in his native country, America; however, in 1863, four years before his death, he took British citizenship.[7] He was the first black actor to play the main Shakespearean parts on the English stage, portraying Othello, Lear, Shylock and Hamlet, and he also appeared in Ireland.

In 1856, Ira was 49 years old and had been performing in England and Ireland for over 20 years. He had already been subject to the prejudices of the white British – when he had played Othello in 1833, newspapers protested about a black actor being allowed to appear at Covent Garden.[8] Yet he was seen by others in the press as a very gifted performer. It was evident that the press was torn between their prejudices towards Ira's racial background and their admiration for his undoubted talent. But it was the former prejudice that they delighted in airing in 1856.

It was in this year that Ira was brought before the Bail Court in an action for seduction, brought by another actor, William Stothard. He argued that Ira had seduced his wife, Emma, and that she had subsequently given birth to 'a nigger'. Stothard was clearly horrified by the fact that his wife had had a child that clearly wasn't his; his action seems to have been an ill-thought out attempt to claw back respectability by getting Ira convicted of seduction. He was obviously unable to accept the fact that his wife may have willingly engaged in a sexual relationship with 'The African Roscius'.

Stothard had originally trained as a surgeon in Hull, but in 1849 had 'had taken a fancy to try his fortune on the stage and, having heard of the celebrity of the defendant, he went to Liverpool, where the defendant was then starring'. He went by the professional name of Stewart, but 'he played "utility" parts in anything, he was a little fair mad', according to Richard Norman, an actor at the Surrey Theatre who had performed with him at the 'minor theatre' in Liverpool.

William Stothard had asked Ira to teach him how to act and paid him £50. He was then sent to perform in Hull, Liverpool, Wales and other places. It was sometime that same year, 1849, that Stothard was introduced to Emma Iggulden by Ira – she was staying at her aunt Jane's house in Bloomsbury, which was where Ira lodged.[9] Although the press stated that Emma was only 18, perhaps attempting to paint her as a young innocent, thus building the picture of seduction, she was actually in her early twenties.[10] Emma and Stothard started courting and were married on 15 August 1849 – with Ira Aldridge even giving Emma away.[11]

The court proved that after her marriage, Mrs Stothard had been 'entirely neglected' by her husband for several years – thus giving her some justification for embarking on an affair. Stothard had performed in Wales straight after his marriage and although initially taking Emma with him, he subsequently found that he 'could not afford to take her the different circuits with him' and so sent her off to stay with his mother in Tunbridge Wells. It was during this separation that Ira was alleged to have seduced her and on 15 March

1853, Emma gave birth at a lying-in hospital. William was not present and Emma's family did not know where he was. Ira then allegedly wrote to Emma: 'If you give me the assurance that the child is "of colour" and that the father is the person you name – you understand me – both you and your child shall not be neglected. Is it a boy or a girl?' Although William Stothard insisted that he could 'prove' that the baby was black, the child in question had in fact died of dysentery by the time the case was brought to court. However, the fact that Emma named the baby boy Frederick Charles Aldridge Stothard was something of an acknowledgement of her child's parentage.[12]

Emma's mother, Ann Iggulden, gave evidence to say that she had been against Emma and William's marriage – 'I objected to the marriage on account of the plaintiff being a performer'. She added that Emma had previously written to William complaining of neglect and that he answered 'that he earned so little he really could not send her money'.

Emma had been lodging with a Susannah Burgess around the time of her confinement and her landlady had later seen Ira and told him that Emma had had his baby.

> He seemed confused and asked me why I said he was the father; I said, 'Because it is so much like you.' He said, 'She is married'; I said, 'I know that, but white men don't have black children.' He said, 'Are you a mother?' I said I had had nine children, but I had never had a black one.

Ira then gave Susannah money, making it clear that it was not for Emma, but for her landlady's family – an attempt to keep Susannah quiet, perhaps; but he stood up in court and argued that 'what he had done was with leave and licence' which, the court heard, was 'adding insult to injury' to William, who was 'entitled to sympathy'. But William's acting career had been disastrous – 'his career was a most precarious one' and he hadn't lived with his wife for six years. The defence counsel went further: 'The wife was delivered of a child and where? In a lying-in hospital; left, deserted by her husband and without a farthing given her by him.' The defence also raised the question of racism:

> Aldridge was not the only man of colour . . . What would they say of a lady who would falls to the arts and devices of a 'nigger'? The moment a woman yielded to those desires which were a curse of her nature, then the word 'seduction' was introduced.

Therefore, it was assumed that Aldridge must be the father simply because the child had been clearly mixed race, despite there being other black men in England; and it was assumed that she must have been seduced by him when actually, her own desires played a part (ignoring the fact that women were seen to be weak creatures who were 'cursed' by desires).

The court still found in favour of Mr Stothard. It is true that Aldridge already had a complex personal life – he was married throughout the course of his and Emma's relationship, his wife Margaret dying in 1864, and the couple had brought up his son Ira Daniel, born in 1847 to another, unknown woman. But he had also expressed willingness to financially maintain Emma's child when it was born; and Stothard had neglected her both financially and emotionally. However, although the judge ordered that Ira should compensate Stothard for the 'loss which he had sustained', he also advised the jury to consider the neglect and the fact that the marriage would have been unsuccessful regardless of the 'seduction', due to Stothard's attitude, in awarding damages. They therefore decided that Aldridge should pay Stothard 40 shillings in damages for sleeping with his wife.

Money was often a factor when it came to relationships in Victorian Britain. Either the man didn't have it and couldn't maintain a wife, or he attempted to find a woman with money who he could make his wife. This was seemingly the case with Percy Mackenzie, the son of the late, well-known actor Henry Compton and an actor himself, who appeared in court in 1886, charged with contempt of court. Percy had been accused to marrying a ward of court, 19-year-old Mary Emily Constance Payter, who just happened to have a fortune.[13] In fact, she had property worth £20,000, in addition to estates at Dinapore in Bengal, India, inherited from her father, an Indian merchant. Percy had failed to get the consent of Mary's guardians, or the courts, prior to marrying her.

The couple had met the previous March, when Mary had been staying at her grandmother's in Brighton. Percy had asked her mother Isabel's permission to pay his addresses, but she refused, stating that he had no means at that time of supporting a wife and that 'she objected to his profession'. Mary's guardians also objected, saying no marriage could occur until Percy was in a position to maintain Mary, 'he being at the time without an engagement'. The solicitor for the guardians informed Percy formally that as Mary was a ward of court, if he married her without their permission, he would be liable to be committed to prison. Percy failed to heed their warnings. On 6 November 1886, at St Mary Abbott's church in Kensington, Percy Mackenzie married Mary Payter. That the two knew that they were doing wrong was clear – the marriage register had Mary's age entered as 22 and her father as 'Charles W. Payter'. Mary's guardians found out and he was charged with contempt.

His defence was that the intimacy between him and Mary had been 'permitted, if not encouraged' by the Payter family, although he did not deny that he had committed the contempt of court. He stated that when he became engaged to Mary, he had been unaware of her fortune, merely thinking that she had an income of £200 a year. He believed himself to be of good character and of suitable rank to be her husband. As to her guardians' concern about his employment – why, he had just entered into an engagement to appear in the Hull Theatre Royal's pantomime, at a salary of ten guineas a week! However, if he was sent to prison, he would lose that job – and so a custodial sentence would actually punish Mary as much as him and 'might materially affect her prospects in life'. Percy insisted that Mary's property should be 'absolutely at her own disposal' and he was even willing to execute a settlement to that account, 'on the most stringent terms that could be devised'.

Unfortunately for Percy, the judge, Mr Justice North, 'did not see how, if he were to accede to the suggestion made on behalf of [Percy] there could ever again be an order for committal for contempt in marrying a ward of court'. Therefore, although he was happy for there to be a settlement with regard to Mary's property, the committal to prison for the unlucky husband was 'a matter of course'. Mary sought and gained a divorce from Percy in 1893, on the grounds of his adultery and cruelty.[14] Two years later, she married again, in Paddington, to James Thomson Currie, a Scottish financial agent who was presumably regarded as a better match for her.[15]

Despite the many advertisements in the late nineteenth century press for condoms –

'sheaths that will last a year or more!' as one 1890s ad put it, attractively – many of the impetuous sexual affairs involving both actors and non-actors resulted in pregnancies and the births of illegitimate children. Although it is commonly argued that Victorian society stigmatised both unwed mothers and illegitimate children, part of the post-1834 move towards branding individuals as 'deserving' or 'undeserving' of help, this was partly to do with the poorest levels of society and in particular, the fear of such individuals applying for poor relief or needing workhouse admission, thus placing pressure on local resources. Although many were undoubtedly 'shamed' by their experiences, it was not a universal experience and in other cases, financial remedy was sought and achieved in rather a prosaic, matter of fact way. Bastardy was common enough that in one nineteenth century newspaper advice column, a woman who had written in asking how she could get a man to pay maintenance towards her child was given the following advice, with no moral comment attached:

'Agnes' must apply to the magistrates of the division in which she resides for an affiliation order. The summons can be served where the reputed father lives; and the application must be made within 12 calendar months after the date of the child's birth, or her remedy would be lost unless he had made payments previously on account of the expense of the child's maintenance.

As in the eighteenth century, there was a focus on the financial maintenance of illegitimate children. This could be a major issue to single actresses, who might be in a precarious situation, dealing with temporary contracts or poor pay and working out how to either maintain a child themselves, or pay for it to be looked after by someone else. When the father of the child then started pleading poverty, there could be a real problem and this is when cases might hit the police courts. In 1899, for example, an affiliation case was heard by the Worship Street magistrates. A 26-year-old tailor from Redditch in Worcestershire, Leigh Mortimer Clarke, was charged with neglecting to pay £30 to a woman named Jessie Benedict.

Jessie was an actress, a single woman. She had been on the stage for at least a decade, having been one of the Five Senses in William Musketry's pantomime of *Lady Godiva* at George Sanger's Ramsgate amphitheatre in 1889 and a 'song and dance' woman in a show at Days' Concert Hall in Birmingham in 1892.[16] Whilst on a tour with an acting company in 1894 and presumably working the midland theatres, she met 21-year-old Leigh Mortimer Clarke. In the genteel language of the nineteenth century press, she was described as having 'made his acquaintance' – to the extent that she became pregnant with his child.

On giving birth, Jessie sought an affiliation order and Mortimer Clarke was duly ordered to pay her 5s a week to maintain their child. For a couple of years, it appears that he paid his money, but then, for the following two years, failed to do so. The £30 mentioned in court was now the amount of arrears due. Mortimer Clarke still tried to avoid paying, offering Jessie just £10. Unsurprisingly, Jessie's solicitor spluttered, 'Why should she take £10 for £30?' Jessie muttered, in response, 'I do not intend to'. Mortimer Clarke's solicitor now threatened Jessie, saying that if his client went to prison, Jessie would get nothing and 'he will be ruined'. But Jessie was an actress, used to negotiating about contracts and payments. 'Why should I care about that? He has ruined me!' The tailor was ordered to pay £30; if he failed to do so, he would be sent to prison for three months. Perhaps unsurprisingly, he went to prison.

One should not make the assumption that men were always in the wrong; in some cases, women accused them of being the fathers of their children when in fact they weren't. However, even in some of these cases, the men failed to act in a decent manner. One actor, seven years earlier, had been dragged into court charged with fathering a child, but still faced jail, despite him not having been proved to be the dad. Matthew Brodie was a 'well-known actor' employed with Madge Kendal's Company in Leeds. He was brought before the City of London Court in November 1892, where a solicitor, George Kebbell, applied for his committal to Holloway Gaol.

It was explained that Brodie had been charged with being the father of an unnamed actress's baby. She had previously brought him to court on a bastardy summons, but Brodie had been successfully defended against the charge by George Kebbell. He then owed Kebbell for his defence costs, which came to £10 18s 6d – but had only paid him £2 to date. Brodie argued that he did not have sufficient 'means' to pay his solicitor; Kebbell, in return, produced receipts signed by Brodie that showed Mrs Kendal had been paying him £8 a week for the previous two months for his acting engagement. It was found that on this salary, Brodie 'could certainly pay this small claim' and he was told to pay within forty days or go to jail.

Sex was, it is clear, very much a part of theatrical life; both within and outside of marriage. Although some sexual relationships were the result of love, others were more to do with money, or simply sexual urges and gratification. When things went wrong, the courts could and did get involved – and so did the press. In terms of bastardy, actors were both fathers and mothers of illegitimate children, but their profession may have made them more of a draw for the newspapers than other individuals fighting over affiliation orders and money. This is not to say that other cases did not make the pages of the newspapers, but the Victorian press knew that its readers would immediately be drawn to a story by mention of an individual's theatrical occupation.

CHAPTER 12

Breaches of Promise

Breach of promise was a similar type of tort to the 'crim con' covered in the last chapter, only it involved couples who had never married. It involved a woman who believed she was going to be married, only to be let down by her young man.[1] There were several cases reported in the press that involved actresses bringing suits against young men. These frequently, although not always, involved actresses who were involved with men of fortune; such relationships guaranteed the actress some financial security while they lasted – but if she was let down, she might attempt to shame the man and regain at least some of that financial security through the bringing of an action for breach of promise of marriage.

This was the case, for example, with an unnamed actress who won her case against 'the nephew of a well-known member of parliament for a Yorkshire borough' in 1894 and with a 22-year-old actress, Rosa Vaile, who brought a case against Herbert Merrion, 28, in the London Court of Exchequer in 1873.[2] Vaile was described as a 'young lady of some personal attractions' who had worked primarily in the provincial theatres – in Birmingham, Manchester and Liverpool. With two of her sisters, she performed under the name of The Sisters Fanchette.[3] Her young man, Herbert, was 'entitled, it was said, to considerable property on the death of his mother and uncle' – in other words, he was heir to a fortune. The couple had met in Kent, when Herbert was undertaking some business for his wealthy uncle in Gravesend and Rosa Vaile was acting at Rosherville. He had visited her at her parents' house and wooed her parents too – telling her mother that he was 'very much struck' with the actress and highlighting his good prospects to Rosa's father, wine merchant Joseph Vaile.[4] He had stressed, apparently, that his mother was 'almost dead' and that when she was, he would have money. They said they regarded him as their daughter's suitor, especially when he turned up with several rings, asking Rosa to choose the one she'd like. However, he was clear that this wasn't a wedding ring, for he said when they married, he would buy her a more expensive one. He called her parents 'Pa' and 'Ma' and when 'Pa' died at Bradford, where his 'Rosey' was performing at one of the local theatres, he promised to 'erect a marble memorial' to remember him by.[5] However, he not only failed to marry her: he married another woman, one Frances Pike, in the summer of 1873 instead.

Rosa duly brought an action against him, where she described how she and her three sisters had been appearing at the Prince of Wales Theatre in Liverpool, when Herbert followed them there and 'renewed his promise' to her. He had then accompanied the sisters and their mother around the country as they toured – to Manchester, Birmingham, Sheffield and other towns. But it also emerged that Rosa's mother had previously sued Herbert, to get him to pay for his board and lodging while he was staying with them (suggesting that he was more a lodger than a fiancé) and she admitted that she had had a second lover, a 'rich merchant at Birmingham' called Fred, who had 'made love to her and promised to present her with a gold watch'. In fact, she admitted that she had had several rich lovers who had visited her and her sisters. It was clear that getting money was the sisters' primary aim, and their mother stressed how Herbert had promised to settle £500 a year on her daughter and another £500 a year on the mother. It was found that although there had been, on balance, a breach of promise, the Vaile family's actions and obsession with money meant that Rosa was only entitled to a 'very small modicum' of damages. Herbert was ordered to pay her just one-fifth of what Rosa had hoped to get as her annual settlement from this rather naïve heir.

In 1884, actress Emily May Finney, known professionally as May Fortescue, got engaged to Arthur Cairns, the Viscount Garmoyle (later the 2nd Earl of Cairns). She was at that time acting as Celia in *Iolanthe* and Arthur had fallen in love with her whilst watching her perform in the play. His friends refused to accept the relationship; May was not only an actress, but the daughter of a coal dealer – she was not seen as an appropriate choice for a future earl. The *Hampshire Telegraph* drily noted that 'the rejoicings at the coming theatrical marriage are probably greater amongst the friends of the fiancée than amongst those of the eligible young man'. May was not allowed to wear jewellery at the Savoy Theatre, where she was performing, and had to wear her engagement ring on a piece of ribbon round her neck rather than on her finger. She did not like this and possibly saw her marriage to a wealthy young man – Arthur was then just 21 – as a way out of the drudgery of the theatre. Arthur agreed that she could leave her theatrical engagement within the next two weeks, which surprised the press, who commented that Arthur had 'already developed such a decided taste for the drama and its fairer exponents' that it was 'surprised to hear' that he had agreed to this. The insinuation was that it was May's profession as an actress that attracted Arthur and that he would not have fallen in love with her had she been in a different occupation. The papers were right to be cynical; Arthur broke off his engagement to May in January 1884.

May then sued him for breach of promise. The case received much publicity, with newspapers repeating rumours spread by other publications and the amount of damages Miss Fortescue might get increasing like Chinese whispers – amounts varying between £5,000 and £50,000. One theatrical manager was interviewed by the *New York Herald* and claimed that Arthur's parents had made a mistake by not letting him marry a 'reputable girl like May Fortescue. He will now fall a victim to some Gaiety nymph of easy morality, who will whisk him off to a registry office and marry him out of hand.' Lord Garmoyle – described as 'one of the cheeriest and best looking of the young men about town' – now won friends in the press by his treatment of May. Unlike many other men in such cases, he declined to defend the action and had paid her damages of £10,000 – nearly half a million pounds in today's money. May Fortescue was clearly adored by the press at this time, who saw her, as Lord Garmoyle once had, as a 'blue-eyed darling'. She was clearly seen as being different from the 'Gaiety nymphs', being a 'pretty and popular young actress, with a personal reputation that scandal had never assailed'.

She also had the last laugh. Arthur died six years later, aged 38, of pneumonia, but May returned to the stage and lived until 1950, using the money she had won from Arthur Cairns to start her own touring theatre company.[6] It was suggested that it was press coverage about May's innocence and Arthur's caddishness that had led to the huge sum being awarded to May; she had 'cried on the shoulder of the famous Frank Harris of the *Evening News*' in order to guarantee the column inches, thus showing how actresses could manipulate public perception of them and influence what the newspapers wrote about them for their own ends.[7] May was a good manipulator if so; there was no criticism of her in later press reports of various relationships, including with art critic Harry Quilter and Ellen Terry's youngest brother Fred.

Four years after the Fortescue case, in 1888, a well-known burlesque and *opéra bouffe* actress, Phyllis Broughton, brought a breach of promise case against her former partner, Lord Dangan, the eldest son of Earl Cowley. He was barely 22 and already had theatrical relatives – his uncle Colonel Frederick Wellesley, a club owner, was married to actress Kate Vaughan, famous for her 'skirt dance', a more modest version of the can-can. It was noted in the press that Miss Broughton's 'engagement to a nobleman was announced some four or five months ago', although strangely, it did not record whether this engagement was to Lord Dangan or another nobleman. Phyllis, it was recorded, had played at the Gaiety Theatre for several years, before becoming 'one of the chief attractions' of a play called *The Old Guard*, currently being performed at the Avenue Theatre. One newspaper implied that Phyllis was bringing the case having seen the success of May Fortescue's 'remarkable' case against Earl Cairns – as Lord Garmoyle had become the year after his breach of promise case – and although Phyllis had not specified the amount of damages she was seeking from her nobleman, she 'probably hopes to get as much as Miss Fortescue'. The paper concluded that if she 'has written so extremely nice and proper a letter as Miss Fortescue sent to Lord Cairns, she may find a very sentimental jury to appraise the value of the wrongs of her heart'. However, in the event, Phyllis won damages of £2,000 – nowhere near May Fortescue's result, but still far more substantial a sum than many actresses received in court.[8]

That these actresses were infamous for their targeting of rich men is evident from the press coverage of such cases. One paper included the tale of a 'sprightly actress' who brought a breach of promise action against 'the stupid son of a Peer' – a tale that possibly owed its origins to the Phyllis Broughton case. The boy's aunt duly called on a local parson who was 'known and respected by many members of the theatrical profession' to use his influence to prevent her nephew from marrying 'this wretched woman': "'I shall do all I can," was the reply, "to prevent this nice girl from marrying your fool of a nephew.""

Although it has been argued that where court cases involved an aristocrat and a woman from a lower class, the courts 'insisted on romanticising the women' and gave them their sympathy, it is not evident that this applied in cases brought by actresses, who were seen almost as a distinct 'species' where the normal rules failed to apply.[9] In another case involving a peer and an actress, in 1896, the Lanarkshire-born actress May Gore – the professional name of Mary Stuart Smith – brought an action claiming damages from Lord Sudley, the 28-year-old eldest son of the Earl of Arran and a commissioned officer in Her Majesty's Horse Guards. May attested in court that 'her age, as far as she knew, was 27'. It was later shown in court that her baptismal certificate showed that she was 31. Lord Sudley denied the alleged promise; not surprising, as May was seeking £15,000 in damages. Queen's Counsel represented both parties in the case, which was heard before the Lord Chief Justice in the Queen's Bench Division.

It was claimed by the plaintiff's lawyer that in 1889, May was living with her sister

– the Honourable Mrs Bingham – and met Lord Sudley. After being introduced to her, he 'proposed that Miss Gore should live under his protection', in other words, as his mistress. May agreed to this. She may have already been sexually experienced; she stated in court that when she had met Lord Sudley, she was known as Mary Sherbrooke, having had to take on a new surname 'after I had gone wrong' on arriving in London from Scotland. One of her sisters had also been living under the protection of a man – possible Bertha, who was also an actress.

Lord Sudley established May in apartments at Ashley House on Shaftesbury Avenue. This relationship lasted for two and a half years and was apparently of 'the closest and most devoted character . . . no married relationship could have been attended with a greater degree of affection' than theirs. In letters, the lord frequently told May that he intended to marry her and made a will in her favour. Unfortunately for May, the letters had not survived – the earl and his family heard of the relationship and apparently put pressure on May to destroy all her correspondence with her lord. Two incriminating letters were given, under duress, to the earl's representative and May was paid £500 to 'acquit Lord Sudley from all manner and causes of action and demands'; she also had to promise not to renew the relationship between her and Lord Sudley. May's argument was that this £500 was not enough money to maintain her and that as a result, Lord Sudley was responsible for the 'great temptation in which she was placed' – in other words, she entered into a sexual relationship with another man, a Mr Sturton, who might help her live the life to which she had become accustomed. It was recognised by May's QC that others might have little sympathy and believe that she should have 'sought by toil to maintain herself in independence. That was doubtless the severe moral view, but was it natural?' In other words, the blame was the man's, Lord Sudley's, for encouraging her into a life of dependence and immorality in the first place.

Despite May's new relationship, which started in August 1893, after she had taken on a professional engagement at the Lyric Theatre, Lord Sudley went again his family's aversion towards the actress and tried to renew their relationship, some fifteen months after it had ended. He knew that she was seeing another man, but had decided that she should go back to him, 'with a view to marriage'. He wanted May to end her new relationship and go back to him. May argued that she had only done so because he had explicitly promised her marriage.

May said that she didn't trust Lord Sudley and wanted some breathing space. She went on tour to America, but while she was away – a matter of a couple of weeks – he wrote almost constantly to her, after having threatened to kill himself if she sailed out there. When she returned, she decided that he must love her, because he had written so much to her despite getting little encouragement. She agreed to marry him. The wedding was apparently set for Christmas 1894; but then Lord Sudley became ill. He was then advised that he needed to go to Cairo on duty; when he returned, he claimed his father and a sister had been trying to get him to 'give up the intention to marry'. May told him in no uncertain terms that he had ruined her life.

In court, there was laughter when the couple's nicknames were revealed – May was 'Puss' or 'Pussy' and Lord Sudley was 'Podge'. An excerpt from one letter, where Lord Sudley wrote, 'Do make up your pussy mind' and another where he referred to May as 'my fattest of pussies', was seen as particularly hilarious. The *Hull Daily Mail* even headline its article on the case 'Puss and Podge', whereas the rest of the press stuck to the usual 'actress sues a nobleman' line.

Podge no longer loved Puss, however. Lord Sudley denied ever intending to marry May – 'I never mentioned the subject to her' – and argued that not only was there no evidence whatsoever that he had intended to, he had already provided for her, as his mistress, giving her an annuity of £100 a year and leaving her a large sum of money in his will. The court found in his favour; the only consolation for May was that Lord Sudley said he would not push her for the costs that he had been awarded.

By bringing breach of promise suits, women were able to gain financial compensation for the their 'investment' into relationships – or, as Ginger Frost has termed it, their 'sacrifice'.[10] In some cases, the women involved claimed to have been seduced at a young age by someone they genuinely thought would marry them and had committed themselves to a long-term relationship in the expectation that marriage would, at some point, follow. For example, in 1893, Dubliner Florrie O'Keefe brought a case for breach of promise of marriage against Henry Elmore Frith, a well-known provincial actor and son of artist and Royal Academy member W.P. Frith, at the London Sheriff's Court.[11] Florrie said that in 1885, she had been performing in a Gaiety touring company at Newcastle. Henry, then aged around 27, had been part of the same company and they started seeing each other.[12] Soon, they became engaged and 'under a promise of marriage the defendant seduced the plaintiff'. They moved in together and continued to live as man and wife for the next seven years, with Henry introducing Florrie to others as his wife.[13] In February 1892, a marriage was arranged at the Manchester register office, but for some reason it did not take place. By Christmas Eve that year, their company was performing in Portsmouth. Florrie had to ask Henry for money to get some food and he became abusive, saying that she would never see him again. He then disappeared to London. After Florrie tracked him down, he said he would pay her 10s a week maintenance; but when she tried to sort this out with his solicitors, they tried to get her to agree to have 10s a week when Henry was between engagements and £1 a week when he was working – but only on condition that she signed 'a paper relinquishing all claims on the defendant'. She refused to sign. By the summer of 1893, Henry had married another actress, Effie Marguerite Kenney and this seems to have finally prompted Florrie's action.[14] Ironically, when she brought the case, Henry was playing in a piece entitled *Lured to Ruin*. Florrie, who was only 17 when she had met Henry, claimed that she had been lured, seduced, by him, and was awarded compensation of £150.

Florrie and Henry were relatively unusual amongst the breach of promise cases detailed by the press in that they were both actors and had met when acting together. In many cases, the man was either nothing to do with the profession, or just a keen theatregoer. In some cases, he may have been in the audience, watching the actress perform and then asked to meet her afterwards; in other cases, both parties might have been in the audience and struck up a conversation. This was the case with one couple in 1900. Lilian Dorothy Gibbons, a 23-year-old actress known professionally as Esme Gordon, brought a breach of promise suit against Charles Edwin Green, 'in business in the City'. They had first met in the stalls at the Empire Theatre in London, being introduced by Lilian's previous gentleman friend (who she had also had sex with, according to the press) and from there, a relationship had developed. Their relationship had progressed to the stage that Lilian had become pregnant, at which point she had broken off the relationship, claiming she had 'not realised her position before'. Rather belatedly, Charles had then promised to marry her, but never turned up to the register office.

Lilian had been in the UK for seven years, having travelled from America at the age of 16. Under cross-examination, she denied having pretended to be a widow when she first arrived in England and also denied having lived under the protection of any other man except for Charles. However, she was soon made to admit that she had been 'intimate' sexually with a man prior to meeting Charles in March 1899. Lilian was painted as a scarlet woman – a young, single American who had had sex with two men outside of marriage and become pregnant by one of them. It was noted in court, however, and later in the press, that Charles was cowardly rather than manly for both trying to blacken Lilian's name and – unlike his former partner – refusing to be cross-examined. Despite Lilian's alleged pregnancy, Charles's counsel contended that she had 'lost nothing' by Charles failing to marry her, so should not get damages; in addition, 'defendant could not afford to pay a large sum'. The judge, though, found in Lilian's favour and awarded her £200 in damages.

These breach of promise cases were fairly common – substantial amounts of money could be fought for in court in terms of damages, so there was a clear motivation for spurned 'Gaiety nymphs' to seek retribution or resolution. In addition, some actresses may have given up their acting work in preparation for married work and faced financial difficulties when they tried to resume their careers. The standards of evidence required in cases could be quite low and so there was opportunity for some actresses to use breach of promise in a fraudulent way, to get money from a man anxious to avoid ending up in court, with the attendant negative publicity.[15] In addition, reputations could be made or ruined on the basis of such cases, for where relationships were broken off, there might remain rumours of 'immoral' behaviour, or of some fault on the part of the woman that led to the man seeking love elsewhere. In a society where professional and personal reputations were important, there was an additional motivation for actresses to seek resolution through the courts to ensure firstly that their reputations remained intact and secondly, that this was publicised through the pages of the newspapers. However, the papers did not necessarily have the actress's interests at heart – what was important was telling an interesting story that appealed to readers. Sometimes, fact was not needed either – the newspapers increasingly relied on gossip and rumour to fill their pages, such as when, in 1888, the *Dundee Courier* started one story about a breach of promise case between a comedian and an actress in New York, where the story started, 'It is rumoured . . .' and contained several similar statements throughout, such as 'The story goes that ...', 'There was a report a few weeks ago . . .' and 'he is said to . . .'. The uncertainty about the story may have been due to it being US-based, but it is clear that rumours were seen as being as good a base for stories as facts and that a juicy breach of promise case was regular fodder for the more sensationalist parts of the press.

CHAPTER 13

Till Death Us Do Part?

Given the common perception of Victorian morality, Victorian society, and Victorian theatre, was a mass of contradictions that reflected the perhaps surprising individuality of people's lives. In much of society, women were expected to give up their jobs and careers when they married, in the expectation that their husbands would support them and that their job would now be looking after their spouse and any children that came along. Although there were plenty of actresses and managers who were married, there could still be an expectation that some would give up their theatrical careers on marrying. However, for every actress who did so, there was another who continued; and there were several husband-and-wife teams of theatrical stars and managers who successfully combined marriage and careers by working together. Other actresses attempted to give up their theatrical ambitions on marrying, often when marrying men outside the profession who were happy to have a lady friend on the stage, but not a wife. This was the case with Eva Sothern, daughter of comedian Edward Askew Sothern and sister of the actors Edward Hugh, Lytton and 'Sam' Sothern.[1] Despite having had a successful career on both sides of the Atlantic for at least a decade and being from a theatrical family, she still gave up her career when she married a Scottish gentleman, John Lionel Smith, in 1891, when she was 21. The 1901 census recorded her simply as 'wife'; and in an article about her family in 1907, she was described as having 'cut short a promising stage career when she married and retired into private life'.[2] Not all women were like Eva, however; they sometimes found the lure of the stage too much and sought to return to it, which might mean putting their career above their marriage, thus ending the latter. Although some actors and actresses were recorded in the press as having affairs with each other, others were more traditional, wanting a conventional wedding and the status of marriage.

The newspapers carried both of stories of actresses marrying others in the profession and those outside it; their coverage could be similar to the stories you get today in *Hello!* magazine, with the couple's weddings and wedding clothes being detailed for eager readers. An actor's status and reputation influenced the extent of the press coverage and so this chapter details those who were recorded in short announcements, those whose romances were reported but whose names were not regarded as an important part of the story – and those whose weddings received whole paragraphs detailing guests, parentage, clothing, honeymoon destinations and past and future professional roles. These stories illustrate the inter-relationships between actors and actresses who performed together in London or the provinces, as part of the same theatrical company. They show how actresses could be wooed by audience members, how they could be disapproved of because of their professional background and how their weddings could be seen as a public event by both press and fans alike. Some of their stories are a cautionary tale for our own society, as this chapter explores.

Mid-century, one marriage took place that was significant in Victorian theatre history and its hierarchy of theatrical figures, but it also highlighted the errors that could occur in nineteenth-century newspapers. In 1859, Mary Keeley and Albert Smith married. Mary was the eldest daughter of actress Mary Ann and comedian Robert Keeley. Together, they formed a famous duo of theatrical managers. Their daughter, whose full name was Mary Ann Lucy Keeley, was born on 21 March 1830 and baptised at the actors' church of St Paul's, Covent Garden, on 24 May.[3] The church was literally a stone's-throw from her parents' home at the time, on Long Acre.

Mary made her first appearance on the stage at the Lyceum, playing Bertha in *The Cricket on the Hearth* in December 1845, at the age of 15. Since then, she had played in numerous farces and burlesques, or parodies and was seen as a 'lively actress', performing largely at the Adelphi theatre in London. By 1859, Mary was living with her parents in Brompton when she married author Albert Richard Smith, the son of surgeon Richard Smith. They wed at the church of St Mark in St John's Wood, the marriage entry signed by the bride's well known father, listed as 'comedian' in the entry.[4]

Their impending marriage had been recorded in the local press, although one newspaper was certainly late with the news. On 25 August 1858, the *Glasgow Herald* had reported: 'We are informed, from the very best authority, that Mr Albert Smith, immediately on his return, will be married to Miss Mary Keeley, the deservedly favourite little actress, of the Adelphi Theatre.' Of course, the couple had in fact wed three weeks earlier, showing that the newspapers were not always first with the news. Presumably, the *Glasgow Herald* had taken its story from another, earlier paper, but had not checked the facts before it published it rather later. If it had checked the *Jersey Independent* and *Daily Telegraph*, for example, it would have realised its mistake, for that paper, copying the *Telegraph* of Tuesday 2 August, noted that 'In confirmation of the announcement in our impression of Monday, we are enabled to state that the marriage of Mr Albert Smith with Miss Mary Keeley was solemnised yesterday [1 August]'.

The love story between Mary Keeley and Albert Smith turned into a tragedy, which again, appealed to the press. In December 1859, the *Belfast Mercury* reported that Albert Smith had suddenly died of apoplexy, just four months after his marriage. It included a long and fulsome obituary, stressing his link to 'the celebrated comedians' the Keeleys and recording that a series of well-known actors had performed in his melodramas on the stage, including 'Mr and Mrs Keeley . . . and other theatrical celebrities of the same stamp'. It also noted that: 'Nine times in every week he went through his entertainment and sung his songs, never allowing any real or fancied illness, or any domestic matter, however onerous or worrying, to interrupt the due discharge of his business.'

The *Belfast Mercury* had taken its story from the *Sun*, which was credited, but unfortunately, there was a slight error with both pieces – in that Albert Smith had not actually died. This event actually took place five months later, in May 1860. Albert really died that time, at home, aged just 33. He was days away from his 34th birthday. His second round of obituaries noted that he had also been a keen traveller, climbing Mont Blanc and visiting China. It was noted that Albert, 'this most celebrated of modern entertainers', had been 'in the height of fame and happiness when, on the day before last Christmas Eve, he was seized with a fit, a curious combination of apoplexy and epilepsy, by which he was prostrated for some three weeks. That attack seems to have made a great inroad upon his constitution, for since that period he has not been the same man.'

Albert was undoubtedly a fascinating and interesting man, being young, talented and adventurous. His link to one of Victorian England's foremost theatrical families made sure that he would hit the headlines and so when he was taken ill in the winter of 1859, the newspapers made sure to cover his case – even if it meant bringing his death forward a few months. In this, it carried on the tradition of covering events in Albert's life in the wrong order, or at the wrong time.[5]

Other marriages and details of actors' personal lives were more accurate, but like the details of Albert and Mary's lives, marriages and deaths, press coverage provided a wide range of information about individuals. For family historians, this is a boon, as it can provide details of the companies and theatres an actor worked in – but it can also say much about wedding fashions and the ceremonies that theatrical couples favoured. Just as the elite had their marriages recorded in newspapers such as *The Times*, with pedigrees and parentage listed, so too did actors have their marriages recorded in *The Era*, with details of their professional engagements. So in November 1870, *The Era* recorded that on the previous Monday, Morris Edmondson of the New Theatre Royal in Stockton had married Sophia Rose Proctor, 'also of Mr Sidney's company' at the Stockton-on-Tees parish church.

This was reported in less flowery, romanticised language than the report in *The Dundee Courier and Argus* in 1893:

> Another romantic marriage has taken place in Glasgow. A week or two ago Mr Cowlard, manager at the Theatre Royal, pledged his troth to Miss Florence Burle, principal girl in 'Dick Whittington'. This example has been followed by Mr Webster Messenger, of the Grand Theatre, who, it has transpired, was on Tuesday married to Miss Rosie Ewart, leading girl in 'Robinson Crusoe'. The bride is a daughter of the Baroness Von Waldech.

In these cases, the brides and grooms were all in the theatrical industry and currently performing locally, hence their newsworthiness. The way the report was written also suggests that the newspaper saw the marriage of men working in the theatres with their principal girls something of a novelty and a curious thing that their readers would appreciate and find amusing. In other cases, it was the parents of a bride and/or groom that were newsworthy. In 1895, Captain Charles Edward Bancroft of the Royal Welsh Regiment married 24-year-old Margaret Catherine Grimston at All Soul's Church in Langham Place, London. This might not have been interesting except for the fact that both parties were the children of 'leading lights in the profession' and thus the marriage was of 'peculiar interest in the theatrical world'.

Charles, it appears, or certainly the press believed, was the eldest son of Squire Bancroft and his wife, Effie Marie Wilton, who had run the Prince of Wales Theatre off Tottenham Court Road and then the Haymarket Theatre – although on his marriage entry, the space for Charles' father's details was left blank and the *Oxford Dictionary of National Biography* states that Squire and his wife only had one son, George Pleydell Bancroft, born in 1868.[6] The Bancrofts, who were great technical innovators and had first incorporate the use of electric light on the English stage, had retired ten years prior to the marriage of their son.[7] His bride, Margaret, was the eldest daughter of William Hunter Grimston and his wife, Margaret – the parties who were far better known as actors William Hunter Kendal and Madge Kendal. The press reported that 'Mrs Kendal, in an interview with a lady journalist after the ceremony, said she had travelled all night after playing at Hull; she only reached London about six o'clock on Sunday morning and after seeing her daughter to Italy, would return to her work again, travelling all night'.

It is clear that it was the Bancrofts and Kendals who attracted the press and not their children per se (one article about the wedding was simply headlined 'Mrs Kendal's daughter') – but this did not prevent the newspaper from describing the bride in detail – 'the bride looked charming in a rich crème satin robe with full skirt; the large sleeves of same material being arranged in classic folds. She was followed by one bridesmaid only, her sister, who was most simply dressed in a crème surah frock. After the ceremony the happy couple left for Dover, en route for Como, the bride's costume being of brown cloth, relieved with soft pink and a picturesque brown hat and feathers to match.' This detail is surely a precursor of the pages of wedding coverage found in today's newspapers and magazines, that focus on the clothes worn by the bride and what designers may have produced them. Mrs Kendal's daughter was the epitome of stylish elegance, it appears, at her rather classy wedding.

Although the press may have got the details of Margaret's parentage correct, were they right in highlighting the 'theatrical' parentage of the groom? As stated, he had left the father's details sections of his marriage entry blank; and there is no baptism of a Charles, son of Squire, either under Bancroft or Squire Bancroft's birth surname of Butterfield. The official marriage entry that was copied in the *Leamington Spa Courier* of 21 September 1895 recorded Margaret's father's name, but did not include the same details for Captain Bancroft. However, in 1906, the *Hull Daily Mail* noted that 'Captain Charles Edward Bancroft, the son of Sir Squire Bancroft, was buried on Wednesday in Brompton Cemetery, London'. Perhaps Charles was reluctant to admit to his 'dramatic' parentage; the same reluctance seems to survive in the contemporary omissions of his name from accounts of his parents' lives.

Another wedding involving the child of a Victorian star received a detailed article in *The Era* in 1876. This time, it involved Amory Sullivan, known professionally as T.S. Amory, who was also the eldest son of 'celebrated' tragedian Barry Sullivan. Amory married Adeline Stanhope, 'the graceful and accomplished young actress, who made her first appearance at the Haymarket Theatre as Miss Edith Gray and who has since played with great success in the leading provincial theatres'. The article was glowing about Amory's personality and career success, noting that 'from the Antipodes to Drury Lane Theatre, Mr Amory Sullivan has made friends and kept them and there will be hearty congratulations on the occasion of his marriage'.

This event was newsworthy because both the parties were actors, because the groom's father was also well-known and because they were seen as respectable members of the profession – Amory's moral attributes were stressed in the article. In this way, *The Era* was attempting to redress the image of actors as morally ambiguous, highlighting Amory's loyalty towards his friends and the conventional relationship between Amory and Adeline. Unfortunately for *The Era*, however, Adeline, who went on to have four children by Amory, committed adultery with actor Nelson Wheatcroft while her husband was touring in America – in 1882, she had been appearing with Wheatcroft in *The Beautiful Russian* at the York Theatre Royal and by the time her English tour had reached Bournemouth, it was noted that 'Mr Wheatcroft was constantly with Mrs Sullivan and paid her marked attention'. Amory divorced his wife on the grounds of her adultery the following year, again making the headlines in the provincial press, which noted, 'practically there was no defence'. She later married Wheatcroft when he had not divorced his first wife, Jane, making the marriage bigamous.[8] After Nelson's death from pneumonia in 1897, both Adeline and Jane made the news for both claiming to be his legal wife.

Theatrical weddings clearly gave the press the chance of going to town on details of their lives and careers, all for the titillation or enjoyment of their readers, who would have their memories jogged by mention of individuals' prior performances and enjoy finding out what they were up to in their private lives. In 1872, the wedding of popular comedy John Clarke and actress Teresa Elizabeth Furtado, which took place in Great Yarmouth, gave *The Era* opportunity to stress their popularity and success. It breathlessly stated that 'thousands who have "many a time and oft" been delighted by their histrionic talent will join us in congratulating the happy couple on so auspicious an event'. It noted that the 'pretty' Miss Furtado had first appeared on stage back in February 1864, appearing as Mercury in a performance of *Izion* at the New Royalty Theatre; meanwhile, her groom had first been on stage at the Drury Lane theatre in October 1852, playing Fathom in *The Hunchback*. This was subdued, though, compared to *The Era*'s article on the marriage of Mattie Reinhardt the following January. It took until the end of the article to find out why Mattie was actually being written about at this time:

> Miss Mattie Reinhardt, of Drury Lane and the Olympic Theatres, whose performances of the Princess in Mr Gilbert's fairy piece so entitled and of the Sister Louise in *Frou Frou*, will be remembered, as well as her later impersonation of Rowena in Ivanhoe and whose recent visit to the Provinces as the representative of Galatea, in *Pygmalion and Galatea*, was attended with a degree of success which more than justified the choice of the author, whose intention had been to invest her in the Provinces with the part of the Fairy Queen Selene in his last work, has quitted [*sic*] the scene of her recent triumphs to become the bride of Mr Elliott, eldest son of Thomas Elliott, Esq, of Sunderland. The marriage was celebrated by the Rector, the Rev [William B] Galloway, at St Mark's Church, Regent's Park, on Thursday, January the 9th.[9]

Mattie's career was justifiably detailed here; she was a popular actress who had, four years earlier, appeared in the play *Little Em'ly* at the Olympic Theatre, with her performance being greatly admired by Charles Dickens.[10] During 1866 and 1867, she had toured both England and Australia with *Antony and Cleopatra*.[11] There was great interest both in her professional and her private life. This interest meant that papers both home and abroad took an interest in her nuptials and tried to find links with her. For example, the *Sydney Evening Herald* noted that 'Mattie Reinhardt, an accomplished actress, said to be a native of Sydney, has been married to Mr Elliott, of Sunderland'. Newspapers were fickle, as were audience interests, however and in 1900, in an article that noted how Mattie had been W.S. Gilbert's 'ideal' of Galatea, she was also seen as theatrical history; she was referred to as 'Miss Mattie Reinhardt, whom old theatregoers will remember in the '70s'.[12]

For artists such as Mattie Reinhardt, or the children of famous theatrical figures such as Charles Bancroft, names and details were important when it came to reporting marriages. Readers clearly wanted as much information and background as possible. But with lesser known actors and musicians, it was the romance, the story, that was wanted and other details – including names – were not necessary. Therefore, in 1892, *The Era* covered one story that failed completely to mention the names of the bride and groom; the marriage was being reported simply because it was 'quite a romantic little story' about a 'theatrical marriage [that] will shortly take place in the North'. It was noted that there had been a man who played the violin with a theatrical company, but the company had been left stranded in a Northern seaport town, perhaps as a result of an unscrupulous manager. Left to their own devices and without income, they had to improvise. The man in question decided to busk and pitched in Redcar, then a 'little seaside resort on the Yorkshire coast'. Dressed as a Neapolitan fisherman, with a mask covering his face, he played his violin 'like a second Paganini' and found that he could make a decent living doing so. A young woman passing by listened to him and was attracted both by his violin-playing and his 'splendid figure'. A while later, they happened to both be at a dinner party, unknown and not recognised by each other. During a conversation, the man revealed his busking past, was recognised by the lady and they fell in love and got engaged. 'They are now to be united in the little village church not far from the scene where they first met under such romantic circumstances.'

Many theatrical marriages were the result of two individuals working in the same business getting to know each other through professional work, but others did involve one theatrical party marrying an individual from outside the business. These appear to have predominantly involved non-acting men falling in love with actresses, such as when Hull merchant Henry Bolton married actress Eliza Marie Durett in 1850, perhaps as a result of initially admiring the female on stage whilst part of the audience.

As discussed in a previous chapter, one way in which Victorian society appears very modern is in the nature of fandom. The fans' fascination with well-known actors was evident when the latter got married and their fans sometimes jostled to get a glimpse of their favourite figures getting wed. This in itself created a news story. In 1896, the British press eagerly repeated a story that was making the rounds in Australia, saying the marriage it reported was 'chiefly remarkable for the extraordinary and outrageous behaviour of the uninvited onlookers'. The Potter-Bellew theatrical company, led by Cora Urquhart Brown-Potter and Kyrle Bellew, had been playing in Sydney, during which time, two of its actors – American Ida Hamilton and Australian-born Scott Inglis – decided to get married. Inglis was incredibly popular and Ida was famed for her beauty. Therefore, on the day of the wedding, an enormous crowd gathered at the Oxford Hotel, where the bride and her guardian, Cora, were staying. A second group crowded round the entrance to St Stephen's Church. As soon as the church doors were opened prior to the wedding, the crowd rushed in and in a few minutes, the church was packed 'from floor to ceiling' with uninvited guests, meaning that few of those who *had* actually been invited could get in, let alone get a seat in the pews. When news went round that the bride's carriage was getting near, there was a scramble – 'women hustled women, children screamed and men elbowed excited girls, who called out angrily as every movement jostled them against their neighbours'. This scramble resulted in the church font – a big stone one – being knocked over and smashed, but this did not quell the crowd and in the end, the bride had to be escorted up the aisle by a group of burly policemen.

These omens were not good and the marriage between Scott and Ida did not end happily. The popular, 'tall [and] handsome' Scott Inglis committed suicide in his boarding house at the age of 35, two years after his marriage. It was reported in the Australian press that 'he had been disappointing the management owing to his absence from rehearsals' in New York and had just been dismissed. 'He was much disgusted and remorseful and today shot himself directly under the heart and must have died instantly.' Both the American and Australian press reported his suicide in detail, despite admitting that 'Mr Inglis's widow does not yet know his fate'. Again, with parallels to some contemporary events, Ida may well have heard about her husband's death from the media.

A love affair in the 1880s between an actress and a member of the elite had long-term repercussions that were still being debated in the press seventy years later. A 21-year-old actress Eva Raines – the professional name of Daisy Evelyn Lyster – was appearing in *Little Jack Sheppard* at the Gaiety Theatre London.[13] At one performance, an audience member was George Charles Wentworth Fitzwilliam, a young Militia officer. He fell deeply in love with the actress. This was not, of course, uncommon. Many young members of the British elite fell in love with actresses. In Fitzwilliam's case, he ran headlong into an affair, which appears to have led to the birth of a son, George James Charles Wentworth Fitzwilliam, in the late spring of 1888. But he then married Daisy, the marriage taking place in the autumn of 1888.[14]

Now we go forward to 1951, where an inheritance case was being heard in the High Court before Justice Pilcher.[15] The action was brought by George and Daisy's son George, now aged 63 and the owner of Goodruffs Farm in Edgdean, near Pulborough in Sussex. He was making a claim of legitimacy, arguing that he should be legally established as the elder brother of the current heir presumptive of the 9th Earl Fitzwilliam. The current heir, who was the earl's second cousin, was Captain William Thomas George Wentworth Fitzwilliam, aged 46 at the time, a bachelor living in Peterborough. The current earl, a 67-year-old with no children, had succeeded his cousin, the 8th Earl Fitzwilliam, who had been killed in an air crash in 1948, aged 37.[16] There were other claimants too, though; Olive Dorothea, Countess Fitzwilliam – widow of the 8th Earl – and their daughter, 16-year-old Lady Anne Juliet Fitzwilliam.

George Fitzwilliam appeared to be arguing that his parents had actually married before his birth, in a secret wedding. He believed that they had been legally married 'at a date unknown to him between September 1, 1886 and his own birth on May 19, 1888'. He agreed that he could not 'fix the date specifically' but believed it to be in either September or early October 1886, 'in Scotland and according to Scots law by mutual exchange of consent'. He had a declaration made by his father in 1930 stating that 'when travelling in Scotland in 1888 he had gone through a form of marriage with his late wife', which they believed to be valid.[17] However, they had later realised that that 'for want of compliance with certain requirements of Scottish law, our marriage was invalid and on December 31, 1888, we were formally married at St George's Hanover Square'. George was arguing that the evidence would show that 'the date 1888 for the Scottish tour was a mistake for 1886'.

George, who was known to his family as Toby, argued that his father had made statements after falling in love with Daisy that he intended to marry her and was going to Scotland with her. The secrecy was necessary because he wanted to get a commission in the Household Cavalry and it was a rule there that 'no officer could be married to an actress'. He was gazetted as a second lieutenant in The Blues in May 1888 and 'from that time kept his marriage secret'. The current heir argued that the Scots marriage had never taken place and that if it had, 'it was not lawful by Scots law and that the only lawful marriage of the parents ... was after Mr Fitzwilliam's birth and took place in an English church'. Unfortunately for Toby, the current earl's view was the correct one – and Toby's argument that a date of 1888 for a marriage was incorrect by two years seems, on the basis of archival information available today, to be merely wishful thinking, to make him legitimate whereas he certainly appears to have been born prior to a legal wedding.

There were added complications in that Toby was a disappointment to his parents, having run up debts amounting to £1,000 at Cambridge University. 'His father's annoyance at this was increased when Toby fell in love with a lady on the stage of whom his parents did not approve.' His father was not understanding of his son falling in love with an actress, even though he had done the same. Toby was removed from Cambridge by his father, who sent him away to Alberta in Canada. He lived there for two years and returned without his parents' knowledge or consent in 1912. He continued to have disagreements with his father that eventually led to George changing his will and his property in Peterborough was left to his other son, William Thomas – known as Tom.

Toby lost his case; his brother Tom continued to hold the title of 10th Earl Fitzwilliam until his death in 1979. As Tom had no children, on his death, the title became extinct. However, the family seat of Milton Hall – where actress Daisy and her husband George had been listed as living in 1901, together with the young Toby – continues to be owned by family members today. This case showed how the love affairs involving members of the theatrical profession and those from the landed gentry could have long-term repercussions, affecting generations of their families and involving issues of legitimacy and inheritance stretching well into the twentieth century.

This is just a selection of reports of theatrical marriages in the British press over the nineteenth century. It is clear that the press varied in their coverage, picking the stories and the angles that they thought would most entertain or interest their readers. They gained their information from various sources, in some cases using official announcements that the individuals had placed in certain papers as their starting point and in others, lifting or adapting stories from the overseas press. In a strongly class-based society, the details of the bride's and groom's parentage was important information, especially when the parties were from different social backgrounds. In other cases, their parentage was important if they came from theatrical dynasties, even if the parties marrying were not in the industry themselves. Background as to career – what plays the individuals had performed in and where they had performed – was also newsworthy, particularly in *The Era*, with its strong theatrical bias. *The Era*, though, also had another function in presenting an image of actors and other performers to the world that showed them to be respectable, moral members of society, unlike more negative perceptions of them that continued to exist, at least to a certain extent or amongst certain sections of society, up to the end of the century. Unfortunately for *The Era*, though, some members of the profession failed to live up to this portrayal of them – and this was manna for other papers, who lapped up the tales of personal drama and recounted them for their eager readership. In such a way, the papers provided gossipy, salacious tales of contemporary stars' private lives that the media today continue to do.

CHAPTER 14

Bigamy

The Victorian newspapers enjoyed a good bigamy story and, judging from the evidence, there were plenty of cases to choose from. Bigamy was fairly common, with there being over 5,000 recorded bigamy trials between 1857 and 1904.[1] It had been a felonious offence in England and Wales since 1603, when the Bigamy Act came into force.[2] But as the number of cases above show, the illegality of bigamous marriages did not stop them taking place – and, indeed, the relative prevalence of bigamy was understandable given the difficulties faced by parties wishing to end their marriage.

Until the mid-nineteenth century, divorce was only possible via a private Act of Parliament, an option not possible for the majority of couples (between 1700 and 1857, there were only around 300 such cases). The Matrimonial Causes Act of 1857 made it possible to divorce in court, but only on a limited number of grounds – and even after the Act was passed, the cost of getting a divorce meant that many preferred informal separations and illegal second marriages to seeking a formal dissolution of their prior marriages; and the limited grounds for divorce meant that simply falling out of love with one partner, and in love with another, was not a sufficient reason for the courts to allow a marriage to end.

The insecure and erratic nature of theatrical work may have made actors more susceptible to trying the 'cheap' way of making a new relationship permanent; and where actors were touring the country, or even the world, they might have thought that they could wed again without their previous partners and families finding out about their deception. Just as in the eighteenth century, when men were able to establish such relationships because of the increased mobility of the era and their greater ability to migrate than women in the nineteenth century, actors, with their peripatetic lives, felt able to take on and commit to new relationships in new places.[3] But they reckoned without the press, who eagerly reported stories about bigamy and scoured the overseas newspapers for stories that they could copy or analyse. Bigamy cases could be thrown out on what seem to be rather trivial technicalities – and the punishments for those convicted of the offence differed wildly.

Then as now, the press went to town on cases involving well-known performers. One of the most notorious cases of bigamy in the nineteenth century revolved around the glamorous actress and dancer Lola Montez. Born the more prosaic Maria Dolores Rosanna Gilbert, or alternatively Elizabeth Rosanna Gilbert, in Sligo, Ireland, in 1821, she intrigued the press during the 1840s, after she was accused of a bigamous marriage. She had eloped and married Lieutenant Thomas James at the age of 16, with the couple separating five years later, before Lola went on the stage. She then had subsequent affairs, including a spell as the mistress of Ludwig I of Bavaria, but had fled Europe at the start of the 1848 revolutions, when Ludwig abdicated.[4]

On arriving in London, she quickly wed cavalry officer George Trafford Heald. But although Lola and her first husband Thomas James had divorced, the divorce terms stipulated that neither side could remarry while the other was still living. Heald's family were horrified at George's marriage to this notorious character and Heald's aunt brought a bigamy action against Lola. The press was captivated and eagerly tracked Lola's movements. *The Examiner* noted that the couple, until recently on a Continental tour, had had to return to London to appear in court in relation to the charge. They arrived in London about 11 pm on the Thursday and 'immediately drove to their resident in Half-moon Street, Piccadilly'. It was reported that Lola was expected to appear at the Marlborough Street Police Court the following Monday, 'to meet the charge of bigamy preferred against her by the aunt of Lieutenant Heald'.

However, Lola and George did not stay to fight the charge, but instead fled Britain – travelling firstly to France. This did not stop the press from speculating as to what might happen next, as they eagerly monitored the couple's movements. Some seven months after Lola decided not to appear at Marlborough Street, *The Examiner* reported that final proceedings were about to take place, with recognizances being made for Lola's appearance – but it appears that Lola never had her day in court. She and George lived in self-imposed exile first in France, then Spain. But under pressure, the marriage broke down – and then George drowned. In 1851 Lola made her last permanent move, to the United States, where she died, aged 39, in January 1861.

Lola's avoidance of a conviction or punishment was not unique. In another case, a well-known composer bigamously married a famous American star, rather innocently believing that nobody at home would get to hear of it – but even when they did, he managed to swagger his way out of trouble. This case revolved around Edward Solomon. Together with his brother Fred, an actor, the Solomons had a fair bit of success in the Victorian theatres. But the Solomon brothers had an eye – or two – for the ladies and a disregard for the niceties of the marital contract. Fred Solomon had been on tour round the provincial theatres with Alexander Henderson's company, performing in the comic opera *Madame Favart*, when he eloped with a fellow theatre company member in Edinburgh. He and 18-year-old Alice Harper wed in an 'unofficial' ceremony before fellow performers in September 1879, the ceremony taking place at a private house in Hill Square.[5] Unfortunately, Fred had forgotten that he was already married, having wed a 16-year-old actress in London five years earlier. The tour moved on to Belfast and then Dublin, with the company performing at the eight-year-old Gaiety Theatre, which at the time took many of its productions from the English stage; but Alice died of typhoid fever at the Royal Dublin Hospital just weeks after her 'wedding'.[6] It took Fred a further six years before he finally got round to divorcing his first wife, Sarah and when he did, it was on the grounds that she had committed adultery while she had been performing in America. At the time Sarah was allegedly committing this adultery, Fred was getting bigamously married – but this was not mentioned in the divorce case.

Fred's brother, Edward, was the better-known Solomon sibling, being a successful musical composer. He had initially married actress Jane Isaacs, known professionally as Lily Grey, at the Strand register office in early 1873, when both were around 16 years old. The couple then later wed again in a traditional Jewish ceremony.[7] In 1882, Jane filed for a judicial separation, later changing this to a petition for divorce, arguing that Solomon had committed adultery with two women – Cecilia Reynolds and the actress

Edith Blande.[8] But in 1885, Jane brought a bigamy action against Edward, accusing him of having married Lillian Russell in America. It was not surprising that Jane had found out about Edward's marriage – Lillian was a famous actress and the wedding had been widely reported (in very fulsome terms and fancy language) in the press.

The case was initially heard at the Marlborough Street Police Court. Edward, described as a 30-year-old musical composer living at Hanover Place in Regent's Park, surrendered to his bail to answer the charge of feloniously marrying Helen Louise Leonard – Lillian Russell's real name – in New Jersey on 10 May 1885, his Jane being alive at the time. Jane gave evidence that she had married Edward, under her maiden name of Jane Isaacs, early in 1873. Edward had then deserted her, before marrying Russell in America. Jane's mother then appeared to state that Jane and Edward had been married in a register office on 15 March 1873, 'the ceremony according to the Jewish rite being performed some months later at her private residence in Russell Street, Covent Garden'. Jane said that Edward had deserted her after two years of marriage, leaving her to support their young child. She and her daughter had lived with her mother, 'except when she [Jane] was occasionally absent on professional tours through the provinces'. A policeman, Detective Sergeant Drew, then declared that he had taken Solomon into custody and that on being charged at the police station, he said: 'I admit that I did get married in America, or anyhow that I went through some ceremony, but I was not aware at the time that my wife was living, as I had not heard anything of her for several years.' The case seemed clear-cut; Solomon had no proof that Jane, who was young and healthy, had died and had known that he was remarrying without any knowledge of where his first wife was. Yet the case went on and on. There was then an argument about whether Solomon should be allowed out on bail. The magistrate was willing to agree to this but only if Edward could find two sureties of £250 each – the equivalent of around £11,500 each today. It was argued that this was prohibitive; but then, Solomon's religion was also used as a reason for why he should be allowed bail; his lawyer noted that the Jewish Day of Atonement was about to commemorated and that Solomon would be subject to 'serious consequences' for the rest of his life if he had to spend that day in prison. The defence then tried a third tactic, arguing that bigamy was not necessarily a serious charge, but could amount only to a 'technical breach of the law'. The former type of offence was only where there had been deceit practised, 'and where, practically, rape has been committed'. The magistrate did not take kindly to this argument and Solomon was removed into custody, the sureties for his bail not being reduced and Solomon unwilling, or unable, to find two people who would risk so much money.

The case may have particularly infuriated the magistrate – not to mention Jane Issacs and her family – because of the publicity that had attended Solomon's second marriage. The *New York Morning Journal*, in particular, had given a fulsome account of the wedding, with lots of hyperbole and flowery language, its headline reading:

> Lillian's hub and bub. Pretty Polly takes a new hubby in Hoboken. With Solomon
> in all his glory she returns to rock the cradle in New York.

The *Journal*'s piece detailed all the arrangements for the wedding, including the 'black enamelled cab' that transported the bride and groom, the location of the wedding at the Dutch Reformed Church at Hudson and Eighth Street and Lillian's outfit – 'a black and white check underskirt, trimmed with black silk and a black silk overskirt. Over her shoulders was thrown a black cape, jetted. On her head sat a jaunty black silk bonnet'. Edward Solomon had worn a broadcloth suit, 'shiny spring hat' and a buttonhole rose.

Solomon had gone so far as to give the newspaper's reporter an interview a couple of hours after the wedding, inviting him into the couple's house:

> 'Yes, it's all over,' said Mr Solomon, rubbing his hands, 'and now we hope to lead a quiet home life, away from the public gaze. Our stage existence will always be open to criticism, favourable we hope and trust.'

Yet even at this point and across the Atlantic, there had been speculation that Solomon was already married. The *Journal*'s reporter had not been shy in raising the 'rumour that Mr Solomon had a wife in England', first talking to the vicar who married the couple, who stated that this incorrect rumour – as he saw it – had simply arisen because Solomon had, two years earlier, visited America with Edith Blande, who had been performing in one of Solomon's operas, *The Vicar of Bray* – the insinuation being that they were a couple. It was stressed that Edith Blande was now 'sharing her heart with a well-known American manager, now resident in London'. Given the naming of Edith Blande in Jane Solomon's divorce petition, suggesting an affair many years earlier, it is likely that the press knew more than they were willing to hint at.

Back in London, *The Era*, covering the bigamy case, tracked down a copy of the New York paper and duly repeated its article verbatim underneath its coverage, thereby drawing attention to the existing rumours and the certainty that the second marriage had taken place, as well as showing its investigative skills and the ability to communicate information about events that had taken place thousands of miles away. But despite the apparently overwhelming evidence, there was one problem. The court needed witnesses to identify Solomon as the person mentioned in the marriage certificate. Specifically, they wanted Lillian Russell to come over from America to give evidence and act as a witness – but she failed to come. There were concerns that if she kept failing to show, Solomon would end up being remanded from week to week, thereby being indefinitely imprisoned when he had not yet been found guilty of an offence. Therefore, on 14 October 1886, the magistrate decided simply to order Edward to provide a surety of £500, which he did and was therefore released. He 'left the precincts of the court accompanied by a number of friends'. Jane Isaacs formally received her decree nisi in 1887, five years after first attempting to file for divorce.[9] Edward then married another actress, Kate Everleigh, in 1889 – but despite the dubious origins of their marriage, Lillian Russell did not seek a formal end to her relationship with Solomon until 1893, so it appears that Solomon either simply claimed to be married when he was actually cohabiting with Kate – or he had again committed bigamy. Two years later, he died in London of typhoid fever, aged 40, having packed a lot of living, loving and marrying into his short life. His obituary noted his 'early' marriage to Jane Isaacs, but omitted to mention his more famous American wife, or the bigamy case, at all.

Solomon's complex personal life received many column inches because of the involvement of a famous American actress – giving more than a smidgeon of glamour to the case. However, you didn't have to be a well-known actor or actress to get press coverage of your private life. The papers covered the unfortunate lives of jobbing actors and their partners, too. These included cases where bigamy had been consciously committed by an individual, knowing he was doing something wrong, but also cases that were due to an inability to gain a divorce from a first spouse. Prior to 1857, divorce was out of the question for those without the means of financing a private Act of Parliament. So what did you do if a marriage was failing, if you did not want to live with an individual any more? You might simply move out, arrange an informal separation whereby both spouses lived separately, perhaps with the wife maintained financially by the husband, particularly where children were involved. This was not an unusual situation in nineteenth-century Britain. Where things got complicated was when a new partner was found. In some cases, the married partner might genuinely believe that his first marriage had ended purely because of the length of time that had elapsed since he had lived with his spouse; or had even forgotten, in the heat of the moment, that the first wife existed! Although such cases could, and did, still reach court, a jury might take such circumstances into account when sentencing. This was certainly the case with a comedian named Peter Cullen.

Peter Anthony Cullen, aged 37, was found guilty of bigamy at the Central Criminal Court on 14 December 1840. The court heard that he had been married to tailoress Mary Ann Mitchell on 23 February 1824 at St Mary's Church, Whitechapel. The couple had not been well off and so after their marriage, which was witnessed by the wife of a Suffolk cow-keeper, they lodged with Mary Ann's father in Houndsditch before finding lodgings with the cow-keeper's wife in Britannia Street, off the City Road. In 1827, the couple were seen at a party at their former landlady's home, but by the start of 1828, they were known to have separated.

Twelve years elapsed, during which time Cullen and Mary Ann remained apart. On 16 November 1840, Cullen married again, at the church of St George's in the East, this time to Jane Bristow. She had met Cullen when he knocked at her door in Lambeth that June to ask for lodgings. He moved into Jane's first floor front room, but on being injured at the beginning of August, when he was struck on the head with a poker by an Irishman, Jane looked after him and the relationship blossomed. Jane told the court that she had over £1,000 in funds and that her four children were entitled to a share of that money. Perhaps encouraged by her money, Cullen proposed. She had heard that he had once been married, but Cullen told her that he had not heard from Mary Ann in eight years and that he believed she was dead.

But Cullen wasn't as innocent a creature as this tale so far suggests. He was certainly not motivated by love towards Jane and her children, who were aged between 11 and 18, when he married again. Within days of the marriage, he turned Jane's eldest daughter out of the house, swore and demanded his new wife's papers. When she couldn't find them, he said 'he would go to the theatre and neither I or he should sleep again in that house till he had seen them – he said he would have it and what did he marry me for but my money'.

Although Cullen had been engaged as an actor at the Surrey Theatre for the past five years, he was still short of money. He had never saved any part of his earnings. Edmund Faucet Saville, an actor who had worked with Cullen, described him as a 'generally useful horse in the team' and, slightly more flatteringly, as an 'exceedingly steady actor' until he had his encounter with the poker-wielding Irishman in the summer of 1840.

While recuperating, in the arms of Jane, he had been unable to work – and thus unable to earn. Cullen was found guilty of bigamy, but 'it having been shown that they had lived separately for a number of years, the Court said the case did not call for an extreme punishment and sentenced him to six months' imprisonment'.[10]

Another case, from later in the Victorian era, also involved a long-running story. In this case, it involved the Bristol-born comic singer William Horace Lingard, who was approaching 40 at the time his case came to the London Divorce Court in 1877. He had married Alice Dunning, then aged 19, in 1866.[11] Alice was also on the stage and known professionally as Alice Dunning Lingard. William and Alice emigrated to America in 1868, where William had a successful career, often appearing on stage in drag.[12] He later became the manager of Wood's Theatre, later known as the Theatre Comique, located at 514 Broadway in New York.[13]

But a decade after the marriage of the two actors, another actress came forward to claim that she was also married to Lingard. Amelia Martha Thomas argued that she had got to know Lingard in Southampton, where they had both been engaged at the local theatre – 'Lingard being then second low comedian'. They were married in Southampton in 1860, said Amelia, with Lingard giving the surname of Thomas at their wedding.[14] In the Divorce Court, Amelia's lawyer, at this point in the story, commented: 'It appears that the respondent is not quite sure what his real name is, for it appears he has amended his name in the answer from Thomas to Needham'. The judge, Sir Richard Phillimore, reiterated this, saying, 'He appears to enjoy three names – Thomas, Needham and Lingard'.[15]

Amelia Thomas then continued her evidence, duly repeated in the newspapers. She said that she had her first child with Lingard in 1861. The following year, Lingard had gone to Portsmouth to perform and Amelia, objecting to being away from her husband, had duly followed him down to Hampshire. On reaching his lodgings, he rather cruelly told her that 'his affections had changed regarding her'. He then offered her £100 to get a divorce, which she refused. The case continued and was clear cut: the Bristol registrar, a Mr Gwynn, appeared in court with evidence of Lingard's marriage to Alice Dunning on 20 June 1866. A Miss Elizabeth Thornton, who had rented rooms to Lingard and another 'lady, certainly not the petitioner in the case', was called on to prove that Lingard had committed adultery on Amelia with Alice. The case was proved; Amelia Martha was given a decree nisi. She was also awarded custody of her child, previously reported to be 'young William Harry Thomas, whom his flinty-hearted father refuses to provide for'.

William and Alice's relationship lasted until Alice's death in 1897 and their union produced a daughter. They had returned to England prior to Alice's death and William continued performing afterwards. In 1911, he was performing in the provinces and the census recorded him as staying in digs in Leamington Spa with a 26-year-old Chicago-born actress named Beatrice Moreau. In the census entry, where there was space to list any infirmities, Lingard had noted, 'None, thank God!' and his obituary in *The Times* noted the he 'retained his activity and ruddy complexion into old age'.[16] He died in 1927, aged 89.

Showing how many of the English actors of the period were connected, in 1869, William Horace Lingard, Alice Dunning and Alice's sister, Harriet – known professionally as Dickie Lingard – had performed a burlesque entitled *Pluto* at the Olympic Theatre in Chicago. It had been written by Henry Brougham Farnie, who was also embroiled in a bigamy case a couple of years after Lingard's.[17] This case was heard as Farnie versus Farnie at the Probate and Divorce Court in 1880 and was eagerly covered by *The Era*. It was brought by Mrs Farnie on the grounds of the bigamy of her husband Henry Brougham, described as 'a well-known dramatic author'.

Alethea Emma Harvey, a singer, had married Henry Brougham Farnie at All Souls Church in Langham Place, London, on 31 May 1865. However, late in 1879, she began divorce proceedings, arguing that her husband had been married before and that no legal steps had been taken to end that marriage before she had been wed. Alethea was correct. Henry had indeed married before, his first wife being Elizabeth Bebb Davies. The couple had married at Llanychaiarn in Cardiganshire, Wales, on 13 August 1861. After their marriage, they moved to Farnie's homeland of Scotland, settling in Cupar, Fife, where Farnie worked as the editor of the *Fifeshire Journal*. However, marital bliss did not last long. He started an affair with an Edinburgh woman, Margaret Whittle and in July 1863, Elizabeth Farnie sued for divorce in the Scotch Court of Divorce. The divorce was granted on the grounds of Henry's adultery on 5 December 1863.

Farnie then married Alethea, but she appears to have been unaware at the time of his earlier marriage. Henry certainly appears to have attempted to cover up his past, by declaring himself a widower on their marriage entry.[18] Alethea found out about his first wife later and then sued for divorce because her understanding of Scottish law was that 'whatever may have been the operation or effect in Scotland of the decree of divorce . . . the respondent did not thereby become free during the life of Elizabeth Bebb Davies to contract a valid and lawful marriage in England'.[19] But Alethea's legal knowledge was deficient. The original divorce, evidence of which was provided by Farnie in court, did not state that he could not remarry. Alethea's petition for divorce was therefore dismissed on 22 April 1880; she appealed and her appeal was also dismissed. Henry Brougham Farnie died in Paris on 21 September 1889, leaving an estate of over £20,000. Almost exactly a year after his death, on 25 September 1890, Alethea Emma Farnie remarried in Primrose Hill, north London. Her second husband was Gino Lofiego, an Italian singer.

Some cases of bigamy only emerged as a result of prosecutions for other offences and even then, sometimes, because of a silly mistake. This was certainly the situation in John Byron's case. John Byron was a 24-year-old clerk, who had been working for merchant Henry Willis at 37 Old Broad Street, London for around ten months. He had suddenly left his employment in August 1847, claiming to be ill – but he had actually swiped his employer's cheque book from a room next to his own office before leaving. On 11 September 1847, in the early afternoon, Byron tried to present a forged cheque for over £911 at Robarts, Curtis and Co, bankers based on Lombard Street.

Robarts was the bank used by Byron's employer, Henry Willis. One of Robarts' clerks, Henry Barham, was not initially suspicious – he genuinely believed that the signature was Willis's. One of the issue clerks, Christopher Windle, changed the notes, giving £50 in gold and a ticket for £40 in notes, which needed to be taken to another part of the bank, to Byron. Byron had lots of experience watching his former employer write cheques and knew how to do it; the subject was always written on the cheque, so Byron had duly written, 'Duty on tea' on his. It appears to have been Willis, rather than anyone at the bank, who realised what had happened and reported it to the police. Byron was apprehended by the police at Newcastle upon Tyne on 4 January 1848, the latter having been notified that Byron was wanted by mean of 'the electronic telegraph', a message being sent by PC James Bradley, who was based at London's Mansion House.[20]

Byron was sent back down to London, where his trial for forgery took place at the Central Criminal Court on 31 January 1848. Here, it emerged that this humble clerk was a man with dreams of making it as an actor – and that he was also a bigamist. In court, his undoing was asking for one Ann Bissett to be a witness for his defence. The first question she was asked was whether she was Byron's wife, to which she replied in the affirmative – she had married John in St George in the East on 31 January 1847.[21] It was then argued that her evidence was inadmissible, as it would be biased. But the judge then recalled another woman who had been called as a witness, one Harriet Little, as saying that Byron had been married to her orphaned sister. Harriet had given a detailed testimony, stating that she had acted as housekeeper for John at his home at 8 Miles Lane while her older sister had been visiting their father in the country for a couple of weeks. She also stated that John had two children by her sister, his wife.[22]

The judge called Harriet Little back and asked when the first marriage had taken place. She said it was five years earlier and that Byron had been courting her for two years previous to that. The judge then argued that Ann Bissett's marriage to Byron could not have been legal and that she could therefore be a witness. Bissett said she had first met Byron at the City Theatre in Bishopsgate Street, where she occasionally went 'for pleasure', on her own. She said that Byron 'attended there for pleasure, not as an actor'. Bissett said that the couple had been in desperate straits, they had no money in the house and that Byron had decided that they should move to Newcastle where he 'expected to obtain an engagement as an actor'. His word was law and so the couple sold their clothes and furniture in order to raise the money needed to journey to the north-east. Byron appears to have had more than pipe-dreams of performing; when he was arrested, it was discovered that he had indeed been engaged to perform at the Royal Newcastle Theatre. But Byron knew he was in trouble; in Newcastle, he and Ann took on the surname of Mason – and it seems to have been only after reaching the north-east that he broke the news to her that he already had another wife still living.

When called to make his defence, Byron came clean about his embarrassing predicament, recognizing that he was in a bit of a double-bind: '[he] said that he could only clear himself from the charge of forgery by admitting that he had committed another offence, that of bigamy.' He explained that after he had been married to his first wife for some time, they became financially distressed – he was unable to provide for his wife and their two children. As a result, they went to live with his father. While continuing to live on his own, ostensibly to start earning money to again support his family, he 'became acquainted with the second wife and was imprudent enough to marry her'. Now things became really complicated. After a fair bit of time had elapsed, his first wife got in touch, getting increasingly anxious to live with her husband again. He tried to put her off – 'he of course did all he could to induce her to remain in the country' – and succeeded for a while. But in early September, other family members got in touch with him to say that his first wife now had suspicions about him and thought that he might be living with another woman. She was determined to 'come to London and ascertain whether her suspicions were well founded'.

Byron panicked and decided to flee to another county, where he thought he might be able to find work as a provincial jobbing actor. He had, previously, 'already performed on one or two occasions at a minor theatre in London' and was confident he would be able to support himself through theatrical work. But he had no money to go and had to sell his clothes in order to get the money to travel. He stated in court that his only reason for leaving London for Newcastle was his 'fear of being taken into custody for bigamy'.

The jury, after a 'very short deliberation', returned a guilty verdict and the prisoner was sentenced to be transported for ten years. However, this was not an unusually harsh punishment for the bigamy. John was convicted of forgery of a payment for money and this is what the sentence of transportation was given for. From the criminal registers, it appears that this punishment was deemed enough and John was not punished for the bigamy he had been forced into revealing.[23] He was duly transported to Australia aboard the ship *William Jardine*, with 260 others, on 9 August 1850 and arrived in Tasmania on 14 November that year.[24] He left behind both wives – Matilda and Ann – but perhaps was relieved that his complicated personal life was now out in the open and there was no need for lies and confusion any more.

Bigamists could use a variety of reasons to excuse their actions. Byron blamed economics, financial necessity splitting his first family up, whilst ignoring the fact that he had then conveniently forgotten about their existence. Edward Murphy, meanwhile, blamed his father-in-law for 'making' him marry his wife against his will. Edward Murphy had married Sarah Jones at the Church of St John the Evangelist in Lambeth on 28 April 1845, when he was around 17 years old. She was a tailor's daughter and he was just setting out in the industry, working for her father, whilst secretly harbouring ambitions to become an actor – something he achieved, both inside and outside of court. According to Sarah's father, listed as tailor Samuel Jones in the Old Bailey Proceedings, they lived together afterwards 'on and off two or three years', not living together all the time as Edward was soon able to find acting work and was frequently away on engagements in provincial theatres around the country. However, they still managed to have three children, one of whom died young. But Edward then took a liking to a young newsvendor's daughter named Elizabeth Ann Stiles or Styles and married the 22-year-old on 12 July 1852. The marriage register of St Philip's church in Bethnal Green recorded his profession as 'traveller' which, in a way, he was.

On 26 September 1852, *Lloyd's Weekly Newspaper* reported that Edward Murphy, aged 25, had appeared at the Central Criminal Court charged with bigamy – 'feloniously intermarrying with Elizabeth Ann Stiles, his wife being alive'. When he had been originally apprehended, Edward had told the police 'that he had been in daily expectation of it [his arrest] and should abandon every hope'. Yet in court, he attempted to excuse his behaviour. *Lloyd's Weekly Newspaper* reported breathlessly:

In defence, he with considerable address pleaded as a mitigation of the offence his having been trepanned, when an orphan, at the age of 16, into a marriage with his master's daughter, whose temper was most inimical to their happiness; that he had consummated the second marriage under the belief that the first was illegal and finally throw himself on the mercy of the court.

The Old Bailey records show that Edward went further in his full address to the court. He stated that he had got Sarah pregnant when he was 16 and her father, Samuel, had made him marry his daughter to maintain her honour. Edward stated that he only agreed to do this on the understanding that that Samuel would then give him 'a better insight' into the tailoring trade, but that he then reneged on this. He stressed that Sarah had brought on her own downfall, because 'her violent temper made my home miserable'. He maintained that he wasn't aware that his second marriage was illegal, because his first marriage was 'when I was under age and my second wife knew that I had been married'.[25] Elizabeth Ann refused to appear in court, but in her absence, the jurors found Edward guilty of bigamy and sentenced him to four months in prison. One can't help feeling that Sarah, who was slated by her husband in court, was better off without him.

These tales of bigamy, lies and obfuscations may suggest that actors were a fickle bunch – dumping or abandoning wives (or, less frequently, husbands) with gay abandon and having few reservations about taking part in marriage ceremonies despite being fully aware of their illegality. Yet they were not alone and the Victorian newspapers often contained tales relating to those in rather humble occupations as well as more affluent individuals – all classes were occasionally guilty of bigamy. But if actors appear to have disdained the usual polite forms of behaviour, their lifestyles may have encouraged it. They were often frequently on the move, touring round the country – or, if lucky, further afield – and never in one place for too long. Theirs was a precarious life. They regularly met new people, in new surroundings, and temptation kicked in. They may genuinely have thought they were doing nothing wrong, or have convinced themselves that nobody would find out what they were doing. And lastly – they were actors. If their moment in court came, they would do their best to perform for the jury. As the newspaper reports show, on occasion, their acting was often not enough to enable them to escape conviction; but in others, it appears that little happened to them apart from a divorce from their first, unwanted, wives.

CHAPTER 15

Divorce

Today, the ending of a celebrity marriage is a guarantee of press coverage – and in the nineteenth century, things were pretty much the same. In fact, divorce was more of a newsworthy story, given its relative rarity. As previously discussed, prior to 1857, divorce was primarily a matter for those with a lot of money to push their case and was particularly difficult for women to obtain. However, even after 1857, the law was biased against women; men could gain a divorce on the grounds that his wife had committed adultery, but women had to prove both adultery and another offence such as bigamy or desertion, or cruelty.[1] This explains the many cases brought by women that detailed violent behaviour on the part of their husbands and their own innocence in the instigation of such violence. Therefore, some of the stories reported by the press have to be considered in the light of this; the wife, in bringing the divorce petition, may have exaggerated incidences in some cases, in order to make her case for cruelty stronger.

The passing of the Matrimonial Causes Act meant an increase in cases that the press could draw on for stories post-1857. As one of the stories shown here makes explicit, some women welcomed the passing of the Act to end marriages that they had long been unhappy with, or where a partner had deserted years earlier. Actors and actresses were not the only occupations represented in the divorce courts, but their stories were of particular interest for the increasingly celebrity-driven elements of the press.

Divorce could be an expensive business and even the money involved in bringing a petition for divorce to the courts could form a story in itself. In 1865, one case was heard that highlighted the difficulties of divorcing when you were an actor. The case of Chapman v Chapman and Wright was brought by an actor, Henry Chapman, who, as *The Era* reported, 'sued *in forma pauperis* . . . and conducted his own case'. He stated that he was an actor and from his marriage in 1854, had lived with his wife in 'different parts of Lambeth'. In 1859, he said that he was 'then obliged to separate from her on account of her violent temper and irregular habits and she has since lived with the co-respondent [Wright]'.

Henry Chapman had married Jane Whitnall on 28 February 1854 at St Mary at Lambeth.[2] At that point, he was officially a coachman – the same profession as his father Thomas. Jane was the daughter of a farmer, John, who had died some time before the wedding; she may have been the same Jane Whitnall who was working as a domestic servant in Lambeth in the 1851 census.[3] It is not known whether Henry was working as an actor at the time of his marriage, but was supplementing his income by working as a coachman, or whether he changed career afterwards. His future, post-marriage, seems to have been generally insecure, though. Jane, he had argued, was bad-tempered and their marital life must have been fractious. She then started a relationship with Mr Wright; but perhaps her husband's precarious financial situation had already becoming something that she found hard to deal with and live with. The lack of facts surviving about Henry

Chapman suggest that his career was not a stellar one. Certainly, by 1864, Henry was reduced to having to file for divorce *in forma pauperis*, as *The Era* had reported. This meant that the court had given him permission to launch a legal action without having to pay any court fees or costs. Henry's status was due to his impoverished financial situation – those who sued in this form were the poor, or prisoners – showing that acting could be a fraught, insecure profession and was not a means of gaining financial prosperity.[4]

The passing of the Act enabled couples who had long been separated to finally gain a formal end to their marriages. However, the distance between them separating and finally being able to gain a divorce could cause further, unexpected problems. In Brighton, in 1844, George Joseph had married Mary Levy Dumont. Mary was still a minor and her father, Alexander Levy Dumont, had to give his consent to the marriage.[5] The young couple settled in Marylebone and soon had a baby daughter. Within two years of the marriage, though, Mary committed adultery with another man, Henry de Vereyen, at the family home. She then left the marital home and disappeared, leaving no clue as to where she had gone. After some time, Joseph started a relationship with another woman – but was unable to marry her because legally, he was still married. In 1858, he was thrilled when the Divorce Act was passed: '[He] was determined to take advantage of the new Act, get a divorce from the faithless woman who had deserted him and pass the rest of his life in domestic peace and conjugal enjoyment.'

Joseph quickly filed his petition for divorce in the Divorce and Matrimonial Department of the Probate Court on 5 October 1858.[6] By this time, he had done some detective work and found that his wife had fled to Europe, where by 1855, she had started a relationship with a German actor named Ferdinand Wenzel.[7] Mary was still living with Wenzel in Frankfurt. George Joseph had proved that she had legally committed adultery and started the process of getting his wife removed to England. While this legal process was underway, the German authorities lodged her in a local prison.

But now, things got really complicated. Joseph returned to England, but before his divorce case could be heard, he received a letter from the thespian Wenzel. He told Joseph that Mrs Joseph had been made so anxious about the divorce case and her imprisonment that she had gone into premature labour with her illegitimate child and she had died as a result. Wenzel attached a document with an official signature, proving the death. Joseph had no reason to disbelieve the letter and so withdrew his divorce petition and, as a widower, promptly married his new love. Two children followed and the family was happy and content. But then, years later, another letter was received by Joseph. This one was even nastier than the previous one:

> Joseph received a letter from his wife's paramour, informing him that Mrs Joseph, so far from dying in child-bed, was alive and the only way to prevent her from interfering with his domestic happiness and claiming her husband, was by sending a goodly honorarium, or fee, to his lawful wife and make a proper arrangement for the periodical payment of a sum of money sufficient to keep the disreputable wife's lips closed during her lifetime.

Joseph immediately went back to court and lay a petition to have his dropped divorce case put once more on the court's register. *The Era* noted that the case showed 'the use and benefit of the Divorce Act in a very significant manner', although it failed to draw attention to the nineteen years it had taken Joseph to end his marriage.

Initially, theatrical divorces received the attention of the press because of their novelty, in the immediate aftermath of the Act being passed. As an increasing number of people sought divorces, one might expect press interest in them to have declined – but this was clearly not the case. Divorces were an easy source of stories and the evidence put before the court was often fascinating, intriguing, or downright salacious, as parties tried to emphasise the dramatic in order to meet the necessary criteria for a divorce. For an increasingly gossipy press, it was manna. This was particularly true of cases involving well-known actresses and the newspapers were keen to include as many details as possible about these. One such case involved the actress and singer Nelly Power – one of the 'earliest female stars on the [music] halls'.[8]

Nelly Power was the stage name of Ellen Maria Lingham. She had started her career aged just eight and was, as an adult, famous for the song *The Boy I Love Is Up In The Gallery*. She had married Roland Gideon Israel Barnett when she was 20, on 1 June 1874, at the Hackney register office. The marriage ceremony was followed two weeks later by a traditional service at the Jewish Church at Paris. They had settled down to married life in Stockwell and various other places around England, lastly at Liverpool. The marriage had been rather tempestuous, as well as short – Nelly had walked out on her husband twice, the second time being on 28 September 1874 when she left their home at Mount Pleasant in Liverpool, before finally filing for a judicial separation on 29 October 1875.[9] The suit received even more publicity than it would otherwise have done after Frederick George Hobson, who Nelly had known for some seven years, appeared in Clerkenwell Police Court accused of assaulting her estranged husband.

In this case, Barnett stated that he had gone to Nelly's mother's house on 8 November 1875, to see the actress. She had not been there, but Barnett then witnessed her return to the house in a hansom cab, accompanied by Hobson. The next day, Barnett went again to the house, in what appeared suspiciously like stalking. He found Hobson in the front room. He walked out, but then turned back towards the house, to find himself accosted by Hobson and some friends. Barnett refused to answer his questions – probably relating to why he kept turning up at his mother-in-law's home – and so Hobson knocked him down.

Barnett stated that he was formerly a financial agent, based on the Strand, with his business apparently based around sending flyers to young college students offering to lend them money. He had been made bankrupt the previous year, had debts of £12,000, no assets and had failed to keep any accounts.[10] Barnett was, according to Nelly's version of events at least, a bit of a ne'er do well. In her separation suit, she graphically described how he suffered from venereal disease and had given it to her. She stated that she was still 'suffering greatly from the effects of such disease and has ever since remained under medical treatment'. She also stressed his 'great pecuniary difficulties' and bankruptcy and that although she had given up her acting career on marrying, her husband's failure to support her had led to her having, in July 1875, to resume her career in order to maintain herself. He had called Nelly a 'bloody bitch' and urged her to commit adultery with a rich man. Although Barnett was painted in the blackest terms and in the assault case had struck the first blow against Hobson, it was the latter who was ordered to enter into recognizances to be of good behaviour for six months.

The papers were full of misbehaving husbands and misbehaving wives and although some motivations for ending a marriage were common to those both within and without the theatrical profession, the stresses placed on actors and other performers, particularly those caused by living away from one's spouse if on a provincial tour, suggests that they may have been particularly prone to marriage splits. It is clear that geographic separations could cause the breakdown of marriages. Living in a different city, meeting different people or being part of a distinct theatrical community away from one's family could soon loosen ties and encourage new lives and relationships. Sometimes, though, it was not the partner who was working away who strayed – it could be those who were left behind. Neighbours and friends were to be as distrusted as much as strangers. For example, in 1878, Thomas Brunton filed a petition for divorce on the grounds of his wife's adultery with a Mr Coulton. Brunton had only been married six years, having married Annie Hoyle at the registry office in Salford on 14 December 1872. They had rented a house in that area and swiftly had three children. Brunton was an actor, engaged at a theatre in Manchester. There, he met Coulton, who was employed as a musician at the same theatre. In September 1877, Brunton started a provincial theatre tour with J.L. Toole and so had to leave his wife and children in their 'comfortable' home at 15 Short Street. He was a good husband and sent her a regular allowance for maintenance. After a few months, he returned home briefly to visit his family; but whilst out locally, he heard some rumours about his wife and Coulton. He went to talk to Coulton about it, but found him 'distant', 'whereas formerly they had been the most intimate friends'. He returned home and accused his wife – she 'partially' admitted it. From then until January, Brunton was again touring the theatres – but then received a letter from his wife. On opening it, he found that it was addressed to Coulton and had been sent to him by mistake – but it was written in 'a most improper character for a married woman to address to a man not her husband'. In February, Brunton wrote to a friend of his in Salford, Mr Walker and asked him to watch the couple. Walker saw the couple together in Ordsall Lane and then later peered through the Bruntons' kitchen window and saw the couple clearly together. He duly reported back. In court, 'the wife's adultery was clearly proved' and the divorce was granted.

Trying to ascertain details of actors' lives in the nineteenth century can be tricky due to the use of varied stage names, which can obfuscate matters. The press could refer to actors involved in court cases by their professional or their real names; and even if a case was brought in an actor's real name, the press might – although not always and not consistently – use the professional name, as it was the name their readers would be more likely to recognise. In one case, from March 1900, all the parties involved had both birth and stage names, which were not used consistently in the subsequent press reports. The press reported that actor Charles Ford Morgan had sought a divorce from his wife, singer Maud Holland, on the grounds of her adultery with 'John Carrington, known on the stage as Dick Neville'. Neville had, appropriately, played Don Juan on stage in Birmingham three years earlier. Charles Ford Morgan was known professionally as Lytton Grey; his wife was born Alice Maud Holland. This was Morgan's second marriage – his first wife, a singer born as Caroline Edith Harper, but known professionally as Edith Grey, had died following a miscarriage in 1887, aged just 26. In 1892, Morgan had married Maud, a schoolmaster's daughter, at Great Yarmouth.[11]

From 1897, Maud had been in actor-manager Edmund Lockwood's company together with Dick Neville. They were part of the cast of the comic opera *La Poupée*, which in December 1897, was playing at the Lyric Theatre in Ealing.[12] *The Era* reported that on 16 December that year, the production had 'met with distinct success, which was in great measure due to the sprightly and exhilarating interpretation of the character of Alesia given by Miss Maud Holland, who has an excellent voice and uses it in good style . . . Mr Dick Neville does well as [the jolly monk] Father Maxime, his voice and bearing are worthy of commendation'. Within four days of this performance, Dick Neville had disappeared, the *Hull Daily Mail* reporting: 'The Ealing Police were yesterday investigating the disappearance of Dick Neville (or John Carrington), an actor attached to "La Poupée" comic opera company.'

The *South Wales Daily News* was more perturbed, noting that 'Richard Neville' was the 'son of a London clergyman and much liked by his confreres, as well as by the audiences'. But a clue might have been in the extra detail the Welsh paper provided – he had gone to 'dine with a medical friend' in London one evening and didn't return to his lodgings; the following morning, his wife telegraphed the friend and learned that her husband had left his company at an early hour. 'Mrs Neville' was herself an actress who was with another touring company; a new reading of the reports suggests that Neville may have been having assignations with his colleague Maud while his wife was away performing with a different company. The *South Wales Daily News*, though, speculated that he had not seen the notice put up stating that his company had been re-engaged for a new tour, starting at the Newport Lyceum on 26 December and that he had therefore left thinking he had finished his work. Neville seems to have been notified, or had returned anyway, for he continued to work with the company, when they returned to London and the Crouch End Theatre by February 1898. By this point, Maud Holland was displaying signs of dissatisfaction at home. The *Illustrated Police News* reported: 'She complained to her husband that she found it very difficult to get from the theatre to her [marital] lodgings at Maida Vale after the performance and he allowed her to take lodgings near the theatre.'

It later emerged from a Crouch End landlady that Maud's lodgings there were actually apartments that she shared with Dick Neville, 'as man and wife'. By the end of the month, the production was due to transfer to Birmingham and Maud announced that she was going to rejoin her theatre company there. She took her belongings and told her husband that she would be 'supping that evening with some ladies of the company and would not be able to get home to sleep'. The next day, she asked her husband to meet her at the Alhambra Theatre, but failed to turn up. That evening, he got a letter from her, 'stating that she had been offered an engagement in America and that she would not have time to say good-bye'.

Maud did go to America, but Charles later found out that she had moved in with Dick Neville on reaching there, the couple renting lodgings at Rist House on East 14th Street. He wrote to her on hearing the rumour that this is what she had done and 'in reply to his letter, she wrote admitting that this was true and that her only object in leaving London was to avoid a scandal. She said that if he obtained a divorce the co-respondent would marry her.' The *Illustrated Police News* added a further part of her unwittingly ironic letter: "'I left you", the letter ran on, "because I thought you would see in my face what I had done. You know I was never deceitful.'"

In a separate case, in 1882, the wife was far more honest than Maud Holland in admitting her guilt. Actor George Curryer duly appeared in the divorce court in January 1882 to seek the dissolution of his marriage. His wife was Mary Anne Curryer, née Wheeler – an actress who was known professionally as Mabel Verner. The couple had married in Walsall in 1874, when George was 25 and Mabel was just 19.[13] They had acted together in various places, but also took roles in different productions, which meant that they might be performing in different cities. However, George stated that when this happened, he visited his wife as often as possible and despite their separations, they managed to have four children together in the space of eight years, although only one survived.

In his divorce suit, George had accused Mabel of having committed adultery with Edward Shelton, who was then the manager of the Globe Theatre in Poole, Dorset. In the autumn of 1880, George and Mabel had both been performing in Scotland, but when Mabel's engagement ended, she accepted one in Edward Shelton's theatre. Shelton was also married with children, but this did not stop a relationship from developing. In April 1881, a witness stated that, whilst engaged at the Grecian Theatre in Islington, Mabel had been living in lodgings with Edward Shelton as man and wife – 'they remained in lodgings till October, on 16 September the respondent gave birth to a child'. Two weeks after giving birth, on 1 October 1881, Mabel was writing to George from Brighton to confess her 'sin' and eleven days later, Shelton wrote to George saying,

> He had read their correspondence, he had known before he had met respondent how little the petitioner valued her and had already condoned three other similar offences, so he felt he was doing no wrong, pledging, 'After twelve months of Mabel's heart, I am willing to entrust my entire happiness in her hands.'

George denied knowing of any 'similar offences' – he claimed to have had no idea that she had previously conducted any affairs. In court, the judge pronounced a decree nisi, with costs awarded to cuckolded George. Mabel's alleged adulteries whilst on tour gave credence to the Victorian press's belief that being an actress and being a wife and mother were incompatible roles; as Kerry Powell notes, 'even the theatrical press and many actors and actresses themselves recognised a deep-seated incompatibility between women performers on one hand and wives and mother on the other'.[14] But there was also the fact that actresses were used to being independent and might feel constrained by the conventional notions of fidelity and dependence that many husbands expected. Mabel had the freedom to live her own life when working away from her husband and – if Shelton's letter to George Curryer is to be believed – she enjoyed that freedom.

There was a dichotomy within the theatre. Were actors supposed to act as moral beacons for their audience and did the audience expect or want that? It appeared that the audience, the theatregoers, were not as bothered by the actors' morality as the newspapers thought they should be and would continue to watch and admire them regardless. And even the newspapers were somewhat ambivalent, wanting to be critical whilst also covering divorce cases in detail and recognizing the talents and ability of the actors to entertain the masses. This dichotomy was also evident in how some actors conducted their private lives. Some were indeed faithful to their partners, at least as far as we can ascertain from this distance in time and a lack of evidence as to the contrary; others tried to conduct clandestine affairs; but others were more open about their relationships. In the case of Mr and Mrs McNamara, who were refused a divorce in 1867, the adultery alleged by the husband was observed by several witnesses.[15]

Edward Kingett McNamara was the proprietor of the Royal Pavilion Gardens at North Woolwich. The gardens were a popular place for entertainment, featuring promenades, a lake, islands, bridges and a ballet stage: in 1859, it was promoting its ballets and singing concerts in the press, as well as firework displays and its proximity to the Eastern Counties and Blackwall Railways. But Edward was also a horse dealer; it was stated that 'he seemed to have been much given to theatrical speculations, somewhat to the annoyance of his family'. His wife Marian Elizabeth Sophia McNamara, known professionally by her maiden name, Miss Marian Taylor, was a singer. He had met her when she was engaged as a concert singer at the gardens, but she later became manager of a London opera company. The married at the church of St Dunstan in the West on Fleet Street in November 1857 and seemed happy until 1863, when they went to Hull for work and first met Edmund Rosenthal, the professional name of Thomas Metcalf, who was the manager of a travelling opera company. Marian Taylor had got an engagement with the company, touring the English and Welsh provinces.

Marian had fallen for Rosenthal by the time they moved onto Cardiff in November 1863 – and the couple were not very good at concealing their feelings. A queue of witnesses appeared in the divorce court to tell of what they had seen. Edwin March Sheam, who had been a waiter in a Cardiff hotel where the couple later lodged, said that he had gone upstairs about 7 am and found Marian in her nightdress in Mr Rosenthal's bedroom, whilst that gentleman was in bed. Sheam also said he had seen them in Rosenthal's bedroom on several other occasions and seen them 'kissing and pulling each other about'. A stage carpenter, George Harvey, noted that they behaved 'familiarly' to each other – 'he had seen them kissing each other. On one occasion at Boston, he entered their room suddenly and found them standing up in a very excited state.'

A chambermaid at Henston's Hotel in Cardiff, by the name of Ann Watson, said she remembered the couple staying there once in November 1863. Although they had booked separate bedrooms in the hotel, which were opposite each other, she had seen Marian coming out of Rosenthal's bedroom in her nightdress, shoes and stockings. A week later, she had taken up some water and seen Marian emerging from the same room and although she was fully dressed, Ann was still shocked as 'she knew that Mr Rosenthal was in the bedroom'. Yet Ann, who seemed to know a lot, also mentioned that Mr McNamara had also sometimes visited his wife at the hotel. To laughter in the divorce court, she said: 'He was very affectionate to her and she retaliated.' 'Reciprocated would have been the better word!' exclaimed the judge. Ann blithely continued that actors and actresses always tended to kiss each other after a curtain went down on a burlesque or operatic performance, if the applause suggested that performance had been successful.

After Ann had finished giving evidence, a comedian named Abel, who was acting manager of the opera company, was called on to give his memories of being with the couple on tour, when they were lodging at The Cock Inn in Halifax. He noted that they had a shared sitting-room and he had seen them 'act there more like two children than a grown man and woman'. At one point, he had gone into the room to find Marian lying on a sofa, whilst Rosenthal sat on a chair next to it, 'with his legs on the sofa and his arms around her neck'. Abel made sure he got a good view; he could 'see her legs and her breast was open'. He saw Rosenthal's immediate rising from the sofa to cover Marian up as an indication of intimacy; to modern eyes, it appears more that Rosenthal was aware of Abel's interest in Marian's body and acted accordingly to protect her.

Another witness, singer William Parkinson, had also seen Marian in her nightdress (apparently, many people had) and that 'she was not abashed at his presence'. He also sniffily said that 'at Shrewsbury he saw Rosenthal put on his slippers and then put his legs up over the respondent's knees'. It was then alleged – after substantially briefer discussion – that McNamara had had an affair with a girl named Fanny and also 'Marie Charles, one of the ballet', who had been said to have drunk champagne with McNamara 'in a quiet part' of the Royal Pavilion grounds. He was said to have taken another girl to a coffee shop in north London for two hours – damning evidence, apparently.

The divorce petition had originally been brought by Edward McNamara on 15 February 1866, with him seeking £500 in damages; it took over a year for the case to be resolved in the Divorce Court. Marian's defence had been firstly to deny the affair, but then to argue that her husband was both 'accessory to and conniving at, the said adultery' and that he 'condoned the adultery complained of . . . if any'.[16] She further added that her husband had frequently committed adultery himself 'with common prostitutes', that he 'wilfully separated himself' from her prior to 'the alleged adultery complained of' and was therefore guilty of 'such wilful neglect and misconduct . . . as would have conduced [*sic*] to the adultery if there had been any'. These allegations, detailed in the divorce petition, appear to have gone unreported in the press, which took pleasure in detailing Marian's behaviour with Rosenthal, but were more reluctant to report allegations of a man having sex with prostitutes. Although witnesses were called to rebut the charges of adultery, *Reynolds's Newspaper* didn't bother to report their testimonies; they were obviously not as salacious as the previous witnesses'. In the end, the jury decided that both Mr and Mrs McNamara had committed adultery – and dismissed the petitions of both for a divorce on the grounds of each other's behaviour.

In conclusion, it is clear that the theatrical industry was a mass of insecurities and contradictions. The press coverage of 'theatrical divorces' reflected the wider debate about the perceived immorality of the profession; whilst some actresses were found to engage in freer sexual behaviour than that promoted by the church and the press, they were only doing the same as some other women from other walks of life and were not representative of all actresses. The majority of divorce petitions brought by actors and actresses involved adultery by the husband rather than the wife and depicted a depressing level of violence, which was borne by women sometimes for a long time before the additional proof of adultery enabled them to legally end their marriage.

The newspapers acted both as gossips and gatekeepers, choosing which salacious details to publish whilst censoring others. They focused, unsurprisingly, on the interesting bits of testimony in court cases and ignored more ordinary details, which could sometimes create a one-sided report of a divorce case. The discussing of sexual behaviour in a legal setting enabled the Victorian press to repeat it as a matter of fact and as a newsworthy incident, giving readers a thrill at the same time; yet by comparing details provided in divorce petitions to the press reports of the same cases, it is clear that there was still some censoring of what detail was reported. The press reports were a sanitised version, offering titillation rather than graphic detail. There was also little discussion of the repercussions of domestic violence; the emphasis was on the drama of it – again, its newsworthiness and ability to sell papers.

Yet, as the press did on occasion point out, the salacious cases could distort the picture of actresses as women of loose morals and not reflect the industry as a whole. *The Era* was keen to stress that the theatrical profession was far more moral than the public might believe and stressed the danger that could face actresses tarred by gossip and rumour. But the fact that the newspapers were one of the primary means for spreading those bits of gossip and rumour made them complicit in the image of the theatre as a hotbed of sexual intrigue.

CHAPTER 16

Death and Disaster

A considerable proportion of theatrical coverage in the press was devoted to the deaths of actors, managers and playwrights – and these were covered more and more and in increasing amount of detail, as the nineteenth century progressed. This reflected the growing importance of the theatre and its performers to the increasingly literate working classes, with stories included to cater for them and their fascination with individual actors and actresses.

Coverage could vary between the commonplace and the exotic and look both at home and abroad. Some reports were about deaths sustained during the course of performers' work, reflecting the conditions of the theatres in which they worked. Others reflected the insanitary conditions of Victorian life, with smallpox and typhoid being diseases that could strike anyone, including thespians. But it was not just the performers whose deaths were commented on. In the Victorian era, there were several disasters involving theatregoers, caused by crushes and panics, and by poorly-built or cramped seating areas. These were also breathlessly covered and the deaths of those who just wanted to enjoy a good performance at their local theatre and who otherwise would have had a pretty anonymous life, gave them a form of immortality in the press.

Theatre disasters were covered in great detail by the press. They provided the opportunity to run a series of articles – from the first breathless accounts, perhaps only able to cover the rumours or the basic facts, through to coroners' inquests and burials. In 1848, on one otherwise normal Tuesday, the Victoria Theatre on Lower Marsh on London's South Bank was the scene for one disaster, which resulted in the death of two boys. The theatre had been busy that afternoon, with many people queuing to get into the theatre gallery prior to a show. Long before the play was due to start, the stairs to the gallery were thronged with people, who became increasingly claustrophobic in the crowded conditions. Some needed fresh air, but couldn't move, wedged in amongst other people. People started becoming short-tempered – 'unruly' – and in their attempts to get out, shoved others who fell down and were soon trampled on by those around them. The problems were most acute on the staircase landing. Six people were identified as needing urgent medical help, but the crowds were such that it took over thirty policemen to help clear a path and get them carried out to the nearest surgeon, Mr Sewell, who practiced at Lower Marsh. With two other surgeons, he managed to help four boys, two of whom were able to be sent home, albeit with severe bruising. Unfortunately, the other two boys were beyond help.

The following morning, the theatre lessee started an inquiry, together with other theatre officials, to see what had happened and how to prevent a similar situation occurring. The surgeons appeared to say that the younger boy, 11-year-old William Phillips, had died from suffocation and had been dead some time – they believed that he had been tightly wedged in amongst adults and 'he would have been as unable to breathe as if a pillow had been put over his mouth'. The older boy, 15-year-old John Castillo, had, they believed, been hit by something heavy on his head, which had stunned him and caused him to slump to the ground. Once there, he had been trampled on and smothered to death. His face showed evidence of having been kicked and trodden on by people wearing 'shoes with heavy nails in them'. A third boy, Henry Fraser, was unconscious when rescued and although he was still alive, he was very poorly. Not surprising, given that the surgeons had applied leeches to him as his main 'medicine'.

Just as the press was interested in what had happened, so too was the public. It was noted that 'several hundred' people applied to view the boys' dead bodies the day after their deaths, 'and it was not until they were owned [claimed] that the churchyard could be cleared'. The same day, workmen were ordered to repair part of a stair rail that had been broken during the melee – 'it is now so constructed that it would be impossible to force it down, no matter how strong the pressure against it might be'. The press also noted that the Victoria Theatre's management had announced that it would construct barriers on the stairs, like the ones that could already be found at Her Majesty's Theatre.

The papers got most of their information from the theatre's inquiry and then from the inquest, which was held at the Hero of Waterloo pub on the Waterloo Road in Lambeth. The coroner, William Carter, heard the jury's view that the lessee should be reminded of the 'necessity of increased ventilation to prevent a similar occurrence' and that he should not open the theatre's doors too early, but wait until closer to the time of a performance.

The Victoria Theatre disaster was found to be an accident, but there were other cases where it was found that individual theatregoers had caused catastrophes by their high spirits – or even by criminal intent. In 1884, for example, James Turner was charged with culpable homicide after shouting 'Fire!' in the Star Theatre of Varieties in Glasgow, causing a stampede. Many could not escape because the exit door was fastened by an iron bolt set into the stone floor. Seven people died and fourteen were seriously injured; the seven funerals were paid for by Mr McKay, the lessee of the theatre.

In 1892, the Gateshead Theatre disaster was also blamed on someone wrongly saying that there was a fire; a panic again ensued and because the exit from the gallery was 'insufficient and dangerous', many died. It was found that if there had been a real fire, 200 people in the gallery would have been suffocated by smoke before a fire even reached them, as it was on the same level as the flies. The gallery exit was also found to be insufficient and the approach dangerous. The licensing authority was criticised for having 'issued no rules whatever to insure safety and, except a couple of buckets, there were no fire appliances'. Problems were also identified as a result of the building not having been designed as a theatre – it had previously been a Methodist chapel and then a concert hall. At the subsequent inquest, the jury 'considered an Act of Parliament should be passed, making it compulsory on the local authorities to place provincial theatres on the same footing as those in London for the protection of the public'.

It was understandable that audiences might panic about the prospect of fire in a theatre. Theatre construction and set construction, invariably involved a lot of wood; and safety measures were rather idiosyncratic in some. Of course, some fires genuinely broke out in theatres, but there could be disaster even if there were measures put in place to deal with them. For example, the Exeter Theatre disaster of 1887 was caused by a fire, or rather by the gaslights that lit the theatre causing a fire, and followed a similar incident there two years earlier; but people died despite Henry Scarborough, the props master, getting the hose on the stage as soon as the alarm was given and fighting the flames until he was forced to leave the theatre. When the alarm was given, many people jumped over the gallery barrier into the upper circle to escape; others ran down the staircase but found that their path was blocked by smoke; the lights on the stairs went out and they were left in dark, smoky conditions, trying to make their way out but finding that they were trampling on fallen bodies to do so. The theatre's lessee, Mr Baring, was later summonsed to court by the Exeter mayor at the request of the family of one of the deceased; they argued that he had ignored justices' regulations. It was the 'worst fire disaster in the British theatre', resulting in 186 people dying.[1]

In 1878, it was a Liverpool theatre that was the location for disaster. Thirty-seven died in the Colosseum Theatre catastrophe of 11 October, with the 'work of identifying the dead . . . completed yesterday afternoon, when the last body, supposed to be that of a seafaring man, was recognised as that of a Norwegian sailor named Petersen'. The theatre re-opened on 14 October, with a numerous audience there to hear the proprietor, Mr Goodman Junior, give a brief address, expressing 'profound sorrow'. He announced his intention to donate the proceeds of two nights' takings, with double charge of admission, to a fund for the 'distressed', after it was 'shown by official reports that the total number left destitute by the death of the breadwinners does not exceed 30'. In Glasgow, six years later, theatre lessee Mr McKay similarly started a relief fund for 'the necessitous bereaved'.

The tone of newspaper reports into such disasters was largely sombre, focusing both on what could be done for the bereaved families, on ascertaining the responsibility of the lessees, managers and staff of the theatres and on repeating the calls from coroner's juries for improved safety at theatres. The publicity newspapers gave to the inadequacies of fire and safety measures ensured that issues got attention and that the wider public became aware of them. In such stories, the Victorian newspapers served the public interest. However, there was also undoubtedly an element of gawking at the unfortunate, with detailed descriptions of the dead given. The coroner's inquest was an invaluable source of information for reporters and they made the most of it.

So Victorian theatres could be constructed badly, or have what we would regard as considerable health and safety issues that could result in large-scale disasters and the deaths of innocent theatregoers. But on a smaller scale, other cases involving performers rather than the audience could highlight safety issues, both in front of and behind the stage. In addition, all sorts of accidents could occur within the confines of the Victorian theatre. This was an age of experimentation, or trying to see how far special effects could be taken and of trying to introduce danger and a type of realism to performances. Victorian audiences were demanding; they wanted novelty, sensation and danger rather than a tame performance. So it is not surprising that in an attempt to keep their audiences riveted to the stage, to keep them paying their pennies and coming to the theatre, that stunts, for example, could be introduced that could go wrong.

One of the most infamous cases involved the ballet girls who were performing at the Princess's Theatre in London on 23 January 1863.The contents of a pan of 'coloured fire' positioned above the stage for lighting purposes fell down onto the dancers. The flames set fire to Anne Hunt's thin, layered skirts; when she ran off stage to get help, she passed

Sarah Smith – known as Sarah Gibson – and set her skirts on fire too. Sarah suffered burns to a third of her body and died of exhaustion caused by burns; at her inquest on 31 January, Anne gave evidence from her bed, 'where she still lies in a weak and suffering state from extensive burns'.²

In another accident, in 1885, an opera was being performed at the Theatre Royal in Leamington that resulted in an injury to a theatregoer rather than a cast member. The opera was *Rip Van Winkle* and it was being performed by Fred Leslie's company. It was the closing scene – a chorus where the actor playing a captain had to strike down several soldiers' bayonets. During the scene, the actor's sword 'broke off at the hilt and the blade struck a lady in the orchestra stalls no the temple, inflicting a severe wound which bled profusely'. Luckily for the poor woman, a surgeon was in the audience and he was able to attend to her wounds straight away. Eight years earlier, at the Drury Lane theatre, the actor playing a harlequin in that season's pantomime was supposed to leap into the air and straight through the trap door in the stage. However, the trap failed to 'give' and his head hit part of the set. Luckily, the performer wasn't seriously hurt and he continued his performance – receiving 'the sympathising cheers of the spectators'. Onza, a gymnast, was less fortunate; whilst taking a flying leap at the Hull Mechanics' Music Hall in 1882, he fell on the stage and fractured his leg. In 1870, George Beckett, an actor taking part in a benefit performance at the New Royalty Theatre, managed to dislocate his knee. This had a severe impact on his earning potential; he was unable to walk for some time after the accident and so was unable to perform whilst he recovered. Another accident, in 1892, involved a young boy named Wilson, who was employed at the Theatre Royal in Coatbridge as a programme seller. He had been backstage during a performance of *Uncle Tom's Cabin* one evening in August and had wandered towards the props room, to watch the props master polish a revolver. A woman then came in and picked up the pistol. Presumably thinking it was a stage prop, she pointed it at Wilson and pulled the trigger. A blank cartridge was expelled and exploded in the boy's face, severely burning it and causing damage to his eye that led to him being sent to the local eye infirmary.

A further accident occurred in January 1880 – panto time in Birmingham. At the Holte Theatre, the production that winter was *The Sleeping Beauty*. The stage for the show was lit by electric light, with the wires transmitting the electric current running along the passage that led from the orchestra pit to the stage. Attached to the wires were two connections made of brass, which were put below the stage. One night, between 8 pm and 9 pm, the band were taking a break and had left the orchestra pit. The euphonium player, an Italian man whose professional name was Mr Bruno and who had the no-less glamorous real name of Augustino Bierdermann, made his way out. Unfortunately, as *The Era* duly reported, 'as he went out, [he] placed his hands upon the connections, presumably to try the effects of an electric shock. Unhappily, as the lights were out, the full force of the current was in the wires'. Bruno received a shock powerful enough to make him fall back, unconscious. His colleagues saw what had happened, lifted him up and sought medical help – but before it had arrived, the unlucky euphonium player had died. 'For a time the occurrence was kept from the audience, but when it became known it caused much sensation and great sympathy was expressed.'

Murders and suicides affected both the theatrical and non-theatrical professions in Victorian Britain, but many suicides, unless they occurred in exotic locations, only merited a line or two in the press. The *Middlesbrough Daily Gazette*, reporting one London case in 1891, simply stated: 'The man who committed suicide in Hyde Park on Thursday night proves to be Henry Charles Prince, an actor.' Such brevity did not permit an investigation into the reasons why Prince may have wanted to kill himself – whether it was professional or personal problems, or something else, remained unreported. Inquests sometimes enabled the press to go into a bit more detail; in 1897, a Chelsea inquest found that actor Lethbridge Beck, who had cut his throat, had been suffering from depression, whilst Decimus La Farque, another actor who had killed himself by drinking laudanum in 1899, had recently been rejected by his estranged wife Jennie, when he asked her to return to him.

Better-known actors, or those working for larger, more successful – often London-based – theatrical companies might merit more of a story. Probert Scott Fishe was a member of Richard D'Oyly Carte's Savoy opera company. He shot himself in Chiswick at the end of August in 1898, apparently in fear of an impending death from consumption. The report of his suicide noted that he had started his career 'as chorister at the Savoy Chapel, took important parts in several productions at the Savoy, including the title role of *The Mikado* in the recent revival'. Fishe had been suffering from consumption for two years and a recent stay in Jamaica had failed to improve his health. The 'extremely popular' singer had therefore taken his own life, 'and will be greatly regretted'. Four years earlier, an Italian actor, Francesco Garzes, had killed himself at 44 after suffering from a 'terrible malady – an incipient progressive paralysis, which was gradually weakening his memory'. And in 1892, actor Frank Nosworthy killed himself at Macclesfield, aged only 25. He left a suicide note addressed to his manager, where he explained that he had an ailment of the eyes that had caused him to give up his previous career as a draughtsman. His eyes were now getting so bad that he realised that he could not keep acting, either. 'Not choosing to become a burden upon my relatives', he wrote, 'I have decided on the step I am about to take.' These men made a decision to choose a quick form of death rather than to wait for the longer, lingering death that they knew would otherwise take them. However, in Nosworthy's case, there was also a financial concern and the feeling that if he had to give up his profession – again – there was no point in continuing to live.

Such cases suggest that personal situations had more of an impact on the mental health of performers than their professional situation. This was the case with another 25-year-old, Percy Spilsbury, who had given up a good career as a civil engineer to become an actor. He had been a member of a theatrical company that had been on a provincial circuit in 1895. On reaching Burton upon Trent, he had robbed another actor, stealing a pair of his boots. He had been sent to prison for fourteen days and on his release, wrote to his friends 'for assistance', presumably financial. He received no answer from any of them and became despondent. He was found dead in bed in his Burton lodgings, after drinking a bottle of laudanum. In another case, 26-year-old Charles Marley, an actor and theatrical manager, had become depressed after having a misunderstanding with his actress fiancée. She had jilted him and as a result, he drank laudanum one night at his lodgings in Liverpool. After his death, it was reported that 'the most painful part of the story is that the young lady to whom he was engaged was most devoted to him and since his death has been in the deepest distress and so prostrated that medical assistance has had to be called in'. Suicides and attempted suicides did not only affect performers, of course, and they were not always attempted outside the confines of the theatre – but some may have used the theatre as a means to kill themselves. One woman attempted to commit suicide at the Theatre Royal, Leicester, in 1882, by throwing herself from the gallery, but survived the fall.

Some actors died somewhat prematurely, at the peak of, or approaching the peak, of their careers in some cases. These deaths were also picked up on by the press. Signor Duvalli was a mid-Victorian tightrope walker, whose feats amazed provincial audiences. Throughout the 1850s, the regional press covered his deeds, which took place across the country. In June 1855, he was performing at the Rosherville Gardens – billed as 'Italy in miniature' – undertaking the 'daring feat' of walking on the tightrope from the Victoria Tower across the gardens' Grand Lawn on a daily basis. In 1859, Signor Duvalli started the year in Surrey, performing in Kingston and Richmond, then by the summer, was in the north-east, where in July, it was reported that he had spent one night undertaking the 'somewhat dangerous and daring feat of walking along a rope across the river Tyne', before a large audience. This feat was considered particularly impressive because of Duvalli's age – he was 'a man of 55 summers, of little stature, bearing traces of poverty'. This poverty was not alleviated by his performances; although Tyneside spectators enjoyed his performance, it was noted that when his friends went round collecting money from them afterwards, 'voluntary contributions were very small, amounting to little more than one pound, including some shillings kindly collected by Mr Rowell at his bar'. A month later, Duvalli nearly ended up in the Tyne after his friends tied the rope incorrectly, leaving it 'imperfectly secured'. Signor Duvalli performed wherever he was asked, largely in the pleasure gardens that still existed in Victorian England, such as the Vauxhall Gardens and Surrey Gardens, as well as the Rosherville Gardens. If he hadn't been asked, he undertook ad hoc performances in the provinces. It was clearly not a comfortable way of life for him in the 1850s and his health may have led to him looking somewhat older than he actually was.

However, the start of the 1860s saw things looking up for him; in April, he was performing in Glasgow, where it was argued that he was more of a star performance than Henry Irving, who was performing on the same bill at the Theatre Royal.[3] He then went to Ireland, where he first performed in the Queen's Royal Theatre, Dublin, in June and Belfast's Royal Botanic Gardens in July, being billed as 'the champion rope ascender of the world'; and in August was found in Malahide, near Dublin. The latter performance could have been a wash-out, for it was noted that 'the Dublin and Drogheda Railway Company ran special trains for the occasion, but comparatively few persons left Dublin to witness the spectacle'. However, there was a 'very large collection of persons assembled along the shore and when darkness set in their numbers increased largely, until the entire surrounding grounds were covered in every part'. The audience was regarded by the local press as being 'of no very select character', but it seems that the entertainment was popular amongst the ordinary workers of Malahide.

In November 1863, when he died, he was now described as being only in his fiftieth year. His death was seen as particularly tragic. His son, named as Edwy Hubert Duvalli, had died in October 1863, aged 19. His father attended his funeral on 28 October, but it was believed that the shock of seeing his son die and be buried at such a young age caused an acceleration of the illness Signor Duvalli had himself been suffering from for a few days. Three days after his son's burial, the tightrope-walking father died in Leeds. He was buried in the same grave as Edwy.[4] When, seventeen years later, American actor J.K. Emmet died, the stress of a theatrical life was recognised as a factor in his premature death at the age of 39. Emmet appears to have been an alcoholic, but it was recorded that he had been on the stage since the age of 18 and had had a demanding schedule of performances on both sides of the Atlantic, as a result of his skill as a 'personator of German immigrants who spoke our language imperfectly' and who also had 'comic talent in dialect and minstrel parts'. He was popular and earned a substantial amount of money, but 'he could not, however, withstand the suddenness of his success and in various ways he destroyed his health and his fortune'.

Although some actors were younger than others when they died, the press saw premature deaths as occurring to any actor, of any age, who was at their peak professionally, or who had been reaching it when they died, or who were deemed to have not enjoyed a sufficiently long career prior to their deaths. This could happen to many, though, especially as some actors went into a theatrical profession after having worked in other fields first and also as there were numerous illnesses and diseases an individual could suffer from that could prove fatal. This was the case with Alexander Brindal. He was the son of a comedian, regularly performing at the Haymarket in the 1830s – but himself set out to be a more serious actor. In 1847, he made his debut at the Lyceum Theatre, again in the capital, playing Poins in *Henry IV, Part 1*, leading one periodical to note: 'We did not see his debut [on Monday week], but we hear that he has taken and that he gave, flattering proofs of eventually becoming a most excellent performer.' He then went on to appear elsewhere in the metropolis, notably at the Drury Lane and Haymarket theatres, but became particularly 'well-known in the provinces'. His career was bright, but short. Nine years after his debut, *The Era* was recording his untimely death, noting that 'for the last six years [he] has been performing in the country with every prospect of attaining a creditable position'. He had just gained employment for the season back at the Lyceum Theatre, where 'his prospects seemed to present their brightest colours' – when he was suddenly struck with a severe attack of smallpox and died, leaving a widow mourning her 'affectionate husband and the profession . . . [missing] the companionship of a sincere friend'.

John Ferguson had a longer career than unlucky Alexander. He had been a comedian 'of some note', working primarily in the north of England and around Scotland. For a long period of time, he was also a stage manager, working with 'the eccentric and well-known' J.H. (John Henry) Alexander, manager of the Theatre Royal in Glasgow. As he got older, he started suffering from the ordinary signs of ageing, including failing sight and other health problems, gradually becoming somewhat incapacitated. He had many friends in the profession, though, and was looked after at his home in Dundee – 'none of the ordinary comforts of life were wanting at his fireside'. This care was no doubt due to his good reputation in stage circles – this 'veteran actor' was respected and known as 'Honest John' by his friends. When he died, at home, aged 70, he was surrounded by his friends. It is notable that *The Era* stressed John's good reputation and honesty. The acting industry was regarded as being socially disreputable, often 'a last resort before unemployment, the workhouse, or enlistment in the services'.[5] It was not seen as a 'profession' but a mercenary occupation, where managers failed to be scrupulous about who they employed and where actors were fighting for the decent roles – or any role. John Ferguson was therefore seen as an anomaly – by the press, at any rate.

Both Alexander Brindal and John Ferguson's deaths were not wholly unexpected. Although Brindal's illness was short, smallpox was sufficiently feared for a fatal outcome not to be a surprise. Ferguson's decline had been slow and associated with ageing and so his death was not a shock. But other deaths were more sudden. In 1843, for example, the celebrated Irish comedian and actor David 'Davy' Rees was found dead in his bed one morning. Rees had been performing around Ireland, having been engaged at Dublin's Theatre Royal, on Abbey Street, in November that year, together with his friend, vocalist Clement White. He was now in Cork and had dined with friends, including White, one evening. Having been regarded as 'rather well, having drunk but a few glasses of Port wine', he needed to be accompanied back to his lodgings in Old George's Street when he left the restaurant between midnight and 1 am. White was his crutch, accompanying him home, undressing his friend and putting him to bed, as Rees was complaining of an 'attack in the leg'. White seems to have stayed over at Rees's rooms himself, as, at 9 am, he was woken by the servant, who announced that she had found Rees lying half on and half off the bed – 'his head on the floor and his legs in the bed'. Both his head and face were swollen and black; it was believed that he had been trying to get out of bed when he had had a fit and collapsed. He had been due to appear that evening in a benefit concert for his manager, Mr Seymour – probably Frank Seymour, who was manager of the Theatre Royal in Waterford in the 1830s – who 'we regret to say, has suffered a considerable loss in the sudden demise of him "who was wont to keep the theatre in a roar"'. A more dubious compliment was also paid to the dead comic – 'his departure has left a blank in the comic walk that is not likely to be readily filled'. Rees was, it seems, Mr Seymour's cash cow; without him attracting theatre audiences, his manager would end up poorer than he would otherwise have done. The Irish papers described Davy Rees as an 'unrivalled comic actor' and even the English press mourned his untimely passing – the *Liverpool Mail* noted that he was simply 'many years ago a very popular member of the corps dramatique, at the Theatre Royal, in this town'.[6]

An even more sudden death occurred the same week as Davy Rees's fatal apoplexy. This time, death came not to a performer, but to a theatregoer. Ferdinando Jeyes, a 65-year-old solicitor described in the press as living in Harper Street, Red Lion Square, Holborn – but listed at Chancery Lane in official records – had decided to take his daughter and two friends, a man and woman, to the theatre for the evening. They reached the Drury Lane theatre and were about to enter. As they walked to the door, Jeyes went to take his money out of his pocket to pay for his admission ticket. The man in his party saw him suddenly stagger and ran forward to catch him in his arms. Another theatregoer, a retired naval surgeon named Hooper, helped to convey Jeyes to a space outside the theatre where 'restoratives could be applied, but without success'. Jeyes died on the spot, in what the *Bristol Mercury* called 'a melancholy instance of the uncertainty of life'. Ferdinando Jeyes was buried at St James' Church, on Hampstead Road, on 8 December 1843.[7]

The newspapers and the public could get it wrong on occasion and publish the details of a death that had not actually happened – which must have been both mortifying and embarrassing to actors who needed theatres and companies to know that they were very much alive in order to get work. One can sense the frustration of American actress

Charlotte Cushman, whose death was prematurely announced in the British press in 1852, nearly a quarter-century before her eventual demise. An apology was duly published: 'Miss Cushman. We are most happy to announce, on the authority of a telegraphic despatch, from the friends of Miss Cushman to a relative in New York, that the disease has taken a favourable turn and that there are now no doubts entertained of her recovery. The report of her death, printed in some of the papers, is, of course, without foundation.' Miss Cushman had certainly been ill; and illness was something that often beset actors and caused concern both to them, the companies depending on their appearances on stage and their public, if they were popular performers.

The Victorian press was interested in all aspects of theatrical life – and death. The nature of a performer's death could shed light on the dangerous nature of their performing lives, working in theatres where electricity was still in a relatively experimental stage, or where their own stunts could be lethal. Press coverage could be extremely useful – in highlighting health and safety issues and helping push for improvements that would make the audience safer – but in other cases, there was simply a desire to gossip, particularly where the class-conscious newspaper reader could learn about an actor's finances and status. In addition, the more dramatic a death, the more newsworthy it was. The lowly bit-part player could get more notice in the papers by dying than he could ever hope to achieve in reviews. Yet the coverage of actor suicides in the press also highlight the insecurity of the profession and the distress that illness could cause those in precarious situations, who feared being unable to work and unable to find an alternative. Although the press was broadly sympathetic to these individuals, prurience still played a part in how newspapers covered such tragedies.

*   *   *

This book has shown how the Victorian press in Britain was as interested in the personal lives of entertainers as they were in the shows they took part in. The era saw the expansion of the press and the concurrent need to use personal stories culled from rumours, gossip, transatlantic newspapers and court cases to fill the newspapers' pages. This coverage of performers' lives broke down the barrier between them and their audiences, making readers feel that they were part of the actors' lives. A very recognizable and modern form of celebrity culture had well and truly arrived, thanks to theatrical gossip.

Notes

Introduction

1. Rosalind Crone, *Violent Victorians: Popular Entertainment in Nineteenth-Century London*, Manchester University Press, 2012, pp. 149–51.

2. Anonymous, 'The Story of Music Hall', The Victoria and Albert Museum, accessed at www.vam.ac.uk/content/articles/t/the-story-of-music-halls.

3. Joel H. Wiener, 'The Americanisation of the British Press, 1830-1914', *Studies in Newspaper and Periodical History*, Volume 2, issue 1-2 (1994), p. 61. Working-class boys' love of 'Penny Dreadfuls' was a cause of concern in the late Victorian era; they were a form of escapism that could give children dangerous ideas (Kate Summerscale, *The Wicked Boy: The Mystery of a Victorian Child Murderer*, Bloomsbury, 2016, pp. 108–14).

4. W.J. MacQueen-Pope described it as taking 'more and more interest in theatrical affairs' by 'degrees' (W.J. MacQueen-Pope, *The Melodies Linger On*, W.H. Allen, 1951, pp. 274–5.

5. Wiener, 'The Americanisation of the British Press, 1830-1914', p. 61.

6. Michael R. Booth, *Theatre in the Victorian Age*, Cambridge University Press, 1991, p. 101.

7. Ibid., pp. 101, 112. Kerry Powell has, however, queried this, stating that a nineteenth-century actress might actually 'earn less money than in any other line of work' (Kerry Powell, *Women and Victorian Theatre*, Cambridge University Press, 1997, p. 5). However, even if it was lower paid, it still offered a combination of economic and personal freedom that might not be found elsewhere.

8. Powell, *Women and Victorian Theatre*, p. 19.

9. 'Prevention of Cruelty and Protection of Children Bill (No 372)', *House of Commons Debate, 14 August 1889, vol 339, cc1284-7*, Hansard, accessed at http://hansard.millbanksystems.com/commons/1889/aug/14/prevention-of-cruelty-to-and-protection.

10. Lord Russell was speaking at a fundraising dinner for the Royal General Theatrical Fund and spoke enthusiastically of his enjoyment of the theatre and his belief that ageing and struggling actors should be helped regardless of what people thought of their morals, or whether they had done enough to 'help themselves' – a rather refreshing perspective for the time (*Evening Standard*, 29 May 1896).

Chapter 1: Licensing the Theatre

1. Russell Jackson, *Victorian Theatre*, New Amsterdam, 1995, p. 79.

2. Ibid., p. 81.

3. The Maskall sisters were spinsters, who lived together at 11 Norland Square in Chelsea for many years; Elizabeth Wadd Maskall died in 1893, aged 62; her sister Mary died in 1919, aged 85.

4. John Wade, *A Treatise on the Police and Crimes of the Metropolis*, Longman, 1829, p. 229.

5. Jacky Bratton, 'Theatre in the 19th century', *Discovering Literature: Romantics and Victorians*, British Library, n.d., accessed at www. bl.uk/romantics-and-victorians/articles/19th-century-theatre.

6. Frederick Burwick, *British Drama of the Industrial Revolution*, Cambridge University Press, 2015, p. 5.

7. For more on this case, see London Metropolitan Archives, ref LCC/MIN/10,803 and Joseph Donohue, *Fantasies of Empire: The Empire Theatre of Varieties and the Licensing Controversy of 1894*, University of Iowa Press, 2005.

8. Donohue, *Fantasies of Empire*, pp. 191–4.

Chapter 2: Theatrical Libel

1. Anthony Slide, *The Encyclopaedia of Vaudeville*, University Press of Mississippi, 1994, rpt 2012, p. 66.

2. Mark Lubock, *The Complete Book of Light Opera*, Appleton-Century-Crofts, 1962, pp. 3–4.

3. Ledger had become editor of *The Era* in 1849 and until at least 1900 was still editing its annual *The Era Almanack*, which he had started in 1868. It has been stated that it was the personal interest of Ledger and his predecessor, Leitch Ritchie, that led to the paper becoming 'exclusively concerned with theatre by the 1850s' (Laurel Brake and Marysa Demoor (eds), *Dictionary of Nineteenth-century Journalism in Great Britain and Ireland*, Academia Press, 2009, p. 206; Claire Cochrane, *Twentieth-Century British Theatre: Industry, Art and Empire*, Cambridge University Press, 2011, p. 278.

4. Anon, *Royal Dramatic College, for the Aged and Infirm Actors and Actresses and for the Maintenance and Education of the Children of Actors*, William Clowes & Sons, 1858.

5. A meeting was held on Monday 19 November 1877 of the governors and subscribers of the college, where they resolved 'that as it is impossible to keep up the Royal Dramatic College . . . there being at this moment no fund for the current expenses . . . the Council do forthwith take such steps as the Charity Commissioners may advise to dispose of the property and to provide for the inmates' (*Morpeth Herald*, 17 November 1877).

6. Although, unsurprisingly, not referred to as such in the Victorian press,

locomotor ataxia, a progressive condition that led to individuals having an unsteady gait, was associated with syphilis. The *Oxford English Dictionary* states that this condition was only identified in the 1850s.

7. It has been noted that Davis (1853–1907), although later a successful theatre critic and librettist who worked under the name of Owen Hall, had less luck with *The Bat*, which was a 'short-lived society newspaper' (Anthony Patterson (ed.), in his notes to George Moore, *A Mummer's Wife*, 1885, republished by Victorian Secrets, 2011, p. 25).

8. A light cavalry corps in the French Army of Africa, it served in the Franco-Prussian War of 1870–1 (Robert Huré, *L'Armée d'Afrique: 1830-1962*, Charles-Lavauzelle, 1977, p. 125).

9. Corlett had been the paper's editor and proprietor since 1865.

10. The newspapers are quiet about Violet after June 1887 (when she was still in the chorus at the Avenue Theatre) until 1915, where there are a few mentions of a Violet Dashwood performing. She sang a couple of songs to the troops at Osterley in October 1915 and sang two Ivor Novello songs 'with fervour' in the St Stephen's Parish Rooms in Middlesex the following March. The gap in press coverage of her may suggest that she never got the 'good position in her profession' that she wished for.

11. David de Bensaude and Violet Lydia Thompson – not the same person as Lydia Thompson, another famous figure of Victorian theatre, but her niece – married on 20 September 1884 at the South Audley Street register office in London, according to David's original divorce petition (The National Archives [TNA], reference J77/364/990). Violet was born in Camden in 1863. The spellings of David's surname differ wildly both in press reports and in official records, but here, the spelling in his divorce petition – de Bensaude – is used. *The Umpire*'s background is described in Mark Clapson, 'Playing the System: The world of organised street betting in Manchester, Salford and Bolton, c1880 to 1939', in Andrew Davies and Steven Fielding (eds), *Workers' Worlds: Cultures and Communities in Manchester and Salford, 1880-1939*, Manchester University Press, 1992, p. 160.

12. In 1888, David appeared in court charged with threatening Violet and had to enter into a recognizance of the peace for six months. A month later, he was in Marylebone Police Court on a charge of breaking the windows of Violet's house, after learning that Lord Lonsdale had visited the actress there on a weekly basis. David had to pay £4 damages – one paper headlined its piece about this, understandably, as 'Mr de Bensaude again'. In 1891, David was again in court – this time the Queen's Bench – where he was accused of stealing £60 from a fellow boarder in a house in Gower Street, London. David described himself as 'husband of Miss Violet Cameron and an undischarged bankrupt'. He lost the case and had to pay £150 damages. He never divorced his wife; in 1911, the 48-year-old Violet was recorded in the census as living in Worthing and having no occupation. Although she was using her maiden name, she described herself as a widow. When she died, in 1919, the papers

did not record her husband's details; the *Derby Daily Telegraph*, for example, simply noted, 'Miss Violet Cameron, the actress and singer, died at Worthing on Saturday after a short illness'. The *Lancashire Evening Post* went into a bit more detail, recording that she made her debut on the London stage at the age of nine and retired in 1903 – but still failed to note the complexities of her personal life, which had given the press such a field day in the 1880s. The only mention of it was in the *Yorkshire Post*, which stated that 'an unhappy domestic life had much to do with Miss Violet Cameron's practical retirement'.

13. Richard Foulkes, 'Cameron, Violet [real name Violet Lydia Thompson] (1862–1919), actress', in David Cannadine (online ed), *Oxford Dictionary of National Biography*, Oxford University Press, 2004, accessed at www.oxforddnb.com/view/article/62581.

14. Elizabeth Lee, 'Merivale, Herman Charles (1839–1906), playwright and novelist', in H.C.G. Matthew and Brian Harrison (eds), *Oxford Dictionary of National Biography*, Oxford University Press, 2004, accessed at www.oxforddnb.com/view/article/34993.

15. Cochrane, *Twentieth-Century British Theatre: Industry, Art and Empire*, p. 53.

Chapter 3: Bankruptcy

1. Booth, *Theatre in the Victorian Age*, p. 31.

2. Jeffrey Richards, *The Golden Age of Pantomime*, I.B. Tauris, 2014, p. 158.

3. As Michael Booth points out, the theatre manager, or lessee, had to maintain the theatre building, pay rates, run the company, take responsibility for the administration and salaries of his actors and staff and arrange provincial and overseas tours (Booth, *Theatre in the Victorian Age*, pp. 28–9).

4. Richards, *The Golden Age of Pantomime*, pp. 139, 160. In 1852, Smith, then manager of the Marylebone Theatre, took on the Theatre Royal in London, having also previously been lessee of the Alhambra, Her Majesty's Theatre, the Lyceum, Astley's and Cremorne Gardens – 'according to the treasurer, Smith was not a person the company would have chosen, but his offer of £3,500 per annum was the only acceptable one'. ('The Theatre Royal: Management' in F.H.W Sheppard (ed.), *Survey of London: Volume 35, the theatre [sic] Royal, Drury Lane and the Royal Opera House, Covent Garden*, LCC, 1970, pp. 9–29, accessed at www.british-history.ac.uk/survey-london/vol35/pp9-29).

5. Marie Studholme was the stage name of Caroline Maria Lupton, who was then aged 25 (Peter Bailey, 'Studholme, Marie [real name Caroline Maria Lupton] (1872–1930), actress', in H.C.G. Matthew and Brian Harrison (eds), *Oxford Dictionary of National Biography*, Oxford University Press, 2004, accessed at www.oxforddnb.com/view/article/74788). The Gaiety Girls were the chorus girls who performed in popular musical comedies of the 1890s.

6. For details about the bankruptcy procedure, see The National Archives, 'Bankrupts and Insolvent Debtors' (www.nationalarchives.gov.uk/help-with-your-research/research-guides/bankrupts-insolvent-debtors/);

for bankruptcy legislation in Victorian England, see Paolo di Martino, 'Approaching disaster: Personal bankruptcy legislation in Italy and England, c1880-1939', *Business History*, 47:1 (2005), pp. 23–43.

7. These details of Brooke's life are taken from W.J. Lawrence, *The Life of Gustavus Vaughan Brooke*, W. & G. Baird, 1892.

8. Jackson, *Victorian Theatre*, p. 80.

9. The Editors of Encyclopaedia Britannica, 'William Charles Macready', *Encyclopaedia Britannica*, accessed at www. britannica.com/biography/William-Charles-Macready.

10. Although occasional nineteenth-century newspaper reports describe J.L. Shine as Irish, he was actually half-Irish, on his father's side. He gave his place of birth as Manchester in the 1881 census. The 1861 census similarly records him as being born in Hulme, a suburb of Manchester. His father, provisions dealer James, though, was born in Ireland in 1828. Although this cannot be corroborated through birth records, despite John being born after civil registration in England started in 1837, this is not surprising, as it was not compulsory to register the birth of a child until after the 1874 Births and Deaths Act came into effect.

11. Christopher Innes, *The Cambridge Companion to George Bernard Shaw*, Cambridge University Press, 1998, p. 278. John L. Shine continued a long career in the theatre after this financial difficulty in 1891.

12. Bernard Ince, 'Spectres of Debt in the Victorian Theatre: A Case Study of Management Failure', *Nineteenth Century Theatre and Film*, 41:1 (2014), pp. 68–84. Ince covers the financial failure of the Torquay Theatre Royal under Charles Collette in detail, putting it within the context of legislative changes during the second half of the nineteenth century.

13. Bernard Ince, 'Natural-born showman: the stage career of Charles Collette, actor and comedian', *Theatre Notebook*, 63:1 (2009), p. 22.

14. Michael Walters, 'A Brief Overview of the Life of Rutland Barrington', *The Gilbert & Sullivan News*, 2:13 (1998), pp. 20–8.

15. John LeVay states that *Citizen Pierre* 'died after three weeks of sparse houses' (John LeVay, *Margaret Anglin, A Stage Life*, Simon & Pierre, 1989, p. 47).

16. Erskine Reid and Herbert Compton, *The Dramatic Peerage, 1892: personal notes and professional sketches of the actors and actresses of the London stage*, Raithby, Lawrence & Co, 1892, p. 197. Contemporaries saw Sugden as a bit of an oddity; he was a graduate of Merton College, Oxford, and went from there onto the stage – 'he once actually played a clown for a week!' according to Reid and Compton. His stage name was also the *stage* surname of his step-father, George Neville, who was also an actor (whose real name was the more prosaic Fred Gartside).

Chapter 4: In Breach of Contract

1. In Ireland, the Irish Court of Queen's Bench was abolished in 1877.

The Queen's Bench Division of the High Court has sat in the Royal
Courts of Justice on the Strand since 1882. In Scotland, civil cases
were heard at the Sheriff Courts and the Court of Session.

2. Booth, *Theatre in the Victorian Age*, p. 117.

3. Four years later, Kendal was on the receiving end of a suit, when he
    was sued by Charles Hannan in Glasgow for failing to pay Hannan
    for a play the latter had written, that he had promised to produce.
    Kendal's defence was that as an Englishman, he did not come under the
    jurisdiction of a Scottish court; although this argument was thrown out,
    it was decided that no formal contract existed between the two men.

4. J. Panton Ham, *The Pulpit and the Stage: Four
    Lectures*, Forgotten Books, 2015, pp. 38–9.

5. By 1881, *The Era* was noting that Pennington was 'the well-known,
    but not too often engaged actor' (*The Era*, 9 July 1881).

6. 'A signed review by Clement Scott, *Illustrated London News*,
    25 April 1891, 551–2', in Michael Egan (ed), *Henrik Ibsen:
    The Critical Heritage*, Routledge, 1972, pp. 225, 228.

7. Lewis Waller was certainly a draw by this time, having first played Buckingham
    in *The Three Musketeers* four years earlier, directed by Herbert Beerbohm Tree,
    before starting up his own theatrical company in various London theatres.

8. The play was written by Oswald with George Thomas; when it was performed
    at the Vaudeville Theatre in June 1887, Frank Oswald also appeared in it.

9. It appears that this case came at the same time as the Sire Brothers –
    Albert and Clarence – were busy waging war on 'scalpers', or ticket
    speculators. Albert was also a lawyer (Kerry Segrave, *Ticket Scalping:
    An American History, 1850-2005*, McFarland & Company, 2007, pp.
    70–1). Nine years later, the Sires had an action brought against them by
    a London firm that found they had been keeping their chorus girls in a
    'system of virtual servitude' (*New York Times*, 8 December 1899).

10. Dyan Colclough, *Child Labor in the British Victorian Entertainment
    Industry: 1875-1914*, Palgrave Macmillan, 2016, p. 39.

11. The 1901 census for Putney gives Clara's birthplace as Chepstow in Wales,
    but states that all four children were born in New Zealand (Garnet Vane
    [*sic*] Butler was born in July 1887 in Auckland, according to the New
    Zealand Birth Index). The daughters were aged between 14 and 17 at this
    time. Clara may have still struggled for money as a young widow with
    children – although all the family had an occupation (as opposed to a job,
    or employment, at the time of the census), they had also had to take in
    three lodgers – a solicitor's clerk, a theatrical wig maker and an artist.

12. This was in 1898, but by 1900, *The Era* was including adverts that simply
    referred to him as 'Master Garnet Vayne' (*The Era*, 1 December 1900).

13. Colclough, *Child Labor in the British Victorian Entertainment Industry: 1875-*

1914, p. 160. The issue had been rumbling on for a while, though; in August 1889, there was a parliamentary debate on child performers, part of the passage of the Prevention of Cruelty to and Protection of Children Bill, in which the MP for Wolverhampton, Henry H. Fowler, stated that the Factory Act had been applied to child performers, stating that under-10s shouldn't be allowed to play for profit, but that at the same time, magistrates had been given the power to licence performers aged between seven and ten! (Source: 'Prevention of Cruelty to and Protection of Children Bill (No 372)', *House of Commons Debate, 14 August 1889, vol 339, cc1284-7*, Hansard, accessed at http://hansard.millbanksystems. com/commons/1889/aug/14/prevention-of-cruelty-to-and-protection).

14. Although in December 1900, Garnet was described as 'the celebrated boy actor, Master Garnet Vayne' (*South Wales Daily News*, 24 December 1900) and was still acting in 1903 (see *The Era*, 28 February 1903), he does not appear to have grown up to be a successful adult actor – perhaps his value was simply in his youth.

Chapter 5: Celebrity Culture

1. Charlotte Boyce, Páraic Finnerty and Anne-Marie Millim, *Victorian Celebrity Culture and Tennyson's Circle*, Palgrave Macmillan, 2013, p. 20.

2. *The World*'s series started in the 1870s and was termed by one reviewer, 'a characteristic product of the present era' (Troy J. Bassett, '"A Characteristic Product of the Present Era": Gender and Celebrity in Helen C Black's *Notable Women Authors of the Day* (1893)', in Ann R. Hawkins and Maura Ives (ed), *Women Writers and the Artifacts of Celebrity in the Long Nineteenth Century*, Ashgate Publishing, 2012, p. 151).

3. Laurel Brake and Marysa Demoor (eds), *Dictionary of Nineteenth-century Journalism in Great Britain and Ireland*, Academia Press/British Library, 2009, p. 103.

4. It was noted back in 1873 that 'many young and pretty actresses' had an 'insatiable love . . . to see themselves portrayed in every possible posture' and this pandering to ego, together with money, meant that advertising was seen as an attractive activity in the theatrical world (*Edinburgh Evening News*, 15 December 1873).

5. This rather snide obituary of an actress was nothing compared to a piece in 1903, when Julia St George died. She was described as having been 'one of the most brilliant burlesque actresses in London . . . whose name was at one time a household word', but she had died, age 79, in the St Pancras Workhouse, having been a 'slave to drink' who 'fell about at times' through drunkenness but could not afford a doctor. When parish officers called at her house to take her to the workhouse, they found her 'lying on the floor in a very dirty and neglected condition' with numerous brandy and whisky bottles lying around. By this time, the early Edwardian era, the press was ready to revel in this comedown of a once-famous actress (*Gloucestershire Echo*, 16 November 1903; *Cheltenham Chronicle*, 21 November 1903).

6.   Catherine Hindson, *London's West End Actresses and the Origins of Celebrity Charity, 1880-1920*, University of Iowa Press, 2016, p. 36.

7.   Ibid., p. 39.

8.   After five years of stalking Mary Fitzpatrick, he was bound over to good behaviour and ordered to pay costs of £2 2s.

9.   In 1880, Cornelie D'Anka went on to marry another theatrical professional, John Edward Ingham, who went bankrupt shortly after their marriage. In 1885, Cornelie was again featured in the press after her stepdaughter, 14-year-old Ethel Maud Ingham, was found drowned in a well, a coroner's inquest finding that she had been very thin, had previously complained of a lack of food and had never attended school. There were allegations that her father had beaten her, but Cornelie gave evidence that she had only ever corrected Ethel 'by words' and that her father had simply sent her to her room. As *The Era* later reported, 'Although the coroner's jury could not ascertain whether Ethel had died by accident or otherwise, they stated that they regretted that 'she should have been for some time exposed to very trying circumstances of solitude and want of the comforts of life'.

Chapter 6: Blackmail

1.   Jackson, *Victorian Theatre*, p. 143.

2.   *The Frederic Dobell Papers, 1872-1916* (Ms 607), University of Massachusetts Amherst Special Collections and Archives, accessed at http://scua.library.umass.edu/umarmot/dobell-frederick/.

3.   Blackmail could also be carried out by hard-up actors. In 1894, William Bawcombe, who described himself as 'an actor out of employ' was fined 40 shillings at Bow Street Police Court, after being found guilty of disorderly conduct. He had followed a local MP, Stewart Wallace, along the street one night and threatened him with violence, saying he was a foreigner and that he had a bomb under his arm.

4.   Irving was speaking immediately after the murder of actor William Terriss, detailed in Chapter 10. The murder had led to heightened fears within the theatrical possession about the lengths to which individuals could go when they felt aggrieved by actors.

5.   John Coleman, *Fifty Years of An Actor's Life, Volume 1*, 1904; rpt Forgotten Books, 2013, p. 242; 1861 census for Egremont, Cumberland (where Paumier described himself as 'tragedian and stage manager').

6.   Marianne Colloms and Dick Weindling, *The Marquis de Leuville: A Victorian Fraud?*, The History Press, 2012.

7.   *The Satirist* featured stories about well-known Londoners and Gregory was not averse to tipping off people that he was about to include them in the next issue, in the hope of getting a bribe not to. As early as 24 May 1831, the *Morning Chronicle* was reporting a libel case brought against *The Satirist* by the Earl of Shaftesbury's son-in-law, which alleged that

his wife had had a baby suspiciously soon after getting married (*Morning Chronicle*, 24 May 1831). *The Satirist* ceased publication in 1849.

8. The previous year, Gregory was found guilty of libelling the Duke by accusing him of having killed Eliza Grimwood, 'an unfortunate woman' in her room (George Clement Boase, 'Gregory, Barnard (1796–1852), newspaper proprietor', in H.C.G. Matthew and Brian Harrison (eds), *Oxford Dictionary of National Biography*, Vol 23, Oxford University Press, 2004, p. 92, accessed at www.oxforddnb.com/view/article/11455).

9. Ibid.

Chapter 7: Assault

1. Crone, *Violent Victorians: Popular Entertainment in Nineteenth-Century London*, p. 130.

2. Ibid., pp. 131–2.

3. Ibid., p. 151. Cave had begun his theatrical career at either the age of 9 or 11 (accounts differ), playing characters such as Tom Thumb, so had a wealth of experience of dealing with difficult audiences. When he died in 1912, aged 89, his obituary read that he was 'the oldest of our theatrical managers . . . [who] came into the world when George IV sat on the throne'.

4. This may be the same Professor Abel [*sic*] who performed with a full military band as part of Hiram Orton's circus in 1858 (see www.circushistory.org/History/BriefO.htm). In 1843, Professor Abel 'of the London theatres' performed at the Windsor Theatre Royal in a play called *My Poor Dog Tray*; Abel played a 'dumb idiot' named Andy and appeared with his dog, Tray. He played to crowded houses and Queen Victoria and Prince Albert were said to be planning to attend a performance.

5. *The Wicked World* was W.S. Gilbert's three-act blank verse play, being performed at the Haymarket Theatre.

6. Marian J. Pringle, 'Hawley, Frederick [performing name Frederick Haywell] (1827–89), actor and librarian', in David Cannadine (online ed), *Oxford Dictionary of National Biography*, Oxford University Press, 2004, accessed at www.oxforddnb.com/view/article/12695.

7. Joseph Knight (rev. J. Gilliland), 'Rousby [née Dowse], Clara Marion Jessie (1848–79), actress', in H.C.G. Matthew and Brian Harrison, *Oxford Dictionary of National Biography*, Oxford University Press, 2004), accessed at www.oxforddnb.com/view/article/24176; 'Daniel Edward Bandmann (1840–1905)' at the *Missoula, Montana* website (www.ci.missoula.mt.us/DocumentCenter/Home/View/739).

8. The first reference by name to Walter Howard as an actor that I can find is in *The Era*, 12 January 1868.

Chapter 8: Theft

1.   George Laval Chesterton, *Revelations of Prison Life, Volume 1*, 2nd ed., Hurst and Blackett, 1856, pp. 134–5.

2.   As Matthew White has written of the first half of the nineteenth century, 'crowded places such as fairs, marketplaces and public executions were particularly profitable for young thieves' – the theatre and its surrounding area, was a more salubrious, but equally crowded place at the right time of day (Matthew White, 'Juvenile crime in the 19th century', British Library, accessed at www.bl.uk/romantics-and-victorians/articles/juvenile-crime-in-the-19th-century).

3.   *The London City Mission Magazine*, Vol V, London City Mission, 1840, p. 159.

4.   James Grant, *Sketches in London*, W.S. Orr and Co, London, 1838, p. 163.

5.   Henry Mayhew, *London Labour and the London Poor, Volume 1*, Cosimo Classics, 2009, p. 40.

6.   See Jeannie Duckworth, *Fagin's Children: Criminal Children in Victorian England*, A & C Black, 2002, p. 25.

7.   Grace Otway is mentioned elsewhere in this book, as four years later, she was accused by her husband of having a child 'of which he could not possibly be the father'. Mabel Harrison was described in 1883 as one of the 'sisterhood of those talented ones who are making this century the "Age of Gifted Women"' – The *Women's Penny Paper*, cited in Kathryn Ledbetter, *British Victorian Women's Periodicals: Beauty, Civilisation and Poetry*, Palgrave Macmillan, 2009, p. 43. Grace Otway and Rose Stapleton had, in 1883, been playing in the Union Street Hall in Cupar as the Otway-Stapleton Company, performing a stage adaptation of *Lady Audley's Secret*. They were described as 'pleasing actresses, who come direct from the London stage'.

8.   *The Falkirk Herald* of 19 November 1890 has Rex Russell appearing in *Pilgrim's Progress* at Falkirk Town Hall, for example.

9.   The only reference I can find to a Jessie Vyner is a girl born in Hackney in the October quarter of 1872, which would make her 16 rather than 19 at the time of this theft (BMDs, Hackney, vol. 1b, p. 494).

10.   For example, between January 1838 and December 1900, there were twelve theft cases involving actresses listed at the Old Bailey. In each case, the actress was either a victim or a witness, rather than the accused. Although this is only a snapshot and obviously focuses on cases in the capital that were brought before the Old Bailey judges, it does help suggest that either thieving actresses were relatively rare, or that their crimes were regarded as more minor and therefore more likely to be dealt with at summary level, where they occurred (source: *Old Bailey Proceedings Online* [www.oldbaileyonline.org]).

11.   Ruth Baldwin, *Outlaws, Outcasts and Criminals of the British Novel, 1800-1850*, PhD thesis, University of California, Berkeley, 2013, p. 143.

12.   There were 155 performances at the Gaiety before it transferred to the Grand Theatre, Islington with a new cast. Most of the Gaiety

cast then took the play around the provinces as part of a touring
company, which only returned to London in December 1886.

13. Baldwin, *Outlaws, Outcasts and Criminals of the British Novel, 1800-1850*, p. 65.

14. Booth, *Theatre in the Victorian Age*, p. 111.

Chapter 9: Prostitution

1. Fraser Joyce, 'Prostitution and the Nineteenth Century: In Search of
the "Great Social Evil"', *Reinvention: an International Journal of
Undergraduate Research*, 1:1 (2008), accessed at http://www2.warwick.
ac.uk/fac/cross_fac/iatl/reinvention/issues/volume1issue1/joyce/.

2. This was *Reynolds's Newspaper*, 3 August 1879.

3. Helen Mathers, *Patron Saint of Prostitutes: Josephine Butler
and a Victorian Scandal*, The History Press, 2014, p. 120.

4. See Margaret Hamilton, 'Opposition to the Contagious Diseases
Acts, 1864-1886', *Albion: A Quarterly Journal Concerned
with British Studies*, 10:1 (Spring 1978), pp. 14–27.

5. Edgar Bruce became the actor-manager of the Prince of Wales Theatre on
Tottenham Street in 1880, produced the highly successful *The Colonel*
and then built a brand-new theatre at Coventry Street in 1884, that became
initially the Prince's Theatre and then the Prince of Wales Theatre from
1886 – see www.arthurlloyd.co.uk/PrinceOfWalesTheatre.htm.

6. Emily Maynard Oldfield was born on 4 June 1859 in Bonn, then in Prussia,
to Charles James Oldfield and Isabella Stinton (FamilySearch, Germany:
Select Births and Baptisms 1558–1898, FHL film number 1052881).

7. Births for Marylebone district, June quarter of 1885, volume 1a, page 619.
On her death in 1959, Viva's birth date was incorrectly given as 7 October
1885 and her place of birth as Ham in Surrey (in the 1891 census, she was
being looked after by a bricklayer and his family in Ham); however, her
baptism record shows that she was born on 13 April and baptised – as the
child of Emily and Charles Bagot – at St Andrew, Ham, on 7 October (Surrey
History Centre, ref 2337/1/1). Viva married Jonathan Edward Knowles at
Bexhill in 1909; however, she was soon widowed as Knowles, a captain
in the Duke of Cambridge's Own (Middlesex) Regiment, was killed at the
Battle of Mons in August 1914 (De Ruvigny's Roll of Honour, 1914–1919).
The couple had three children – Jonathan Maynard, Nina Mary and Viva
Joan – aged between 22 months and 4 years when their father died.

8. TNA, J77/442/3469, dated 1890.

9. A Morton Selton, actor and comedian, is listed in passenger-ship records as a
frequent visitor to the UK from New York throughout the 1890s and up to at
least 1911. He would have been 25 at the time of Viva Bagot's birth (sources:
TNA BT26/109/4, TNA BT27, National Archives (Washington), T715/1720).

10. Charles had given his occupation as journalist and the *York Herald* stated that

he was 'formerly stage manager to Mr Edgar Bruce at the Prince of Wales Theatre and also a special war correspondent for the *Standard*', so he was likely to have been reporting from these countries, rather than holidaying!

11.   National Probate Calendar, 1858–1966, date of death 6 May 1935. Her death was registered as 'Emily Maynard Palmer Saunders, otherwise Emily Grace Maynard Palmer, otherwise Grace Maynard Palmer, otherwise Grace Maynard'. She was described as a widow who had died at Whitehill Chase, Bordon, Hampshire; probate was granted to her daughter, Viva Brabazon Knowles, and her effects were worth nearly £11,000. The BMD index lists her as Emily M. P. G. Saunders, aged 74 (Alton district, June quarter of 1935, vol 2c, page 208). A 'Grace M. Oldfield', also known as Grace M. Evans or Grace M. Evans-Freke had married Henry S. Saunders in Kensington in 1911 (December quarter, volume 1a, page 448), suggesting that Grace may have been married four times in total (to Bagot, Evans, Freke and Saunders, unless Freke had been hyphenated to Evans by her third husband's family).

12.   TNA J77/250/7167.

Chapter 10: Murder, Murder!

1.   Michael Baker has commented that there was a 'gradual change in social attitudes to the stage which was taking place after 1860' (Michael Baker, *The Rise of the Victorian Actor*, Croom Helm, 1978, p. 88).

2.   The British newspapers got their story from an account in St Petersburg's *Russian Gazette*.

3.   The *Dundee Evening Telegraph* of 21 August 1890 made clear it got much of its New York news, including the following murder case, via telegram; the *Yorkshire Evening Post* similarly reported a story involving an American actor named Curtis, charged with the murder of a policeman in San Francisco in 1892, including in its report, the phrase 'says a New York telegram'.

4.   This was the second McVicker's Theater in the city – the first had been destroyed by fire in 1871 and rebuilt the second year on the same site on Madison Street (Bryan Krefft, 'McVickers [*sic*] Theater', *Cinema Treasures*, accessed at http://cinematreasures.org/theaters/1798.).

5.   Although the newspaper article implied that Booth had been murdered, he actually was fine and lived until 1893 (see Eleanor Ruggles, 'Edwin Booth, American Actor', *Encyclopaedia Britannica*, 2016, accessed at www.britannica.com/biography/Edwin-Booth.

6.   Although not mentioned in the British press, apparently Arthur had intended to shoot both himself and Amy, but then discovered there was only one bullet left in his gun and so had to cut his own throat instead. He was still alive when he was discovered by his landlady's son, a maid and another lodger in his boarding house, but died shortly afterwards. Amy had died instantly (Leann Richards, 'Amy and Arthur Dacre 1895', *History of Australian Theatre*, accessed at www.hat-archive.com/Dacres.htm).

7.   This article, in the *Bath Chronicle* of 21 November 1895, was cobbled together from a *Times* article of 18 November 1895. This *Times* piece detailed the telegram from a Sydney exchange company verbatim and included far more detail about the couple's theatrical engagements over the previous years.

8.   Account of the murder taken from the *Peterhead Sentinel*, 21 December 1897

9.   Terriss had, prior to taking up acting as a profession, been in the Merchant Navy for two years, working along the coasts of China, Japan, California and the South Sea Islands, until he realised that the job was 'ill-suited to his impetuous temperament and enterprising disposition', according to the *Peterhead Sentinel* of 21 December 1897. Richard Foulkes has suggested, however, that Terriss had exaggerated his seagoing career and that he had only been in it for two weeks, at the age of 16 (Richard Foulkes, 'Terriss, William (1847–97), actor', in H.C.G Matthew and Brian Harrison (eds), *Oxford Dictionary of National Biography*, Oxford University Press, 2004, accessed at www.oxforddnb.com/view/printable/27144).

10.   *Old Bailey Proceedings Online* (www.oldbaileyonline.org), January 1898, Richard Arthur Prince (t18980110-113).

11.   Madeleine Bingham, *Henry Irving and the Victorian Theatre*, Routledge, 1978, rpt 2016, p. 284; Summerscale, *The Wicked Boy*, pp.182, 197.

12.   Richard Foulkes, 'Terriss, William (1847–97), actor', in H.C.G. Matthew and Brian Harrison (eds), *Oxford Dictionary of National Biography*, Oxford University Press, 2004, accessed at www.oxforddnb.com/view/printable/27144.

13.   This was the murder of music-hall star Thomas Weldon Andersen, known professionally as Thomas Atherstone, who was found shot at the back of a block of flats in Battersea in July 1910. This gathered column inches not because Andersen was as well-known as Terriss, but because the circumstances of his death were seen as peculiarly mysterious – he was found outside in his carpet slippers, and his son had been dining in his flat with a young woman at the time of the murder. The 'young woman', a drama teacher named Miss Earle, was alleged to be Andersen's lover – but she had also, apparently 'had other men' at her flat while she was supposed to be seeing him. The murder remains unsolved.

14.   The murder of Maria Marten by her lover William Corder, in Polstead, Suffolk in 1827. Corder sent Maria's family letters saying that she was fine, but her body was discovered in the Red Barn by her stepmother, after the latter had dreams that Maria had been murdered. Corder was executed at Bury St Edmunds the following year. Thomas Harry Jones' argument that he had though he was re-enacting this crime was problematic, given that Corder had shot his lover, whereas Jones had stabbed a complete stranger.

Chapter 11: Sex and Seduction

1.   *Old Bailey Proceedings Online* (*www.oldbaileyonline.org*), 12 May 1856 and 16 June 1856 (t18560512 and t18560616).

2.   Bingham, a senior magistrate, resigned in July 1860. The newspaper noted

that he had been a legal reporter at the Court of Common Pleas and Recorder of Southampton and Portsmouth before becoming a magistrate at Worship Street and then, in 1846, a senior magistrate at Marlborough Street. The 1851 census recorded Peregrine Bingham, police magistrate, as living at 35 Gordon Square – he was then aged 62. He died in 1864, with press obituaries noting the 'death of an ex-police magistrate' and stating that he had resigned 'owing to ill-health', having been called to the bar at Middle Temple back in 1818 and having been a law reporter in the Court of Common Pleas between 1819 and 1840.

3.   William Beadon died in 1862, aged only around 50. The *Oxford City and University Herald* noted in its deaths column, 'March 30, at Stratford Place, Piccadilly, London, William F. Beadon, Esq, Senior Magistrate at the Marlborough Street Police Court'.

4.   Ginger S. Frost, *Living in Sin: Cohabiting as husband and wife in nineteenth-century England*, Manchester University Press, 2008, p. 23.

5.   'Crim con' was abolished in England and Wales under the Divorce and Matrimonial Causes Act of 1857. Diane Urquhart has argued that although some have claimed that suits for criminal conversation were considered 'very rare' in Ireland by 1816, in fact, cases continued to be brought in the south until the 1980s (Diane Urquhart, 'Ireland's criminal conversations', *Études irlandaises*, 37:2 (2012), p. 2, citing Lawrence Stone, *Road to Divorce: England, 1530-1987*, Clarendon, 1990, p. 255.

6.   Thomas E. Blum (ed), *The Secret Lives of Richard André (1834-1907): A Lecture given at the Osborne Collection of Early Children's Books, November 2, 1989*, Toronto Public Library, 1990, cited in 'Richard André Papers', de Grummond Children's Literature Collection, The University of Southern Mississippi, accessed at www.lib.usm.edu/legacy/degrum/public_html/htm/research/findaids/DG0028f.html.

7.   Victoria and Albert Museum, 'Black and Asian Performance in Britain 1800-1899', accessed at www.vam.ac.uk/content/articles/b/black-and-asian-performance-in-britain-1800-1899/.

8.   Ibid.

9.   The papers called Emma's mother Ingledew, but the BMD records give her name as both Iggulden and Igguldon (marriages for St Pancras, volume 1, page 344, Sep 1849).

10.   Baptism of Emma Iggulden on 1 July 1825 at Speldhurst, Kent, daughter of James and Ann (*England, Births and Christenings, 1538-1975*, FamilySearch, 2013, film number 1469565).

11.   The 1851 census for 22 Judd Place, St Pancras. It records Emma Stothard, niece, living with her aunt Jane Wathurst, a widow and annuitant. Both were born in Speldhurst, Kent.

12.   BMDs, births for St Pancras, June quarter of 1853, vol. 1b, p. 106; death also recorded in BMDs for St Pancras, June quarter of 1853, vol. 1b, p. 102.

13.　She was referred to in the press as Miss Payter or Miss Pater, but Mary
Emily Constance Payter was baptised on 12 August 1867 at Holy
Trinity, Paddington (*England, Births and Christenings, 1538-1975,*
FamilySearch, 2013, film number 804224) and is clearly named on her
marriage licence from 1 November 1886 (Mary Emily Constance Payter
of the parish of St James, Paddington and Percy Mackenzie Esquire
of St Mary Abbots Kensington (LMA ref MS 10091/263, part 4).

14.　In her divorce case, Mary argued that Percy drank and had a violent
temper throughout their marriage. He had been sick over her when drunk,
had tried to cut her throat and, on one occasion, pulled her out of bed
and stripped her naked. He had also frequently left her without money
– mocking the fact that he had insisted he would not take any of Mary's
money from her (divorce record from TNA, ref J77/517/15782).

15.　BMDs, marriages for December quarter of 1895, Paddington, vol. 1a, p.
130. In 1901, Mary was living in Surrey with her husband and two young
daughters, Constance and Harriet (1901 census for Lingfield, Surrey). In 1911,
James was listed as a company director (1911 census for Rye, Sussex).

16.　Days' Concert Hall had two proprietors, George and William Day,
and was managed by J. Gregory. Although Jessie was described 1899
as an actress, at the start of her career, she was more of a variety act,
appearing with musical palmists, gymnasts, a 'transformation dancer'
and 'bar performers'. She was at the bottom of the bill, although she
appears to have performed solo rather than as part of a chorus.

Chapter 12: Breaches of Promise

1.　For more on the history of breach of promise actions, see
Denise Bates, *Breach of Promise to Marry: A history of how
jilted brides settled scores*, Pen & Sword, 2014.

2.　The press often spelled Herbert's surname as Merriman – but his
marriage record has him clearly recorded as Herbert Merrion and
signing his name that way (marriage of Herbert John Merrion
and Frances Pike, 5 August 1873, St John's, Waterloo).

3.　A review of their appearance at the Queen's Theatre in Belfast in 1870 gives
their professional names as Nellie, Rosina and Katty and states that they
performed the can-can 'with a modesty and grace'. Although they played fast
and loose with their ages, the records show that the sisters were Catherine Fagg
Vaile (Kate or Katty), born in 1844; Ellen Lavinia Fagg Vaile (Nellie), born
in 1846; Rosa Laura Fagg Vaile (Rose or Rosina), born on 3 August 1847 in
Holborn; and Emeline Amy Sarah Fagg Vaile (Amy), born in 1854, who also
seems to have performed with The Sisters Fanchette, although possibly not
at the same time as Nellie. There was also one much younger sister, Florrie
(1881 census for 7 Grosvenor Terrace, Falcon Lane, Battersea; baptisms for
St Saviour Southwark, St Andrew Holborn and St Mary, Cheltenham).

4. Joseph's occupation was given on the baptism record for his daughter Catherine in 1844 (baptism record for Catherine Fagg Vaile, 27 March 1844, St Mary's, Cheltenham, Gloucestershire Archives, P78/1 IN 1/14).

5. Joseph Vaile died in Bradford in the spring of 1873, aged 73 (BMDs for Bradford, June quarter of 1873, vol. 9b, p. 73).

6. David Stone, 'May Fortescue', *The D'Oyly Carte Opera Company*, 2014, accessed at http://diamond.boisestate.edu/gas/whowaswho/F/FortescueMay.htm. May died aged nearly 92 on 2 September, 1950 (The National Probate Calendar records her as Finney, Emily May, otherwise Fortescue, May, of 46 Roland Gardens, London SW7, spinster. She died on 2 September 1950, with probate being granted on 14 November. Her effects were worth £6,866 2s 4d. Although Wikipedia records her date of birth as being in February 1862, Emily May Finney was actually born in the Kensington district of London in the March quarter of 1859 (BMDs, Kensington, vol. 1a, p. 16) – an earlier date corroborated by her entry in the 1891 census (1891 census for 15 Church Street, Windle, St Helen's, Lancashire) and in the death indexes, which actually record her age as having been 92 (BMDs for Kensington, September quarter of 1950, vol. 5c, p. 772).

7. Mark Riddaway and Carl Upsall, *Marylebone Lives: Rogues, romantics and rebels – character studies of locals since the eighteenth century*, Spiramus Press, 2015, p. 100.

8. Don Gillan, 'Phyllis Broughton (1862-1926)', Stagebeauty.net, accessed at www.stagebeauty.net/broughton/broughton-p.html.

9. Frost, *Living in Sin*, p. 22.

10. Ibid., p. 164.

11. Florence Ida O'Keefe was born on 12 August 1865 in Donnybrook, Dublin, the daughter of Vivian O'Keefe and Eliza Mary Partridge (*Ireland Births and Baptisms, 1620-1911*, FamilySearch, c. 2011).

12. The 1901 census for 6 Clare Street, Halifax, records Henry's age as 42; the 1911 census for 7 Grove, Hammersmith, states that Henry Elmore Frith was an actor aged 51. He had recently married, to an actress – Isabella – who was twenty-five years his junior. However, the baptism records for St Peter's, Notting Hill, show that he was baptised on 4 May 1858 (LMA, DL/T/048, item 001).

13. The 1891 census shows Henry E. Frith and 'Florence I. Frith' boarding at 28 Quay Street in Manchester, with several other actors. They are described as married.

14. BMDs for Pancras, June quarter of 1893, vol. 1b, p. 249. Florrie herself married Horace Houlston in the winter of 1901 (BMDs for Camberwell, December quarter of 1901, vol, 1d, p. 1671). She and Horace, who described himself as being 'of private means' settled in Faversham; she appears to have stopped acting, but never had children (1911 census for 10 Belmont Road, Faversham, Kent). However, again, she appears to have lived with Houlston before being legally married, being listed on the 1901 census – which was taken on 31 March – as being Houlston's wife (1901 census for 83 Banstead Road, Camberwell; date given at www.nationalarchives.gov.uk/pathways/census/events/census1.htm).

15. Denise Bates, 'Hell hath no fury! How jilted 19th century brides used marriage laws to settle scores', *Daily Express*, 24 February 2014.

Chapter 13: Till Death Us Do Part?

1. Heidi J. Holder, 'Sothern, Edward Askew (1826–81), actor' in David Cannadine (online ed), *Oxford Dictionary of National Biography* (Oxford University Press, 2004), accessed at www.oxforddnb.com/view/article/26041.

2. Eva, like her brother Edward, was born in America; she was baptised in Liverpool on 19 October 1863 (Liverpool Record Office, ref 283 CHY/2/1). She married at St George's Hanover Square in July 1891 (LMA, MS 10091/268). 1901 census for 2 Pelham Street, South Kensington.

3. Register of Baptisms, St Paul's Covent Garden (LMA, DL/T/098, item 029).

4. BMDs, marriages for Marylebone, September quarter of 1859, vol. 1a, p. 755; marriage entry for 1 August 1859, St Mark, St John's Wood (LMA, P89/MRK2, item 007).

5. Albert's widow, the young actress Mary Keeley, did not live a long life herself. The *Morning Post* of 21 March 1870 recorded the death of Mrs Albert Smith at the age of 39, from consumption, noting, 'Mrs Albert Smith was the daughter of the greatly esteemed favourites of the stage, Mr and Mrs Keeley and, as Miss Mary Keeley, her name will be remembered by playgoers'. Her death was sudden and apparently came as a great shock to both her mother, Mary Ann and her sister Louise, wife of lawyer and playwright Montague Williams, who herself died just seven years later.

6. All Souls, Langham Place register of marriages (LMA, P89/ALS, item 075); George Taylor, 'Bancroft [née Wilton], Marie Effie, Lady Bancroft (1839–1921), actress and theatre manager', in David Cannadine (online ed), *Oxford Dictionary of National Biography*, accessed at www.oxforddnb.com/view/article/30570. The 1871 census has Charles Bancroft, born 1864, London, as a school pupil in Marylebone; in 1881, he was at Eton College, so his relationship or parentage is not revealed by the census.

7. William Baker and Andrew Gasson (eds), 'Marie and Squire Bancroft', *Lives of Victorian Literary Figures, part V, volume 2*, Pickering and Chatto, 2007, pp. 235–46, accessed at www.wilkie-collins.info/plays_bancrofts.htm.

8. June Faulkes, 'Nelson Wheatcroft: Actor and Bigamist?' (n.d.), accessed at http://btckstorage.blob.core.windows.net/site10718/christopher%20 wheatcroft%20booklet.pdf and http://wheatcroft.btck.co.uk/Publications.

9. The BMDs for Pancras, March quarter of 1873, record the marriage of Martha Reinhardt and Thomas Elliott (vol. 1b, p. 75). Their marriage entry shows that Mattie, of 15 Regent's Park Terrace, was the daughter of George Frederick Reinhardt and was marrying Thomas Elliot, a merchant of The Green, Bishopwearmouth. The press mistakenly recorded the vicar of St Mark's as being a Reverend A. Galloway; however, the

incumbent at the time was William B. Galloway and his named is clearly recorded as such on the marriage register (LMA P90/MRK/006).

10. Karen E. Laird, *The Art of Adapting Victorian Literature, 1848-1920: Dramatising Jane Eyre, David Copperfield and The Woman in White*, Ashgate Publishing, 2015, p. 101.

11. Richard Madelaine (ed), *Antony and Cleopatra*, Cambridge University Press, 1998, p. 55.

12. Malcolm C. Salaman, 'William Schwenck Gilbert: The Man, The Humorist, The Artist', *Cassel's Magazine*, 20 March 1900, pp. 413–21, in Harold Orel (ed), *Gilbert and Sullivan: Interviews and Recollections*, (University of Iowa Press, 1994), accessed at http://diamond.boisestate.edu/gas/gilbert/interviews/cassells.html.

13. This production was discussed in more depth in Chapter 8, on theft.

14. BMDs (births) for St George Hanover Square, June quarter of 1888, vol. 1a, p. 414 (a three-year-old George is also listed on the 1891 census for 11 Hyde Park Street, Paddington, with his parents); BMDs (marriages), December quarter of 1888, St George Hanover Square, vol. 1a, p. 723.

15. Presumably, this was Sir Gonne St Clair Pilcher (1890–1966), who became a High Court judge (Queen's Bench Division) in this year (Gordon Charles Cook, *The Incurables Movement: An Illustrated History of the British Home*, Radcliffe Publishing, 2006, p. 173).

16. The 9th Earl, Eric, died in April 1952 (see www.cracroftspeerage.co.uk/online/content/fitzwilliam1716.htm)

17. Daisy died, aged 58, in 1925 (BMDs (deaths), March quarter of 1925, Peterborough, vol. 3b, p. 288).

Chapter 14: Bigamy

1. *Parliamentary Papers: The Judicial Statistics of England and Wales*, HMSO, 1857–1906, cited in Frost, *Living in Sin*, p. 72.

2. David J. Cox, '"Trying to get a good one": Bigamy offences in England and Wales, 1850-1950', *Plymouth Law and Criminal Justice Review*, 1 (2012), p. 2.

3. Bernard Capp, 'Bigamous Marriage in Early Modern England', *The Historical Journal*, 52:3 (2009), pp. 547–8.

4. Bruce Seymour, 'Montez, Lola [real name Elizabeth Rosanna Gilbert] (1821-1861), adventuress', in H.C.G. Matthew and Brian Harrison (eds), *Oxford Dictionary of National Biography*, Oxford University Press, 2004, accessed at www.oxforddnb.com/view/article/10697.

5. *The London Gazette*, 1 February 1910, pp. 828–9. Fred and Alice's illicit marriage was referred to in an item placed after her mother's death in 1909, which sought information in case the couple had had children who could claim on the mother's estate. The item included an extra note: 'The said Fred Solomon is believed to have gone to New York some years ago and to have

been engaged at the Casino, New York. It is believed that previous to the marriage above mentioned the said Fred Solomon was married to an actress who was known by the name of Plimsoll.' This was a reference to Sarah.

6. Henderson's company played at the Princess's Theatre in Edinburgh from 22 September to 5 October 1879; then Belfast's Theatre Royal from 6 October to 11 October and then Dublin's Gaiety Theatre from 13 October to 25 October. Alice Harper died three days before the Dublin performances ended, on 22 October 1879. Christopher Morash has noted of the Gaiety – which opened in November 1871 – that 'contemporary plays from the London theatres toured and the time lag narrowed steadily between London and Dublin openings . . . it is true that much of what appeared on the Gaiety stage originated in England' (Christopher Morash, *A History of Irish Theatre 1601-2000*, Cambridge University Press, 2002, pp.106, 107).

7. BMDs (marriages), Strand district, March quarter of 1873, volume 1b, p. 669 and December quarter of 1873, vol. 1b, p. 973.

8. On 16 May 1923, *The Era* reported Blande's death, from acute bronchitis: 'Miss Blande, who came to this country from Australia some 30 odd years ago, was at one time a favourite actress of melodrama in the provinces'; on 27 November 1875, *The Graphic* had described her as 'lively and prepossessing' in a performance of the burlesque *Black-Eyed Susan* at the Opéra Comique. Edward Solomon deserted Jane, his wife, in 1875, leaving her to maintain their daughter (TNA J77/282/8326).

9. TNA J77/282/8326.

10. *Old Bailey Proceedings Online* (www.oldbaileyonline.org), December 1840, trial of Peter Anthony Cullen (t18401214-390), later reported in *The Era*.

11. Alice was born in 1847 and died in 1897. Although some reports state that she was buried in Brompton Cemetery, DeceasedOnline shows that Alice Anne Needham Lingard was buried in Hampstead Cemetery on 29 June 1897 (www.deceasedonline.com, Hampstead Cemetery, grave ref K10/79). William Horace Lingard was buried in the same plot on 15 January 1927, aged 87; the records also show a third person buried with them – their daughter, Louise Emily Marie Dunning Atkinson, née Needham, who was buried on 28 September 1926, aged 59 (her death was recorded in the BMDs for Pancras, September quarter of 1926, vol. 1bm, p. 63; her birth was registered in Pancras in the June quarter of 1867, volume 1b, page 68).

12. 'His youthful, drolly pixyish face immensely enhanced his comic flair', it has been said (Gerald Bordman and Thomas S. Hischak, *The Oxford Companion to American Theatre*, Oxford University Press, 2004, p. 389.

13. This was Wood's Minstrel Hall, later the Theatre Comique, which was converted by the New York mayor's brother, Henry Wood, from a Jewish synagogue; Lingard and Alice had performed there in 1869, in a burlesque – entitled *Pluto* – written by David Braham and Henry B. Farnie (also mentioned in this chapter).

14. This is how the Southampton newspaper recorded it, but, in

fact, William Thomas married Amelia Martha Flint in Stepney in 1860, not Southampton (BMDs, vol. 1c, p. 897).

15.   William married Alice Dunning in Bristol in 1866, under the name of 'William Nedham' (BMDs, vol. 6a, p. 165).

16.   The obituary, in *The Times* of 14 January 1927, noted that his wife was 'Miss Alice Lingard, a popular musical comedy actress', but she had predeceased her 'husband', dying in London in 1897.

17.   John Franceshina, *Harry B. Smith: Dean of American Librettists*, Routledge, 2003, p. 9.

18.   Marriage entry for Henry Brougham Farnie, journalist and Alethea Emma Harvey, at All Souls Church, Marylebone, on 31 May 1865.

19.   *Farnie (Alethea Emma) v Farnie (Henry Brougham)*, Civil Divorce Records, 1858–1911, on www.ancestry.co.uk.

20.   *Old Bailey Proceedings Online* (www.oldbaileyonline.org), January 1848, trial of John Byron (t18480131-616).

21.   BMDs for St George in the East, vol. 2, p. 41.

22.   John Byron married Matilda Wilkinson Little on 22 April 1842, in York. Matilda was just 20 at the time (*England, Marriages, 1538-1973*, FamilySearch, 2013, film number 1470404).

23.   *Middlesex Register of all Persons charged with Indictable Offences at the Assizes and Sessions held within the County during the Year 1838*, 31 January 1848. Accessed at Ancestry (www.ancestry.co.uk).

24.   Convict Records, accessed at www.convictrecords.com.au/convicts/byron/john/25054 and www.convictrecords.com.au/ships/william-jardine).

25.   *Old Bailey Proceedings Online* (www.oldbaileyonline.org), September 1852, trial of Edward Murphy (t18520920-938).

Chapter 15. Divorce

1.   Frost, *Living in Sin*, p. 16.

2.   Marriage register for St Mary at Lambeth, 28 February 1854 (LMA P85/MRY1/424, X102/061).

3.   1851 census for Champion Place, Cobb Lane, Lambeth.

4.   Henry's case is saved in The National Archives' Contentious Probate Case Files and Papers (TNA J121/848 (1864)).

5.   Marriage register for St Nicholas, Brighton, 7 November 1844 (East Sussex Record Office, PAR255/1/3).

6.   TNA J77/29/J8.

7.   I can't find any evidence that this was the famous German pianist and piano teacher of the same name; the name does not appear to have been very unusual in Germany at the time.

8.   Peter Bailey, *Popular Culture and Performance in the Victorian City*, Cambridge University Press, 1998, p. 121.

9.   TNA J77/166/4077.

10. When he appeared before the Court of Bankruptcy in 1876, it was heard that he had been 'playing with the Court for 12 months', 'riding about town in a carriage, setting his creditors at defiance'.

11. The couple had two daughters – Maud Lytton Grey Morgan in 1893 and Eva Lytton Grey Morgan two years later, their middle names reflecting their father's professional persona and name. Elder daughter Maud made the headlines herself when she became the private secretary of 46-year-old widower Lord Alvingham, a chronic invalid, and married him ten years later. She had already been divorced twice. As his secretary, she was said to have written 4,000 letters a year for him (*Lincolnshire Echo*, 1 August 1936). Her sister Eva briefly had her own stage career and in 1920 was appearing in *Broadway Jones* at the New Theatre in Cambridge (*Cambridge Daily News*, 16 January 1920).

12. Lockwood had joined forces with Charles P. Levilly for this production; in an interview with the latter in 1908, the *Daily Chronicle* (whose interview was duly repeated by the *Otago Witness*), had noted that he had been presenting *La Poupée* 'for nearly ten years to provincial audiences' (*Otago Witness*, 25 March 1908).

13. BMDs (marriages) for Walsall, March quarter of 1874, vol. 6b, p. 823.

14. Powell, *Women and the Victorian Theatre*, p. 19.

15. TNA J77/70/241.

16. Ibid.

Chapter 16: Death and Disaster

1.   See also Jonathan Law (ed.), *The Methuen Drama Dictionary of the Theatre*, Market House Books, 2011, p. 185.

2.   The memorial to Sarah Smith at Postman's Park in London, part of G.F. Watts' Memorial to Heroic Self-Sacrifice, states that she was of the Prince's Theatre; however, the contemporary newspaper reports of her death and inquest all confirm that she was performing at the Princess's Theatre at the time of her death. The details of what happened, as recorded by Watts, also differ from press reports.

3.   Charles Hiatt, *Henry Irving: A Record and Review*, George Bell & Sons, 1899, p. 61.

4.   This was not the same 'Signor Duvalli' who was performing in 1878, under the nickname 'The Demon Wizard' (*New Zealand Evening Post*, 5 August 1878) or the 'Signor Duvalli and his trained canaries' who performed in the US in the mid-1870s (Donald Z. Woods, 'Playhouse for Pioneers: The Story of the Pence Opera House', *Minnesota History*, 33:4 [Winter 1975], p. 175) – the repeated use of the name suggests that it was a fairly common stage name of performers seeking to sound more exotic and certainly, I have been unable to find the deaths of either father or son in the registers under the name of Duvalli.

5.   John William Cole, *The Life and Theatrical Times of Charles Kean*, Richard Bentley, 1859, p. 15, rpt in Baker, *The Rise of the Victorian Actor*, p. 27.

6.   In 1858, it was reported that an Englishman named Clement White had just arrived in New York and had set words by actor John Brougham to music, creating a 'hymn of Peace' that was performed at the Crystal Palace (Vera Brodsky Lawrence, *Strong on Music: The New York Music Scene in the Days of George Templeton Strong: Volume 3: Repercussions, 1857-1862*, University of Chicago Press, 1999 , pp. 208–9.

7.   Ferdinando had several daughters and the papers didn't specify which one saw her father die. The 1841 census for Highgate Rise, London, lists Marianne, Hannah and Jane Jeyes all living at home.

Select Bibliography

Books

Anonymous, *Royal Dramatic College, for the Aged and Infirm Actors and Actresses and for the Maintenance and Education of the Children of Actors*, William Clowes & Sons, 1858.

Anthony, Barry, *Murder, Mayhem and Music Hall: The Dark Side of Victorian London*, IB Tauris, 2015.

Bailey, Peter, *Popular Culture and Performance in the Victorian City*, Cambridge University Press, 1998.

Baker, Michael, *The Rise of the Victorian Actor*, Croom Helm, 1978.

Baker, William, and Andrew Gasson, *Lives of Victorian Literary Figures, part V, vol 2*, Pickering and Chatto, 2007.

Barrington, Rutland, *A Record of Thirty-five Years' Experience on the English Stage*, Grant Richards, 1908.

Bates, Denise, *Breach of Promise to Marry: A history of how jilted brides settled scores*, Pen & Sword, 2014.

Bingham, Madeleine, *Henry Irving and the Victorian Theatre*, Routledge, 1978, rpt 2016.

Booth, Michael R., *Theatre in the Victorian* Age, Cambridge University Press, 1991.

Boyce, Charlotte, Páraic Finnerty and Anne-Marie Millim, *Victorian Celebrity Culture and Tennyson's Circle*, Palgrave Macmillan, 2013.

Brake, Laurel, and Marysa Demoor (eds), *Dictionary of Nineteenth-century Journalism in Great Britain and Ireland*, Academia Press, 2009.

Burwick, Frederick, *British Drama of the Industrial Revolution*, Cambridge University Press, 2015.

Chesterton, George Laval, *Revelations of Prison Life, Vol 1*, Hurst and Blackett, 2nd ed., 1856.

Cochrane, Claire, *Twentieth-Century British Theatre: Industry, Art and Empire*, Cambridge University Press, 2011.

Colclough, Dyan, *Child Labor in the British Victorian Entertainment Industry: 1875-1914*, Palgrave Macmillan, 2016.

Cole, John William, *The Life and Theatrical Times of
    Charles Kean*, Richard Bentley, 1859.

Coleman, John, *Fifty Years of An Actor's Life, Volume
    1*, 1904; rpt Forgotten Books, 2013.

Colloms, Marianne, and Dick Weindling, *The Marquis de Leuville:
    A Victorian Fraud?*, The History Press, 2012.

Cook, Gordon Charles, *The Incurables Movement: An Illustrated
    History of the British Home*, Radcliffe Publishing, 2006.

Crone, Rosalind, *Violent Victorians: Popular Entertainment in Nineteenth-
    Century London*, Manchester University Press, 2012.

Davies, Andrew, and Steven Fielding (eds), *Workers' Worlds:
    Cultures and Communities in Manchester and Salford,
    1880-1939*, Manchester University Press, 1992.

Diamond, Michael, *Victorian Sensation: or the Spectacular, the Shocking and
    the Scandalous in Nineteenth-Century Britain*, Anthem Press, 2003.

Donohue, Joseph, *Fantasies of Empire: The Empire Theatre of Varieties and
    the Licensing Controversy of 1894*, University of Iowa Press, 2005.

Duckworth, Jeannie, *Fagin's Children: Criminal Children
    in Victorian England*, A & C Black, 2002.

Egan, Michael (ed.), *Henrik Ibsen: The Critical Heritage*, Routledge, 1972.

Franceshina, John, *Harry B. Smith: Dean of American Librettists*, Routledge, 2003.

Grant, James, *Sketches in London*, W.S. Orr and Co, 1838.

Frost, Ginger S., *Living in Sin: Cohabiting as Husband and Wife in
    Nineteenth Century England*, Manchester University Press, 2008.

Hawkins, Ann R., and Maura Ives (eds), *Women Writers and the Artefacts of
    Celebrity in the Long Nineteenth Century*, Ashgate Publishing, 2012.

Hiatt, Charles, *Henry Irving: A Record and Review*, George
    Bell & Sons, 1899, rpt Forgotten Books, 2013.

Hindson, Catherine, *London's West End Actresses and the Origins of
    Celebrity Charity, 1880-1920*, University of Iowa Press, 2016.

Hischak, Thomas S., *The Oxford Companion to American
    Theatre*, Oxford University Press, 2004.

Huré, Robert, *L'Armée d'Afrique: 1830-1962*, Charles-Lavauzelle, 1977.

Innes, Christopher, *The Cambridge Companion to George
    Bernard Shaw*, Cambridge University Press, 1998.

Jackson, Russell, *Victorian Theatre*, A & C Black, 1989.

Laird, Karen E., *The Art of Adapting Victorian Literature, 1848-1920: Dramatising Jane Eyre, David Copperfield and The Woman in White*, Ashgate Publishing, 2015.

Law, Jonathan (ed.), *The Methuen Drama Dictionary of the Theatre*, Market House Books, 2011.

Lawrence, Vera Brodsky, *Strong on Music: The New York Music Scene in the Days of George Templeton Strong: Volume 3: Repercussions, 1857-1862*, University of Chicago Press, 1999.

Lawrence, W.J., *The Life of Gustavus Vaughan Brooke*, W & G Baird, 1892.

Ledbetter, Kathryn, *British Victorian Women's Periodicals: Beauty, Civilisation and Poetry*, Palgrave Macmillan, 2009.

LeVay, John, *Margaret Anglin, A Stage Life*, Simon & Pierre, 1989.

Lubock, Mark, *The Complete Book of Light Opera*, Appleton-Century-Crofts, 1962.

Mathers, Helen, *Patron Saint of Prostitutes: Josephine Butler and a Victorian Scandal*, The History Press, 2014.

Mayhew, Henry, *London Labour and the London Poor, Volume 1*, Cosimo Classics, 2009.

Morash, Christopher, *A History of Irish Theatre 1601-2000*, Cambridge University Press, 2002.

Orel, Harold (ed.), *Gilbert and Sullivan: Interviews and Recollections*, University of Iowa Press, 1994.

Partridge, Eric, *The Routledge Dictionary of Historical Slang*, Routledge, 6th edition, 2006.

Patterson, Anthony (ed.), *George Moore, A Mummer's Wife*, 1885, published by Victorian Secrets, 2011.

Powell, Kerry, *Women and the Victorian Theatre*, Cambridge University Press, 1997.

Reid, Erskine, and Herbert Compton, *The Dramatic Peerage, 1892: personal notes and professional sketches of the actors and actresses of the London stage*, Raithby, Lawrence & Co, 1892.

Richards, Jeffrey, *The Golden Age of Pantomime: Slapstick, Spectacle and Subversion in Victorian England*, I.B. Tauris, 2015.

Riddaway, Mark, and Carl Upsall, *Marylebone Lives: Rogues, romantics and rebels – character studies of locals since the eighteenth century*, Spiramus Press, 2015.

Rowell, George, *The Victorian Theatre, 1792-1914*, Cambridge University Press, 2nd edition, 1978.

Segrave, Kerry, *Ticket Scalping: An American History, 1850-2005*, McFarland & Company, 2007.

Slide, Anthony, *The Encyclopaedia of Vaudeville*, University
    Press of Mississippi, 1994, rpt 2012.

Stone, Lawrence, *Road to Divorce: England, 1530-1987*, Clarendon Press, 1990.

Summerscale, Kate, *The Wicked Boy: The Mystery of a
    Victorian Child Murderer*, Bloomsbury, 2016.

Thompson, Paul, *The Edwardians*, Routledge, 2002.

Wade, John, *A Treatise on the Police and Crimes of the Metropolis*, Longman, 1829.

Journals

Capp, Bernard, 'Bigamous Marriage in Early Modern England',
    The Historical Journal, 52:3 (2009), pp. 537–56.

Cox, David J. '"Trying to get a good one": Bigamy offences in England and Wales,
    1850-1950', *Plymouth Law and Criminal Justice Review* 1 (2012), pp. 1–32.

di Martino, Paolo, 'Approaching disaster: Personal bankruptcy legislation in Italy
    and England, c1880-1939', *Business History*, 47:1 (2005), pp. 23–43.

Hamilton, Margaret, 'Opposition to the Contagious Diseases Acts,
    1864-1886', *Albion: A Quarterly Journal Concerned with
    British Studies*, 10:1 (Spring 1978), pp. 14–27.

Ince, Bernard, 'Spectres of Debt in the Victorian Theatre: A Case Study of Management
    Failure', *Nineteenth Century Theatre and Film*, 41:1 (2014), pp. 68–84.

Ince, Bernard, 'Natural-born showman: the stage career of Charles Collette,
    actor and comedian', *Theatre Notebook*, 63:1 (2009), pp. 20–38.

Joyce, Fraser, 'Prostitution and the Nineteenth Century: In Search of
    the "Great Social Evil"', *Reinvention: an International Journal of
    Undergraduate Research*, 1:1 (2008), http://www2.warwick.ac.uk/
    fac/cross_fac/iatl/reinvention/issues/volume1issue1/joyce

Urquhart, Diane, 'Ireland's criminal conversations', *Études
    irlandaises*, 37:2 (2012), pp. 65–80.

Walters, Michael, 'A Brief Overview of the Life of Rutland Barrington',
    The Gilbert & Sullivan News, 2:13 (1998), pp. 20–8.

Wiener, Joel H., 'The Americanisation of the British Press, 1830-1914', *Studies in
    Newspaper and Periodical History*, Vol. 2, issue 1-2 (1994), pp. 61–74.

Woods, Donald Z., 'Playhouse for Pioneers: The Story of the Pence Opera
    House', *Minnesota History*, 33:4 (Winter 1975), pp. 169–78.

Theses

Baldwin, Ruth, *Outlaws, Outcasts and Criminals of the British Novel, 1800-1850*, PhD thesis, University of California, Berkeley, 2013.

Index

Theatres without a specified location are in the West End of London. *illus* indicates a plate. Names in parentheses are performers' real names except when preceded by *pn* (professional name).